PERPETRATORS

Stanford Studies in Human Rights

Perpetrators

Encountering Humanity's Dark Side

Antonius C. G. M. Robben

and

Alexander Laban Hinton

Stanford University Press
Stanford, California

Stanford University Press
Stanford, California

Printed in the United States of America on acid-free, archival-quality paper

Library of Congress Cataloging-in-Publication Data
Names: Robben, Antonius C. G. M., author. | Hinton, Alexander Laban,
    author.
Title: Perpetrators : encountering humanity's dark side / Antonius C.G.M.
    Robben and Alexander Laban Hinton.
Other titles: Stanford studies in human rights.
Description: Stanford, California : Stanford University Press, 2023. | Series:
    Stanford studies in human rights | Includes bibliographical references
    and index.
Identifiers: LCCN 2022022364 (print) | LCCN 2022022365 (ebook) |
    ISBN 9781503630673 (cloth) | ISBN 9781503634275 (paperback) | ISBN
    9781503634282 (epub)
Subjects: LCSH: Crimes against humanity—Case studies. | Political
    atrocities—Case studies. | Crimes against humanity—Cambodia. |
    Crimes against humanity—Argentina. | Political atrocities—Cambodia.
    | Political atrocities—Argentina. | Genocide—Cambodia. | Argentina—
    History—Dirty War, 1976-1983.
Classification: LCC HV6322.7 .R63 2023 (print) | LCC HV6322.7 (ebook) |
    DDC 364.15/109596—dc23/eng/20221021
LC record available at https://lccn.loc.gov/2022022364
LC ebook record available at https://lccn.loc.gov/2022022365

Typeset by Elliott Beard in Minion Pro 10/14

Cover design by Derek Thornton / Notch Design
Cover image: Shutterstock 208029595

We dedicate this book to our fathers,
Ladson Hinton and the late Antonius Johannes Robben

Contents

List of Illustrations

Foreword

TONY ROBBEN AND ALEX HINTON'S *Perpetrators* is a multifaceted, unsettling, and intellectually and ethically powerful encounter with "humanity's dark side," with the authors' individual and collective quest for practical wisdom, and with the limits of human knowledge in the face of psychological and social suffering. Inspired by a not-so-random meeting in Buenos Aires, where Tony was conducting research on crimes against humanity and Alex was attending a genocide studies conference, the two senior scholars began a comparative conversation—about methodology, the underlying drivers of mass violence, and the nature of perpetration itself, among other topics—that matured over the years through various iterations. That conversation ultimately became the basis for this extraordinary book.

As the authors explain, *Perpetrators* can and will be read by different people for different purposes. For some it will be a primer of sorts on the critical social-scientific study of those who design, organize, and facilitate mass violence. For others it will be a collective and deeply felt reflection on the destabilizing and finally unresolvable tensions that ensnare genocide researchers. For still others, it will be a window into the professional and personal consequences that come from making the decision to devote a career to a "polyphonic" encounter with those whose all-too-eager "willingness to commit horrendous acts" is readily justified by a "sense of duty to a greater cause."

These consequences have become particularly acute in recent years within a range of academic disciplines, including anthropology and law, which have nurtured epistemological reorientations that call attention to what Nancy Scheper-Hughes described as the "primacy of the ethical," that is, the privileging of the ethical implications of research over the search for truth, meaning, or understanding. As Robben and Hinton note, Scheper-Hughes (in)famously put her call for a "militant" approach to social research to the test when she went undercover to conduct a covert study of organ trafficking, research-activism that led to the arrest and incarceration of a number of traffickers.

Although they are sympathetic to the "good intentions" behind ethically militant social research, the authors of *Perpetrators* reject it as a basis for perpetration studies, a stance that they acknowledge puts them at odds with a powerful moralism at the center of various contemporary social, political, and legal sciences. Instead of "undercover" studies of perpetrators of mass violence that might likewise yield evidence of crimes and culpability, the authors argue for something radically different: an approach to the unbearable complexity of genocide and mass violence that is grounded in what they describe as a "shared humanity," a grounding that must reckon with the fact that perpetration is often animated by politics and practices that manifestly deny the humanity of genocide's victims.

Despite the risks of elevating the search for a "shared humanity" above the prevailing demands for engagement, militancy, and "collaboration with . . . organized groups in struggle for social justice," as another scholar has urged, what is crystal clear is that Robben and Hinton are not promoting a kind of ethical detachment masquerading as better social science. Rather, their call to privilege dialogue and the multiplicity of things that bind together the participants in history's darkest moments—including the researcher—should be understood as an alternative ethics, an alternative form of scientific militancy whose enduring value should be, but likely isn't, obvious to most people.

For that is perhaps the most wide-ranging lesson to be drawn from

Perpetrators, one to which the authors themselves can only allude. By centering the book's narrative on the figures of Alfredo Astiz, Argentina's "Blond Angel," and Duch, the commandant of S-21, the Khmer Rouge's notorious "security center" where—according to Duch—new arrivals were treated as already-dead people whose ends were temporarily deferred, Robben and Hinton shed light on an essential political truth. Astiz was merely among the most iconic of the many who believed they were waging a necessarily ruthless fight in an existential battle against the dark forces of communism; Duch, by contrast, oversaw one of history's worst atrocities as part of the same existential battle, yet on behalf of communism, revolutionary change, and what might anachronistically be described as "social justice."

In other words, the road to genocide and crimes against humanity leads through the politics of both the right and the left, at least in their most extreme, most fundamentalist, and most authoritarian versions. Although *Perpetrators* will serve first and foremost as a guidepost to future researchers who likewise will make the perilous journey that is required to understand humanity's dark side—its meanings, its roots, its lasting consequences—it also sheds critical historical light on the danger of radical politics as such, the ways in which processes of dehumanization are always unleashed for what its proponents claim are the noblest of reasons.

Mark Goodale
Series Editor
STANFORD STUDIES IN HUMAN RIGHTS

Preface

THIS BOOK IS BASED ON several decades of research in Cambodia and Argentina that was financed by many foundations. Alex Hinton would like to thank the Foundation for Psycho-Cultural Research, Institute for Advanced Study at Princeton, Institute for the Study of World Politics, Mellon Foundation, National Science Foundation, National Institute of Health, Rutgers Research Council, Southeast Asia Summer Studies Institute, Social Science Research Council, and United States Institute of Peace. Antonius Robben wants to thank the Harry Frank Guggenheim Foundation, National Science Foundation, David Rockefeller Center at Harvard University, and Netherlands Foundation for Scientific Research for their generous grants. The ideas expressed, of course, are those of the authors.

We cannot list the hundreds of research participants who made our research in Cambodia and Argentina possible and the numerous colleagues who contributed to our work with critical questions and constructive comments. We thank them collectively. Nevertheless, we do make a few exceptions. Two anonymous reviewers improved the book substantially with their astute observations and helpful suggestions. We are equally grateful to Uğur Ümit Üngör for reading the first draft and posing provocative questions in an extended email exchange. We have presented portions of this correspondence in the book. Finally, we want to thank series editor Mark Goodale and editor-in-chief Kate Wahl for encouraging this book project, and acquisitions editor Dylan Kyung-lim White and assistant editor Sunna Juhn for guiding us through the publishing process. Thanks also to Gigi Mark for her work on this manuscript during the production process. Alex would also like to thank the Documentation Center of Cambodia for granting permission to use several images in this book.

PERPETRATORS

Approaching Perpetrator Research

THIS BOOK BEGAN with the Blond Angel. In March 2010, we were in Buenos Aires. Tony was conducting fieldwork on the aftermath of the mass violence that had been inflicted by a military dictatorship (1976–83) known for its forced disappearances. Alex was participating in a genocide studies conference. At the time, he was conducting research on the UN-sponsored Extraordinary Chambers in the Courts of Cambodia. This tribunal was established long after the genocide to try senior Khmer Rouge leaders for atrocity crimes committed during the Cambodian genocide (1975–79), which took place at roughly the same time as the political violence in Argentina.

In both countries, justice had been long delayed. At the time, a domestic tribunal was underway in Argentina. One of Alex's conference hosts suggested that he attend the Argentine tribunal before the start of the conference. As it happened, the person on trial that day was Alfredo Astiz, a notorious military officer who the Mothers of the Plaza de Mayo nicknamed "the Blond Angel" and "Blondie." He had infiltrated their group under the pseudonym "Gustavo Niño" on the pretext of searching for his disappeared brother. Astiz was very much a "spectacular perpetrator," known for his good looks, playboy lifestyle, and involvement in a series of high-profile disappearances. He was also accused personally of torturing some of the victims. During the trial

1

session Alex attended, Astiz proclaimed his innocence, arguing that strong action had to be taken to confront the dire threat posed by subversives seeking to overthrow the Argentine state.

Afterward we met for coffee, as we had known each other for years. We strolled to the Recoleta neighborhood, trying to maintain a conversation but frequently interrupted by the noise of the dense traffic. Our destination couldn't have been more appropriate, because the neighborhood was named after the Recollects, an order of reclusive monks who spent the day in spiritual reflection when they lived there in a convent two centuries ago. Calm finally descended over the afternoon when we ordered coffee at a sidewalk café in a large pedestrian area.

"What struck you most about this morning's testimony by Astiz?" asked Tony, as we waited for our coffee.

"Well," Alex replied, "he reminded me of Duch, the former Khmer Rouge commandant I'm writing a book about. Duch was in charge of S-21, an infamous security center that is a sort of Cambodian 'Auschwitz' or 'ESMA' [a notorious detention and torture center in Argentina]. Duch's the first person to be tried at the UN-backed tribunal in Cambodia. Over twelve thousand people were executed under his watch, many after being tortured into making forced confessions."

"Which kind of similarities are you thinking of?" Tony followed up. "Can you really compare the commander of a torture center to a low-ranking officer, like Astiz, who belonged to an operational task group that hunted down political opponents and guerrilla insurgents?"

"There are a bunch of similarities," Alex responded. "Both were part of a machinery of mass murder that had chains of command even as people had leeway to act within them. And both seem to still believe in the original cause. Duch expressed remorse for the deaths during his trial, but you can tell he thinks the fight against 'hidden enemies burrowing from within' was just. Astiz seemed to be saying something similar during his hearing today. What did you find during your research on him?"

"Astiz, unlike Duch," Tony replied, "never had any moral misgivings about torturing and killing people. He is already serving a life sentence in prison and still believes that the Argentine military were fighting a just war against leftist revolutionaries threatening to take over the country. He was a loyal, low-ranking navy officer following the daily orders to track down and either kill or abduct guerrilla insurgents and political activists." Tony added: "The freedom of action and improvisation was appealing to Astiz. Apparently, he was good at the play of deception, considering his infiltration among the Mothers of the Plaza de Mayo, and his covert operations in Chile and the Falkland/Malvinas Islands. Duch and Astiz differed in rank and ideology but shared the sense of duty to a greater cause and the willingness to commit horrendous acts."

The photo in figure 1 was taken in 1985 at an appeals court hearing. Alfredo Astiz had been accused of the disappearance of the Swedish teenager Dagmar Hagelin but was acquitted by a military court. The Federal Court of Appeals asked him to appear in a lineup as a civil-

FIGURE 1. Navy Lieutenant Alfredo Astiz, alias "the Blond Angel." Source: Wikimedia Commons.

ian, but he refused.[1] He presented himself to the court in his navy lieutenant's uniform to emphasize that he had operated under orders during the military dictatorship.

For hours, our conversation continued in this manner as we discussed our years of research with perpetrators. If Astiz and Duch provided a starting point, our conversation ranged far and wide and touched on areas of research that were understudied, especially anthropology's lack of methodological reflection on encounters with perpetrators of mass violence in the field.

In 2018, we decided to continue the conversation and help fill this key gap by writing this book. Our thinking had developed considerably since our meeting in 2010, and perpetrator studies—which, as Alex notes in the next chapter, dates back to attempts to account for Nazi atrocities— had evolved into a full-blown interdisciplinary field of research with a journal, conferences, and an interdisciplinary network.[2] Perhaps most important, there were many students and scholars, both emerging and established, who were undertaking research on perpetrators.

As the subtitle of this book suggests, our goal is to deepen the study of perpetrators with the insights we have acquired through decades of on-the-ground research into genocide and mass violence committed by authoritarian states. Our lessons learned extend to fieldwork with perpetrators who operate in security forces, revolutionary insurgencies, terrorist organizations, and racist supremacist groups. We examine the challenges of interviewing those violent actors and processing the accompanying emotions. We also consider how the personal and interpersonal impact of this sort of research informs the writing process.

This book is the outcome of our efforts, which encompass everything from the researcher's dreams to the dangers of ethnographic seduction when perpetrators try to make the interviewer accept their account as the only truth. We focus on our fieldwork relations with perpetrators and show how ethnographic knowledge is constructed intersubjectively. And we analyze our research practices in Argentina and Cambodia, and we examine each other's ideas to draw general lessons for the benefit of other scholars.

In this book we work to shed light on fieldwork with perpetrators based on the practical wisdom we have gained through years of research on them—what the ancient Greeks called *phronesis*. Each of the chapters and interludes in this book is informed by this phronesis, a point we return to in the book's conclusion. So, too, are our writing strategies. Each of us began writing about perpetrators through conventional ethnography. Over time, we both became convinced of the importance of writing about perpetrators in more experimental ways, a conviction that informs this book from start to finish.

Thus, we began this introduction with remembered dialogue from our 2010 discussion at a coffeehouse in Buenos Aires. The remainder of this introduction, in turn, intersperses expository prose with dialogue reflecting the conversations we had as we wrote this book—in a manner that echoes the creative interludes we intersperse between the three sections of this book.

Perpetrators: Who and What Are They?

Perpetrators seldom regard themselves as such because perpetrator is an indeterminate concept. Etymologically related to the Latin term *perpetrāre*, *perpetrator* (and its verb form *perpetrate*) connotes performance and execution in the sense of denoting someone who "carries out" an action, particularly one that is "evil" or "criminal, immoral, or harmful."[3] Indeed, the term, which is rooted in a Judeo-Christian genealogy, has come to have a strong legal inflection while also suggesting boundary transgression (e.g., against another person, a social community, a legal order, the state). This book is therefore not about perpetrators in the legal sense as everyday offenders of civil and criminal law but about actors involved in mass violence.

The term *perpetrator* is deeply intertwined with a mirror term, *victim* (and here again our focus is on victims of mass violence as opposed to victims of ordinary crimes). The term has an implied sense of innocence that relates to its early biblical meaning of victims as offerings to a deity or as scapegoats sacrificed to atone for a great harm, such as an epidemic or a war.

The semantic association of perpetrators with victims influences fieldwork. Regarding research participants as perpetrators—instead of patriots, idealists, revolutionaries, or bureaucrats—may have an impact on interviews and provoke strong emotional reactions. A further complication is that perpetrators may be victims. For example, child soldiers may be considered legally accountable for their violent acts, but the circumstances of their forced recruitment into an army or militia attenuates their moral responsibility. In other situations, perpetrators may come under suspicion and be arrested, as was the case with many of the prisoners in the Khmer Rouge security center Duch ran. Even as we note some of these complexities, connotations, and limitations to our *perpetrator* keyword, however, we argue that there are good reasons for using this key concept, in part because it offers valuable analytical affordances.

Who are perpetrators? We begin with a working definition inflected by our concern with perpetrators of mass violence and the emerging literature in perpetrator studies. Perpetrators are active participants in state institutions and repressive organizations or informal associations and networks who carry out genocide, mass killings, or violent acts for the presumed greater good of the state, a people, or an ideology.

Our definition is deliberately broad because perpetrators are active in various types of organizations and have therefore varying degrees of involvement and responsibility for the violence committed. The command-and-control procedures of standing armies and police forces imply that officials of different ranks may be responsible for the same violent act, whereas a loosely organized white supremacist group often consists of members who don't need orders from above to act violently and often communicate through social media technologies.

These differences complicate the conceptualization and identification of perpetrators. For example, low-ranking officers or police may argue that they are not responsible for the violence because they were following orders, whereas their superiors claim that their legitimate orders were not carried out to the letter. Likewise, the founders and spokespersons of supremacist and racist groups may dissociate themselves from violent acts committed in the group's name, saying that they have no control over the actions of their sympathizers.

The closer they are to the violent act, the easier it seems to identify perpetrators. Perpetrators harm and kill people, but not everyone who takes a life is a perpetrator. The murderer, the hangman, and the physician who performs euthanasia are not perpetrators. The first acts out of personal motives and circumstance, the second carries out a verdict, and the third fulfills an authorized request. However, the assassin who eliminates political enemies, the executioner who takes partisans to the gallows, and the physician who administers lethal injections in a eugenics program are perpetrators. But what about a policeman who kills a nonviolent street protester at a political rally, or members of the Ku Klux Klan who lynch a Black man? We regard them also as perpetrators, rather than criminals, because they committed violence as members of respectively a state institution and a formal organization. Perpetrators of mass violence, in other words, are embedded in institutions, associations, or networks.

Scholars have developed different typologies to distinguish perpetrators of mass violence, each with strengths and weaknesses.[4] We find the tripartite model of Üngör and Anderson to be useful for the purposes of this book because it differentiates architects, organizers, and killers who correspond to "different layers of authority, different motives of involvement, different rules of engagement, and changes in these factors over time."[5] While there are other ways of categorizing perpetrators, Üngör and Anderson's three levels make analytical distinctions that acknowledge real-world fluidity as individual perpetrators move between levels or combine several positions within the same level.

For example, militias that operated during the civil wars of Liberia and Sierra Leone were run by commanders who allowed their combatants to commit horrendous acts of violence and involved them also in the trade of blood diamonds. Danny Hoffman shows how these militias did not constitute hierarchical military organizations but consisted of patron-client relationships between ruthless, powerful men who provided protection, food, shelter, and weapons to their armed men and then demanded loyalty and labor in return. As in other loose associations, these dependency relations could be challenged by ambitious combatants who tried to become patrons themselves by luring away clients from weakened commanders.[6]

Perpetrator-architects refer not only to the Hitlers, Stalins, and Pol Pots of this world but also to the leaders and prominent members who serve under them as part of the inner circle of decision-making. They help justify the violence of their own subordinates on ideological or strategic grounds, but they do not formulate detailed plans. The study of these architects requires sufficient historical knowledge because such violence generally occurs during wars or civil strife with public expressions of racist, supremacist, anti-Semitic, and anti-Muslim sentiment. These circumstances result in definitions of individuals, groups, and organizations as enemies whose annihilation promises to create a better society.

This targeting is a process of priming society for violent action against people who are portrayed as posing an existential threat to society. The political situation in Cambodia in the mid-1970s illustrates this process.[7] Against the backdrop of an enormous socioeconomic upheaval (the Vietnam War, civil war, foreign incursion, economic stress, and US carpet-bombing), a genocide emerged in Cambodia that upended systems of meaning and ways of life. The Khmer Rouge offered a vision of renewal that appealed to many, even as it demonized certain groups that were targeted for elimination after the Khmer Rouge took power.

Mid-level organizers operationalize destructive doctrines and objectives as specific procedures and killing methods. The organization of violent death can take the form of a bureaucracy with a clear task division and chain of command, but it may also consist of spontaneous actions taken by lower-level groups and actors. Procedures are developed as the perpetration unfolds because the killing is improvised in response to the unpredictable reactions of executioners, victims, witnesses, bystanders, prosecutors, foreign governments, and human rights organizations.

Scholarly attention is often focused on what Üngör and Anderson have called perpetrator-killers because they are most directly involved in the violence. We prefer the term *perpetrator-facilitators* because the social category of "killers" is not restricted to perpetrators who physically kill people but also includes interrogators, guards, and physicians who have contact with, harm in ways large and small, and help facilitate the violence and killing.

The study of perpetrator-facilitators raises questions about agency, motivation, and dehumanization. We touch upon these issues in this book, but the research of Martha Huggins and her collaborators about police violence in Brazil during the military dictatorship (1964–85) is instructive here. The researchers distinguish torturers from executioners on the basis of the different practices of each. To be most effective, torturers try to understand the psychological makeup and vulnerabilities of their victims. They build personal relationships based on complete dependency in order to extract information with torture methods adapted to each individual victim. One person breaks down through humiliation, while another fears waterboarding and threats to family members. Torturers who cause the accidental death of a victim consider it a failure that angers their superiors because they do not obtain the sought-after information. In the case of Brazil, executioners instead acted fast. They knew little about their victims and did not face the moral dilemmas of torturers who had some kind of personal relationship with their captives.[8]

The division of tasks of repression was standard practice in Brazil, but there and in other places, the roles of executioners and torturers are often not so clearly defined. A manual for Khmer Rouge interrogators gave the following instruction: "Thus we beat them to make them afraid but absolutely not to kill them. . . . Don't greedily want to quickly kill them—bring them to death."[9] The same combination of roles occurred in Argentina, where an interrogator told his victim: "If you talk I'll offer you an easy death, a shot; if not, a pig's death through torture."[10]

We want to emphasize that there are also violent abusers who do not go to the extremes documented in dictatorial Argentina, Brazil, and Cambodia. Beatrice Jauregui conducted fieldwork among police in the Indian state of Uttar Pradesh, showing that officers continuously wavered between authoritative control and coercive violence to enforce the law. Much depended on the situation. For example, if outnumbered by a violent crowd, they might resort to excessive violence to disperse the rioters or keep crime rates down. Police officers were involved in illegal detentions and extrajudicial killings, but at other times they worked by the rules. Jauregui concludes that Indian officers negotiated the maintenance of public order through legal and extralegal means.[11] This vacillation is a challenge to researchers, because perpetrators are likely to situate themselves at a far end of the spectrum from force to violence.

Such perpetrators are also often depicted as either monsters and perverted sadists or ordinary human beings trapped in repressive organizations. Similarly, the scholarly debate over the Nazi bureaucrat Adolf Eichmann was about his humanity, not about whether he organized the mass deportation of Jews to concentration camps. The Israeli prosecutor contended that Eichmann was coldhearted and evil. Hannah Arendt argued the opposite: "The trouble with Eichmann was precisely that so many were like him, and that the many were neither perverted nor sadistic, that they were, and still are, terribly and terrifyingly normal."[12] Eichmann positioned himself as a victim whose virtuous obedience had been exploited by his superiors: "I am not the monster I am made out to be."[13] Many perpetrator trials have been informed by the opposed characterizations of monster versus human being, and similar lines of defense as Eichmann's have been heard from terrorists, abusive police, and racist offenders: they were following orders or believed themselves to be fighting for a greater good and a better world.

The Soviet writer Vasily Grossman, referring to the calamitous rise of German fascism, believed that human beings contain both good and evil. "There's a great deal in all of us that is false, coarse and primitive, an unholy mixture of stuff usually kept under wraps," he wrote. "Many people living in normal social conditions have no idea of the cellars and basements of their own being. But there has been a catastrophe—and vermin of every kind have escaped from the cellars. Now they are at large, scuttling through rooms that were once bright and clean."[14] Grossman was suggesting that we all have darkness lurking in the recesses of our interior. We may see ourselves as morally upright, but our baseness is always ready to burst forth under extreme circumstances.

The assumption that human beings harbor good and evil is often related to moral agency. The Christian belief that people choose to act in either moral or immoral ways, while allowing for some forgivable shades in between, and the notion that right or unjust acts stem from a personal disposition in a receptive environment, are commonly held opinions in the Western world. These viewpoints don't necessarily exist in cultures with other moralities and may not apply to situations in which people's existence is at stake. Moral codes and war conventions, for example, can be violated as a last resort. However, as the political philosopher Michael Walzer has argued, a just war doesn't exempt the belligerents from their responsibility for unjust deeds.[15] This question of accountability is relevant to research with perpetrators. What are the ethical concerns and obligations of ethnographers toward perpetrators? How should fieldworkers prepare themselves for research interviews with different types of perpetrators?

We didn't have any clear answers in mind when we wrote those rhetorical questions. More questions were raised by the leading scholar of genocide and perpetrator studies, Uğur Ümit Üngör, during a Q&A about the book's first draft. Large parts of this correspondence have been incorporated throughout this introduction. New issues arose once we finished the final manuscript. We decided to explore them further by email, and thus continue the conversation we had begun in Buenos Aires. We have inserted these exchanges throughout this book, using our familiar names, Alex and Tony. The dialogue allowed us to reflect in more general terms on our fieldwork experience and offers readers an opportunity to rethink our conceptualization of mass violence and perpetration.

———

ALEX: How do you fit the indeterminacy of perpetrators into Üngör and Anderson's tripartite model [i.e., architects, organizers, killers], and how would you compare such diverse perpetrators as Argentine intelligence officers operating in a dictatorial state and Indian police officers working under democracy?

TONY: This is a tough question because of the major status differences among the three types of perpetrators and the cultural, historical, and political variations between the two countries. Perpetrators are not one-dimensional violent actors but have particular functions, personalities, social backgrounds, and goals in life. Yet as the tripartite model shows, perpetrators can nevertheless be classified from high to low on the organizational scale, irrespective of the national circumstances. Perpetrators make those distinctions themselves. Once, I told an Argentine general that I had interviewed a lieutenant-colonel who had tortured captives. I forgot to say that he was a first lieutenant during the dictatorship. The general burst out: "A lieutenant-colonel? Then he must be a sadist!" It was obvious to him that low-ranking officers may torture people but not when they move up the ladder. This prompts the question what low- and mid-level perpetrators have in common. Can we compare the Holocaust's principal organizer Adolf Eichmann to the concentration camp guard John Demjanjuk?

We should be careful not to concentrate exclusively on violence. A framework that centers narrowly on, say, genocide or hate crimes ignores the gradual process through which perpetrators are coaxed into acts of violence on behalf of the state, a terrorist organization, or a racist group. A singular focus on violent action leads to a biased portrayal of perpetrators. Instead, we must give thought to the multiple facets of perpetrators that emerge under complex personal and political circumstances.

Researchers need to extend the meaning of the term *perpetrator* to those who are participants in atrocity crimes that are committed to serve a greater cause at whichever organizational and operational level. This includes guards, physicians, informers, and hate preachers without whose support the atrocious crimes would not have taken place. I'm aware that this delimitation is debatable. There are no universal criteria. Researchers need to weigh each and every case. Still, I maintain that the type of perpetrators we are discussing in this book are always political actors, in the sense that they don't act primarily for personal motives. Perpetrators exercise power over others in positions organized and approved by their comrades or superiors. They may steal for personal enrichment, but theft is an ordinary criminal act.

How do you see this, Alex?

ALEX: One common move is to deploy analytical difference to distinguish between micro-, meso-, and macrolevels or the parallel scheme of killers, organizers, and architects developed by Üngör and Anderson. While these schemes can be used in different ways, including dynamic ones, they may also lead to the assumption that the killers are somehow categorically different from the architects. And even these terms inflect our attention in a particular direction, foregrounding and backgrounding issues—such as the "killer" category, which erases related forms of violence, ranging from torture to those who detain and guard victims, which is not in line with the executioner connotations of killers, which is why we prefer the term *facilitators*. So, to return full circle, I would urge researchers to focus on process and be very careful with typologies, even as they can, when used with care (as Üngör and Anderson do), be useful analytical containers and facilitate research. The problem arises when we get stuck in the language of these perpetrator containers and can't see out of them.

The issue of culture speaks further to this point, since the very idea of perpetrator is enmeshed in a particular linguistic tradition and intellectual genealogy. What would it mean if we began our research with local glosses for perpetrator? It would, I would wager, disrupt our disciplinary assumptions and enable us to see the perpetrator in different sorts of ways. Like you, of course, I'm biased in this regard as an anthropologist, and I always ask myself how global or transitional justice is understood by people on the ground, for whom such imaginaries may not be very relevant at all.

TONY: Another commonality among perpetrators is that they dehumanize people. When people are regarded as "cockroaches," as happened to the Tutsis during the Rwandan genocide, or as class enemies who pose an existential threat, as was common in the Soviet Union and communist Cambodia, then perpetrators feel morally justified to harm others. The same is of course true for policemen who regard migrant workers and homeless people as "animals," or for Islamist jihadists who defend indiscriminate attacks on Jews and Christians considered "infidels."

ALEX: This issue of dehumanization speaks directly to the notion of difference you mention, but in terms of process. Perpetrator studies too often get stuck in static typologies due to the figurations that inform the field. One of these is to juxtapose the perpetrator as a "monster" to the perpetrator as "an ordinary human being." Another figuration that has had much influence on the field is Hannah Arendt's portrayal of Eichmann as the embodiment of the banality of evil. There is, of course, great diversity in the field, and some scholars focus on dynamics and process. But quite a bit of perpetrator research is informed by "the perpetrator" figuration with its criminal overtones—and by implication the objectivity and rationality of perpetrator research.

Interviewing Perpetrators

Perpetrators are clearly not of a singular kind. The different positions and functions of architects, organizers, and facilitators therefore affect their relationship with the ethnographer and influence the form and content of their interviews. Leigh Payne, who spoke with perpetrators in Argentina, Chile, Brazil, and South Africa, argues that perpetrators create scripts that do not necessarily correspond to what happened, and they adjust those scripts according to changing personal and political circumstances. They draw on a broad range of accounts that include "remorse, heroism, denial, sadism, silence, fiction and lies, amnesia, and betrayal."[16] Payne points out that research interviews are performances intended to foster a favorable impression in the other. Inspired by the dramaturgical approach of Erving Goffman, she regards people as social actors who erect a personal front that includes choice of clothing, hairstyle, speech pattern, and body language. A soft-spoken interviewee, reclining on an old sofa in his living room, leaves a very different impression from that of a retired officer in uniform who sits upright at his shining hardwood desk and speaks in a strong, decisive voice.

Fieldworkers and informants alike try to project favorable self-images onto each other and conceal any conduct that can harm that impression: "The ethnographer seeks access to back-region information; the subjects seek to protect their secrets since these represent a threat to the public image they wish to maintain."[17] Goffman has described how groups protect their secrets.[18] Such defensive practices are also common among perpetrators. They cultivate group solidarity and maintain pacts of silence. Fieldworkers will try to breach those defenses in interviews but may run up against solid personal fronts.

Like Eichmann, perpetrators want to erase the monstrous image created of them in the media. A welcoming reception and a courteous demeanor are common ways to put an apprehensive ethnographer at ease. Appearing caring and morally upright instead of threatening and authoritarian can undo some of the interviewer's negative preconceptions. Payne punctured the impression management of her interviewees by analyzing their performance in terms of the following aspects: "who tells the story of the past (actor), what they say (script), how they say it (acting), and where (stage) and when (timing) they say it."[19] A concentrated attention to the construction of a performance helps prevent fieldworkers from allowing their thoughts to wander toward speculating about the atrocities the interviewee might have committed. Much depends, of course, on the type of perpetrator the fieldworkers are facing. Jessee and Anderson point out that fieldworkers should always ask themselves why perpetrators are collaborating with them, what's at stake for them, which revisionist and self-interested narratives are promoted, and how their comrades and peers look upon the interviews.[20]

Perpetrator-architects are far removed from the actual violence. Mainly concerned with strategic issues, they have little to offer researchers in terms of knowledge about torture and execution but can provide insight into the worldview that informed the stigmatization and persecution of people defined as enemies. As part of this priming process, architects often propagate their convictions publicly in pamphlets, books, and speeches, on websites, and in conversations with journalists. In an interview, they may downplay the influence of their public words and belittle the violence for which they are considered responsible. They may justify the violence as inevitable to reaching goals such as protecting the public order, enforcing the law, preserving racial "purity," and combating revolutionaries of whatever utopian ideology. It is hard for researchers, especially foreign ones, to avoid being dragged into ideological discussions with architects who have a superior knowledge of their country's history and raise moral dilemmas and common-sense arguments to answer critical questions such as, "What would you have done if revolutionaries killed your wife, assassinated policemen, and threatened to forbid people's freedom of religion?" These architects owe their position to communications skills that handicap researchers from the start and require a concentrated attention to the interview's content and form.

Perpetrator-architects pursue the destruction of people regarded as enemies. The translation of this objective into an actionable design depends on the means at their disposal. Totalitarian states have repressive forces in place that can execute the mass violence through organizational channels, whereas the architects of political movements may delegate the violence to local groups. Al-Qaeda exemplifies the latter. This political-religious movement was designed by Osama bin Laden as a global network of locally emerging clusters of operatives. Bin Laden maintained his influence by furnishing or withholding funds for their operations. The clusters had different organizational characteristics; some were hierarchical, and others more bottom-up and flexible.[21]

Of course, violent jihadists are unlikely research participants, but we mention al-Qaeda because its networked organization is also found in other loose associations. A more recent development is the resurgence of racist and supremacist groups that are not part of a national or supranational network but organize more loosely through social media, where hostile sentiments and conspiracy theories circulate. Their networks are structured more rhizomatically and are symbiotic with local circumstances. These movements do not have identifiable architects, which obliges researchers to compose an organizational design from the violent practices of diverse but like-minded groups. The research emphasis lies then entirely on the meso- and micro-levels of perpetration.

Perpetrator-organizers often claim that they only carried out the directives from above and were unable to oversee their implementation below them. They managed the repressive organization and assigned the personnel but cannot be blamed for any atrocious acts. They may have trained operatives in arming car bombs but do not consider themselves responsible for the civilian deaths caused by a poorly executed detonation intended for a military convoy. This defense is too facile. How the violence is organized—centralized, decentralized, divisional, networked—influences the type, degree, and delegation of perpetration. Organizers who create a structure that gives members at the grassroots level great freedom of action continue to be responsible for the violence by having decided to relinquish their direct oversight.

Knowledge about the organization of violence is important to improve the quality of the research interview, although the organizational structures of still-active groups are hard to locate because they contain crucial information about the coordination and execution of violence. In postconflict situations, researchers can often gain access to declassified documents about these organizational structures to help them ask the most effective questions to organizers.

Perpetrator-facilitators seldom admit that they chose to kill and are therefore the hardest interlocutors to interview—unless they have remorse and decided to renounce their past actions. They often present themselves as reluctant perpetrators who carried out orders but disliked harming their victims. Indeed, some portray themselves as victims as well and dismiss the cruel treatment of captives as excesses committed by a handful of sadists. In the absence of direct oversight, they decided when and where to strike and how to improvise the exercise of violence in given situations. Before interviewing them, researchers should consult readily available sources, such as newspapers, court records, truth commission reports, and the published confessions of penitents. Nevertheless, facilitators are unlikely to supply detailed information about their violent acts. Ethnographers should therefore interview victim-survivors to sharpen the questions posed to facilitators, even as they also need to be aware of the intersubjective dynamics with and framings of victim-survivors.

Like other professional academic codes of ethics, the American Anthropological Association's Principles of Professional Responsibility states that the pursuit of knowledge must never override the ethical obligations to research participants, which include acquiring informed consent and protecting their privacy, dignity, and safety. However, there are anthropologists who argue that our moral duty to victims of injustice is greater than the duty of loyalty to the professional code of ethics. Nancy Scheper-Hughes is the principal proponent of this stance. She conducted undercover ethnography to expose the illegal trade of human organs, donning various disguises to infiltrate networks of organs traffickers and providing criminal evidence to authorities.[22]

Whether fieldwork with perpetrators is conducted in covert or transparent ways, there will always be unknowns. Witnesses are killed and archives incinerated after the violence has ceased. Yael Navaro has argued that anthropologists must pay more attention to the gaps of knowledge left in the wake of mass violence. She proposes a counter-methodological approach that examines absences in the evidence of mass atrocities.[23] For example, the destruction of the gas chambers and the exhumation and cremation of the Jews murdered at the Treblinka extermination camp were acts of erasure intended to conceal incriminating evidence. The gas chamber's subsoil foundation is a material trace of the camp; it was discovered in 2010 through a noninvasive archaeological survey. Its functioning can be reconstructed through the testimonies of the few survivors and a comparison with the Majdanek camp captured intact by Soviet troops.

Another example of how absences can reveal mass violence is shown in the memorialization of the Holocaust. The Holocaust can be conveyed by the remaining barracks and ruined crematoria of Auschwitz-Birkenau but also by making the annihilation of the Jewish people visible through the small brass "stumbling stones" (*Stolpersteine*) placed in sidewalks throughout Europe before homes whose residents were deported to their death in extermination camps. Navaro mentions the study of the forensic and traumatic afterlives of mass graves and enforced disappearances, of ruins and rubble, and of the human and material remains of undocumented migrants as other examples of a negative methodology that examines the traces of the missing victims of mass violence instead of focusing only on the survivors.[24]

We would like to add the study of perpetrators as an additional research subject for a negative methodology, because perpetrators often try to destroy incriminating evidence and persist in denying indisputable criminal facts. An ethnographer who interviews convicted perpetrators may be confronted with denials, evasions, and silences that are just as much acts of erasure as the physical destruction of a torture center. The perpetrator's obfuscation of a dark past creates a void in the data collection.

Still, the denials are traces of violence that can be examined by an interviewer sensitive to the interviewee's discourse. This line of questioning will help the researcher delineate the contours of the knowledge gaps—the perimeter of what cannot be pronounced and the point at which questions meet silence. These voids can then be explored indirectly with archival material and testimonial evidence, truth commission reports and trial records, and the confessions of a few repentant perpetrators. This approach provides a way of grappling with the particular challenges of perpetrator research while adhering to professional codes of ethics. Perpetrators are given the opportunity to speak their minds freely, including the denial of legal evidence, and are not deceived about the fieldworker's identity and research objectives. Such interviews should not be regarded as failures, because they set the fieldworker on a path toward new research questions that can be examined in other ways.

The intersubjective construction of ethnographic knowledge has convinced some anthropologists that fieldwork is a collaborative undertaking in which informants are treated as partners in research and writing. Such a positioning is problematic in fieldwork with perpetrators. Perpetrators have too many personal and political stakes in the outcome of the research. The denials, silences, and evasions of confirmed perpetrators disguise mass atrocities. The ethnographer's emotional reactions to the difficult content of interviews with victims of mass violence can serve as additional causeways into such concealed pasts.

———————

ALEX: How have you grappled with such perpetrator denials and deceptions in your research? And more broadly, do you think, as some ethnographers hold, that it is acceptable in such situations to carry out

undercover fieldwork or secretly tape interviews to gather information that cannot be obtained in any other way? Some people also ask
whether researchers should give perpetrators the respect and ethical
concern they never showed to their victims? What are your thoughts on
these charged issues?

TONY: Perpetrator researchers face interlocutors who, with some exceptions, seek to hide their darkest secrets because they want to leave a favorable impression and certainly don't want to incriminate themselves.
Circumventing this deception may seem an attractive option. However,
it's not a foregone conclusion that covert research will yield unique information and insights.

Scholars have a tendency to attribute much value to data that are
hard to get. Anthropologists have submitted themselves to painful initi-
ation rituals to learn secret knowledge. This raises questions about how
we can access the darker side of perpetrators and what we have learned
once we do.

Let me give an example. On one occasion, an Argentine officer ges-
tured that I should stop the tape recorder. He then told me something
off the record which later turned out to be completely false. It makes
me wonder about the reliability of confidential information and whether
covert ethnographic research will yield data that could not be obtained
otherwise.

I believe that, aside from discovering the proverbial smoking gun, a
great deal of information can be acquired in other ways. This has been
shown for decades by Amnesty International and Human Rights Watch
and by the investigative journalists of Bellingcat who have used the internet to document human rights violations by the Syrian government.

At the same time I realize that undercover ethnography may sometimes
lead to shocking revelations that help provide a better understanding and
may even provide legal evidence of serious crimes. Nancy Scheper-Hughes
succeeded in putting several organ traffickers behind bars thanks to her
covert work. In no way do I condemn her or have any doubts about her
good intentions, but I worry about the wider consequences if this approach
becomes common practice. Will the secretly taped perpetrators ever talk

to the ethnographer again after discovering they were tricked, and for that matter, will other perpetrators ever talk to any researcher again? Is the veil of suspicion cast over researchers worth the short-term gain? Please, don't misunderstand: I'm not against public and engaged anthropology, providing expert testimonies in court or sharing information with human rights organizations, but I do have grave doubts about covert fieldwork because I continue to believe in the ethics of transparency. We should do our utmost to uncover the violence ordered and inflicted by perpetrators, but we are not criminal investigators or human rights monitors. I don't feel any moral obligation to protect the reputation of proven perpetrators, as I show in this book, but I do feel ethically obligated to my colleagues and our discipline for not jeopardizing future research projects. What are your thoughts on this, Alex?

ALEX: It's hard to know where to begin since the dilemma you raise about undercover fieldwork has so many layers to it. But perhaps I can start with the chimera, the imaginary of the perpetrator as monster that stands as a first obstacle to research, covert or not. Let's set aside the question of professional ethics for the moment and just consider how having an already coalesced view of the person being interviewed—as a perpetrator-monster—skews research.

A key to perpetrator research is to try to understand such preconceptions we might have and seek, as best as we are able and while being aware of the dynamics of the interview situation, to meet our interviewee, regardless of what they have done, on the ground of shared humanity. It's a bit ironic, I know, given that perpetrators destroy the humanity of their victims. But it is only on this ground, I have found, that we can begin to better understand perpetrators and perpetration.

I'm not one to condemn others on the basis of institutional ethics. After years of research on genocide and mass violence, I'm very wary of moralisms and the way they are too often bound up with ideologies of hate. But it's important to bear in mind the history of human subject protections, which, despite their bureaucratization, excesses, absurdities, and enmeshment with the fear of lawsuits, are meant to serve as a buffer against harming other human beings. These concerns emerged out of a backdrop of research that damaged the subjects in the name of science—not just the Nazi and Japanese medical experiments during World War II but also situations like Philip Zimbardo's Stanford prison experiments in the 1970s.

All of this is a long way of noting that there are good reasons to be cautious about surreptitious research methods that are claimed to be legitimate because the other is "a perpetrator." That's a loaded set of assumptions that may lead to a few good quotes but often bad perpetrator research. The research encounter is never neutral, but we can strive to meet on the grounds of humanity, where understanding hopefully emerges from dialogue. Along these lines, I'm reminded of the US debate about torturing suspected terrorists after 9/11. Harsh and deceptive interrogation techniques rarely worked. Instead, the best information was achieved through patiently built-up rapport, although a rapport of acknowledgment (of humanity) though not one of emotional closeness.

Emotions and Dreams during Fieldwork with Perpetrators

Fieldwork relations are mediated by emotions. Their impact on the intersubjective construction of ethnographic knowledge reaches into and beyond face-to-face meetings. In our case, perpetrators manipulated our interviews and entered our dreams. A reflexive examination of these social processes is essential to discern the constitutive force of emotions in fieldwork and allow researchers to improve the analysis and interpretation of perpetrators and perpetration.

Anthropologists may be the conductors of fieldwork, but they are not always the masters of their emotions. They pursue a good rapport with their research participants but often cannot control the emotions evoked in them by these encounters. It is important for the research not to repress or ignore these emotions, and their study can disclose new layers of cultural understanding. This point was underscored for the first time by two candid ethnographies published in the 1960s. Hortense Powdermaker described how she had been profoundly shaken by the attempted lynching of a wrongly accused Black man in Mississippi. Jean Briggs, in turn, explained why she was ostracized from an Inuit camp in the Canadian Arctic for openly displaying anger. Both contemplated the significance of their emotions in the local cultural context and were able to manage them through self-reflection.[25]

The awareness of such turning points allowed Powdermaker and Briggs to interpret their emotional reactions and resolve the tense relationships with their hosts. Along these lines, some anthropologists have more recently undertaken autoethnographic and autobiographical studies as well as intimate ethnographic studies about fieldwork crises.[26] Other scholars have focused on emotions, feelings, and affects to understand the formation of their professional identities.[27]

The close contact between fieldworkers and perpetrators may be as disturbing as their emotional encounters with victim-survivors. Fieldworkers may experience strong negative emotions (e.g., discomfort, depression, anxiety, fear, anger) and bodily sensations (e.g., nausea, insomnia, lack of appetite) that are provoked by an empathic grasp of the suffering. As the anthropologist and psychotherapist Ivana Maček has observed: "Integrating the emotional impact of these events and experiences and the insights that awareness creates into our work can open the doors to new levels of understanding of mass political violence."[28]

Dreams are another manifestation of the emotional dimension of ethnographic encounters. Not confined to the workings of the unconscious with its deep-lying wishes and internalized conflicts, dreams are tied to people's everyday lives. This "continuity hypothesis" assumes that "patterns in dream content have meaningful continuities with people's concerns, interests, and activities in waking life."[29] Furthermore, cross-cultural studies show that people in many societies assume a relation between the waking world and the world of dreams. Rejecting a strong separation of states of waking and states of dreaming, some people even believe it is possible to intervene in dreams to change their daily reality.[30] In sum, dreams are invested with multiple emotions that percolate night and day through people's lives and whose interpretation may change their conduct.[31] Recent concerns and emotions, what Freud called day residues, appear in a disguised form in dream accounts.

Nightdreams are related to daydreams, which are "fantasies in which one consciously imagines something while fully awake."[32] Both types of dreams contain fantasies that give the illusion of fulfilling a deep wish or a temporary liberation of fears and anxieties in a flight of imagination. Both types are also manifested in distorted thoughts and mental images, but daydreams undergo less repression and revision than nocturnal dreams. Anthropologists like Borneman and Gammeltoft have examined the daydreams of research participants to uncover unconscious and conscious wishes, fears, and anxieties as well as hopes and ideals.[33] They paid less attention to the presence of day residues in the daydreams of their informants and ignored their own daydreams in the field.

We realize that fieldworkers may not remember their nighttime dreams when they awake in the morning and that the self-analysis of the dream narratives is difficult. The advantage of daydreams is their greater accessibility. Ethnographers search continuously for more effective research methods and evaluate the effectiveness of their fieldwork encounters. Daydreams may arise when fieldworkers worry about their research and experience a malaise that saps their energy. They fail to gather the intended data or find that people are unwilling to talk to them or give evasive answers when they do. The ensuing daydreams, then, should be approached not as obstacles but as creative invitations to think outside the methodological box. These fantasies can help fieldworkers disentangle themselves from the strictures of their ethnographic interviews and enable them to come up with new means to engage perpetrators. This has certainly been true with our research when dream traces demonstrated worries and anxieties about our encounters with perpetrators.

––––––––

TONY: How did your dreams about perpetrators affect you and change your understanding of them?

ALEX: There is a direct way in which perpetrator researchers are in a sense "wasted" by who they study and what they grapple with each day. So too, I imagine, are people working in emotionally challenging places ranging from forensic crime scenes to emergency rooms—as dramatically revealed by those working on the front lines of the COVID-19 pandemic. For many in such fields, like those working on perpetrator research, bad dreams come with the turf. But difficult dreams, even those that chill you upon waking from sleep or that emerge as full-blown nightmares, also provide a path to self-growth and a greater understanding of the human condition.

In terms of your question about how I have dealt with dreams throughout time, I have to return to my childhood. My father is a Jungian psychiatrist and dreams were a part of daily conversation. In our household, it was normal to write down, analyze, and talk about dream symbolism. This childhood attention to psychic process has stuck with me into adulthood and has informed my ongoing interpretation of dreams, including those I have had while undertaking fieldwork. But it's not easy. And while doing perpetrator research, I have had awful, violent dreams. Sometimes I go through phases where I don't remember my dreams at all, the battle we all wage with repression and the processing of difficult emotions.

Whatever the state of my dreams, they remain a sort of analytical, ethical, and psychological compass that helps guide me through perpetrator research. I'm curious to know how you dealt with your dreams about perpetrators.

TONY: Alex, I think that your lifelong affinity with dreams is highly unusual in the anthropological and perpetrator researcher communities. Few anthropologists are interested in dreams—neither the dreams of the people they study nor their own. This was very different during the first half of the twentieth century. Especially American anthropologists were influenced by Freud's dream theory and searched for cultural patterns in the dreams of their informants. The study of the unconscious received a boost during the Second World War. Anthropologists such as Ruth Benedict, Margaret Mead, and Geoffrey Gorer collaborated with psychologists like Erich Fromm and Erik Erikson to help the war effort by interpreting the "national character" of their enemies and allies. Other scholars studied Hitler's personality. These national character studies continued into the Cold War. I guess that the growing critique of this too-often-reductionist approach and its neglect of intracultural diversity led most anthropologists to turn away from the study of dreams, which Freud hailed as the royal road to the unconscious.

So even though dreaming about violence and perpetrators during field-work might be inevitable, as you suggest, this doesn't mean that anthro-pologists are in the habit of examining or even remembering their dreams. It was only after I entered psychoanalysis in Buenos Aires to understand its cultural significance through participant observation that I developed the ability to recall my dreams in the morning and write them down for the next consultation hour. I never dared ask Argentine perpetrators about their dreams. To do so was too personal and suspect in a country where dream analysis is common.

Fortunately, unlike you, I never had nightmares. I assume that the writing of fieldnotes and figuring out people's tragic lives, aside from seeing my analyst three times a week, helped to avert the harmful con-sequences of studying violence. I continued recording dreams related to my fieldwork after I left Argentina, but they dropped off very quickly. Oc-casional dreams about perpetrators emerge when I'm writing, but their content revolves mostly around concerns about the writing process.

Writing about Perpetrators

The emotional dynamics of fieldwork complicate the collection and analysis of ethnographic knowledge because the conversion of field data into a text is "an intricate process that moves between different levels of abstraction and makes use of different expressive and rhetorical tech-niques in order to transform one type of information into another."[34] A reflexive examination of the emotions evoked by interviews and field encounters is therefore as necessary to writing as to research.

Andrew Beatty has argued that anthropologists can properly de-scribe their emotions, and those of their research participants, only with a narrative approach, because "ethnographic writing, by design, gets emotion wrong. The methods—analytical, linguistic, experimen-tal, or illustrative—systematically filter out what for actors is of princi-pal significance: namely, history, character, implication, strategy, and plot."[35] Beatty considers Bronislaw Malinowski responsible for the long-standing practice of sifting out the circumstantial aspects of people's lives to arrive at enduring structures, laws, and functions. We do not embrace Beatty's radical position, as we will explain, but his critique shows that the debate about ethnographic writing that began in the 1960s has not died down.

In the 1920s, Bronislaw Malinowski set down the standard for ethnographic texts as objective accounts based on long-term fieldwork and informed by an understanding of people's perspectives on the world. During the 1960s, this ideal of the ethnographer as an omniscient observer and Olympian author was critiqued for muting the informant's voice and disregarding the intersubjective construction of ethnographic knowledge.[36] Clifford Geertz proposed "thick description" as an alternative. Thick description acknowledged people's multiple perspectives and conflicting understandings of their culture and society, even though in this practice the anthropologist remained the authoritative arbiter who interpreted and weighed the various cultural meanings during the process of crafting the ethnographic text.[37]

Geertz successfully displaced Malinowski's experiential mode of ethnographic authority until his interpretive approach was criticized in 1986 by the influential book *Writing Culture*. *Writing Culture* galvanized the spate of reflexive fieldwork accounts and dialogical and polyphonic ethnographies that were appearing under the rallying cry for a "new ethnography."[38] According to James Clifford, the coeditor of *Writing Culture*, the contributors "assume that academic and literary genres interpenetrate and that the writing of cultural descriptions is properly experimental and ethical. Their focus on text making and rhetoric serves to highlight the constructed, artificial nature of cultural accounts."[39] In a rear-guard defense, Geertz responded disparagingly that the "new ethnographers," alternatively called "postmodernists" because of their rejection of grand theories and metanarratives, were suffering from emotional discomfort, one "of estrangement, hypocrisy, helplessness, domination, disillusion."[40]

A more sustained critique came from feminist anthropologists. They stated that feminists had for decades written in imaginative, experimental, and literary styles to expose the subjecthood of women. Feminist anthropologists pointed at the gender bias of the nearly all-male cast of *Writing Culture*, writing from a position of masculine subjectivity and superiority about an "other" who had been exploited during centuries of

Western domination and hegemony. Instead, they were more sensitive to the politics of othering for having been silenced and subjugated in patriarchal societies and universities. They also questioned the sincerity of the mea culpa about anthropology's involvement with Western colonialism and neocolonialism. Postmodern anthropology was demanding a moral reckoning of anthropology, but its mostly male advocates were ill suited to decolonize the discipline without taking heed of the feminist critique of male-authored and male-centered anthropological texts. Finally, feminist anthropologists raised a finger at themselves for falling into the trap of the male-female dichotomy while ignoring the position of women of color and the othering of non-Western women.[41]

The heterogeneous opposition of reflexive, postmodern, feminist, and postcolonial anthropology to conventional and interpretive anthropology had a great impact on the discipline's epistemology and methodology. It legitimized new forms and styles of writing. Current genres include ethnopoetry, blogs, travel accounts, op-eds, memoirs, biographies, autoethnographies, satire, Twitter posts, ethnographic fiction, creative nonfiction, and graphic narratives.[42] A discussion of these genres is beyond the scope of this introduction, but we nevertheless want to clarify our position in the ongoing debate about the merits and drawbacks of experimental ethnographic writing. We do not believe that conventional realistic ethnographic writing should be the golden standard or that one genre is preferable to another. Different genres and styles reveal other cultural realities which together form a composite whole that is superior to any singular representation. We therefore disagree with Beatty that only a narrative approach can adequately represent the emotions of fieldworkers and research participants, especially when the latter are perpetrators.[43]

Given the difficulties of researching perpetrators, it doesn't make sense to dismiss everything besides a narrative approach beforehand. Just as there are different literary narrative styles, each with its expressive strengths and weaknesses, so too do ethnographic writing styles differ in their ability to describe cultural realities and address certain research questions. The narration of personal histories, as recommended by Beatty, will certainly help to apprehend their emotions and intimate experiences in context but will also encumber comparisons and risk making unique what is general. How can ethnographers use creative nonfiction in their writing? Kirin Narayan has written an insightful manual that focuses on four elements to tell a compelling ethnographic story: place, person, voice, and self. She is inspired by the Russian writer Anton Chekhov, who described the tsarist prison colony on Sakhalin Island in the Pacific Ocean with an eye for ethnographic detail. His nonfiction book is situated in a specific place that is much like an ethnographic field site.

Drawing in part on Chekhov, Narayan argues that a detailed, sensory-rich description of the field site, preferably reinforced by an opening scene that unifies place, time, and action, draws the reader into the narrative. Creative ethnographies work best when they highlight specific individuals with fully elaborated personalities whose lives illustrate the research topic. How these individuals speak and hold a conversation further fills out their character. A voice's timbre and the timing of the pauses between words further influence the performance staged before the fieldworker. The way something is said, in turn, informs the meaning of *what* is being said. Very much in line with the reflexive and literary turn, Narayan stresses that fieldworkers should also include themselves into the ethnographic narrative and describe how they changed during the field research.[44]

Where Clifford and Marcus's *Writing Culture* broke new ground by legitimizing experimental styles of ethnographic writing. *Writing Off the Shelf*, edited by Alisse Waterston and Maria Vesperi, takes an additional step, examining the transition from ethnographic writing to creative writing for a nonacademic audience. Waterston and Vesperi note that most of the contributors struggled to free themselves from the academic writing taught in graduate school that is necessary to establish one's professional career. The conventions of providing extensive references, engaging with the scholarly literature, and embedding an argument in a theoretical debate with the anthropological concepts and language in vogue—in addition to having to fit an article's structure into a journal's requirements—usually force ethnographers into a stylistic frame that discourages a popular audience.[45]

Creative ethnographic writing, in contrast, involves making imaginative connections that are not always supported by existing scholarly findings, may not respond to the rigors of what counts as empirical evidence, and often do not fit the conventions of academic journal articles. However, breaking the rules of expository reasoning does not imply that anything goes, since experimental texts are still grounded in fieldwork.

Ethnographic writing about perpetrators poses a distinct set of challenges, including the often-restrained personal contact that ethnographers have with them. Participant observation is rare, though not impossible, as fieldwork among police and armed militias shows, and creating friendships with perpetrators are less likely than with victims and their relatives. Still, this should not deter researchers from writing in imaginative ways. On the contrary, when the limits of fieldwork have been reached, literary experimentation and creative nonfiction become means to extend the lines of reasoning and narration into a world hidden from empirical scrutiny.

Accessible texts about perpetrators give an audience of readers an intimate look into the personal processes that prepared them for committing atrocious acts. Paradoxically, this perspective enhances sympathy for victims by exposing the moral and political justifications of their mistreatment. Narratives about perpetrators also serve to undo stereotypes about evil, animal-like monsters and sadists, and make readers reflect about their own darker sides and thresholds to committing violence. There is a fine line here between self-examination and identification, though. Ethnographic writers must prevent readers from overidentifying themselves with violent characters, and therefore need to analyze their relationship with perpetrators, as we are doing in this book, to make conscious stylistic choices.

———

ALEX: Which styles of ethnographic writing do you think are most useful for writing about perpetrators and mass violence?

TONY: At Berkeley, I was taught that a detached writing style was the right way for academic knowledge production. *Writing Culture* had not yet been published, and Paul Rabinow's *Reflections on Fieldwork in Mo-*

rocco was not considered "real" anthropology. How was this for you, and what do you think about the use of creative writing in work about perpetrators?

ALEX: I was trained in much the same way. If, when I was a graduate student, the grounds of anthropological research were shifting due to postmodernism, which included experimental writing strategies, it was still for many, if not most, anthropologists "research" in the end—even if there were demands for reflexivity and positioning that became standard.

If I was wary of some of the more extreme entailments of postmodernism, especially given my commitment to what is now called public anthropology, I was influenced by postmodernism's experimentation and disruptiveness in the sense of unsettling assumptions. I started off writing in a more traditional ethnographic style and undertook these last two dimensions of postmodernism in some of my more recent work. These influences also undergird this book to an extent. It weaves together different sorts of writing, both more traditional academic expository prose and literary forms, which are underscored by the interludes. It is this sort of open-ended and dialogic style of writing, as opposed to the door shutting of detached analysis, which is more needed in much of academia but especially in perpetrator studies, given the acts that are the focus of its attention.

I would suggest that, along with traditional exposition, which has its place, we very much need to write in ways that mobilize the imagination and promote critical self-awareness in the sense of Adorno and the Frankfurt School. Seemingly detached "scientific" analysis often impedes such critical thinking. We should impart knowledge and insight but in a way that doesn't foreclose thinking but instead opens new doors that readers step through on their own, making their own creative and imaginative act. Our scholarship needs to unloosen and unfreeze, not petrify.

TONY: I agree with you to a certain extent, but not entirely. Whether we are astrophysicists, historians, or anthropologists, scientific work inevitably involves imagination, which I understand as the leap of interpretation beyond a limited grasp of reality. We draw inferences from our theories and generalize on the basis of a partial knowledge of what is in our research principally a human-made reality. Writing about perpetrators and perpetratorhood is challenging because mass violence is overdetermined. It has personal, psychological, social, political, and cultural ramifications that interact with one another. This is why genocide and mass violence can sometimes traumatize entire societies.

A common characteristic of traumatized societies is the compulsive remembering of indelible atrocities in a desperate effort to give them meaning. This search will run up against representational difficulties. Even such formidable writers as Tadeusz Borowski, Primo Levi, and Elie Wiesel had to admit defeat when describing their experiences in Nazi concentration camps. At the same time, there are authors such as Martin Amis and Jonathan Littell who have provided impressive literary accounts of the Holocaust and its perpetrators. Or think of the devastating film *Son of Saul* about Auschwitz, made by László Nemes when he was only in his thirties. Such artistic expressions hover over and inspire our writing. At the same time, artistic creations rely very much on the testimonies of survivors and the systematic work of scholars.

Until recently, I have been reluctant to incorporate literary sources in my work and have shied away from experimental writing. I tried to remain as close as possible to my oral and written sources whose more conventional narration involves already sufficient ethnographic imagination. Writing as a scholar about mass violence based on face-to-face encounters with perpetrators and victim-survivors requires an ethical responsibility to truthfulness—partial though it may be—that reduces the room for interpretational freedom. At the same time, I acknowledge that creative writing can convey emotions and experiences that expository writing cannot. I have tried to do so in ghost writing this book's interludes about Argentina, by including a bit of family history in the analysis of my dreams about perpetrators, and by drawing on the novel *The Stranger* by Albert Camus to show how perpetrators can be represented as contradictory human beings instead of immoral, one-dimensional figures.

About This Book

We have drawn on literary texts as sources of inspiration and have used several styles of writing to communicate our methodological and conceptual contributions to the study of perpetrators, one centered on our many years of research on this topic—our perpetrator research phronesis, or practical wisdom. In our view, a heterogeneous approach does the most justice to this fieldwork experience, the inner complexities of perpetrators, and the challenges we faced as ethnographers. Accordingly, and in keeping with the way we wove dialogue into the introduction, this book is composed of interlinked ethnographic essays, methodological and theoretical reflections, experimental prose, and dialogues in which we reflect on our research experience with perpetrators.

The book is organized into three parts and two sets of interludes. Part I, "Interviewing," discusses our ethnographic encounters with perpetrators. After providing background on the Cambodian genocide, chapter 1, "Spectacular Perpetrators," addresses the intersubjective tensions of ethnographic encounters through the metaphor of spectacle. Alex discusses the different optics that informed his interviews with "spectacular perpetrators," a chimera of the ethnographic and popular imagination. Alex notes that he, in turn, was a "spectacular anthropologist" about whom his informants and the perpetrators also made assumptions. It is at this point that researcher and interviewee are able to speak to each other with openness and recognition of the other's humanity that the best sorts of ethnography can emerge. Along the way, Alex also discusses a variety of logistic and methodological challenges he faced while conducting his fieldwork research in Cambodia in the mid-1990s.

Chapter 2, "Seductive Perpetrators," examines the challenge of understanding the actions, emotions, and lived experiences of Argentine perpetrators from their perspective. Tony pursues this understanding through cognitive and affective empathy, and examines the conscious and unconscious dynamics of ethnographic encounters. Empathy is a subjective capacity that allows ethnographers to put themselves in the place of others, but without losing a sense of self: cognitively, by adopting people's mental representations of the world, and emotionally, by imagining how they sensed that world. Tony questioned perpetrators about their position and function in the repressive organization as well as their ideological justification of the violence against Argentine revolutionaries.

Part II, "Dreaming," focuses on dreams as manifestations of field emotions. Dream interpretations uncover unconscious personal conflicts and resolve fieldwork anxieties. Chapter 3, "The Night Stalkers," describes how Tony's free associations about dreams during nearly two years of psychoanalysis in Argentina—and the interpretations of his analyst—helped to improve his fieldwork. The analytic interventions addressed recent worries in dream accounts and uncovered personal ambivalences that influenced his research. A foundational force in the unconscious consists of the authority models internalized early in life when children identify with their parents. The unconscious reworking of Tony's identification with his father sparked his research interest in the disappeared. This internalized paternal authority also shaped the fieldwork relations, serving as a template for the perpetrators interviewed in Argentina, who were authority figures in their own right. This transposition resulted in fieldwork anxieties that were resolved through dream analysis.

Chapter 4, "Ruin," begins with a dream Alex had in Cambodia the day after he attended the final judgment in the trial of Duch, the commandant of the S-21 security center and first defendant at the Khmer Rouge Tribunal. The dream, involving a menacing presence in the bleak ruins of a fortress, arrived at a key juncture in his research process, one that signaled a transition from research to writing. Alex uses his dream and the metaphor of ruin as a way to think about the impact of doing research on mass violence and perpetrators. In a way, such research "ruins" the researcher by creating a sense of disorder, abjection, and dirtiness that the researcher struggles to contain as he or she excavates the ruins and begins curating, the focus of his chapter in part III.

Part III, "Writing," takes on the thorny issue of writing about perpetrators. Chapter 5, "Nearing the Paradox," lays bare the ethnographic struggle to represent perpetrators as contradictory figures instead of one-dimensional evildoers. The novel *The Stranger* by Albert Camus provides a literary example of how to portray a paradoxical perpetrator. The story's protagonist, Meursault, is tried for murdering a man on a beach in Algeria. The killing is indisputable, but was it caused by conscious intent, external circumstances, or personal character? Camus leaves the reader hanging in reflection about the meaning of intention, agency, context, responsibility, and human nature. These issues are also raised by a polyphonic rendition of the massacre of sixteen Argentine guerrillas in 1972. Several perpetrator-facilitators were convicted in court forty years later. Though historic, the verdict focused narrowly on their culpability. A broader understanding of the massacre requires knowledge of the lived experiences of everyone involved and of how their contradictory accounts continue to convince their political sympathizers. A polyphonic approach to such conflicting renditions makes ethnographic sense but doesn't excuse the author from thinking through its moral implications.

Chapter 6, "Curation," picks up the metaphors of spectacle and excavation from chapters 1 and 4, extending it to the notion of curation, which connotes healing (cure) as well as a sort of guardianship in the contemporary sense of curation as formal display. Alex uses this idea as a springboard to describe how he used experimental writing forms to better represent Duch, the commandant of S-21 security center. In seeking new ways of writing about perpetrators, Alex sought techniques that could contain ambiguity and be evocative instead of freezing analysis in more turgid expository prose. He concludes by offering readers the metaphor of a Medusa in the room as a guide to their own attempts to grapple with the complexity of perpetrators, an issue that Tony took up in the previous chapter.

The three parts are interspersed with interludes of creative nonfiction and literary forms of writing. In the first set of interludes, Alex presents an essay about a Cambodian victim, perpetrator, and witness, and Tony an imagined monologue by an Argentine mother whose three children were disappeared. In the second set of interludes, Tony narrates how an Argentine general would justify his participation in the military dictatorship, and Alex offers a poem about perpetrators who worked at the S-21 security center.

We end by considering some of the book's general lessons, ones that reflect the practical wisdom we have gained during decades of field-work with perpetrators. We hope this perpetrator research phronesis will help other researchers make better choices as they move forward with their explorations of this important topic of study.

Part I

INTERVIEWING

ONE

Spectacular Perpetrators

THE SPECTACULAR PERPETRATOR is a chimera: fierce, slightly gro-
tesque, and spewing the fires of hate. Mythic, dramatic, legendary. The
fancy of the perpetrator researcher's eye. But also slippery. Glimpsed
for a moment, then gone. A trace.

I first faced off with this chimera while doing my doctoral research
in Cambodia from 1994 to 1995. I went there to try to find answers to a
question so many people asked after the Khmer Rouge genocide: why?

They had good reason to ask. After seizing power in April 1975, the
Khmer Rouge sought to completely transform Cambodia, which they
renamed Democratic Kampuchea (DK). They wanted to outdo even
Mao's China in catalyzing a "Super Great Leap Forward." Everything
was collectivized. Money and markets were abolished. Religion was
banned. Freedom of speech, movement, and assembly were curtailed.

People worked in labor teams for long hours and on meager rations.
Some starved. Others fell ill and died. And then there were the disappearances and executions. By the time the Khmer Rouge were deposed
in January 1979, almost a quarter of Cambodia's eight million inhabitants had died. Perhaps half the dead are thought to have been executed.
The victims were often dumped in mass graves, a practice that gave rise
to the phrase "the killing fields."

In "Banyan," the rural village where I did much of my research, a few farmers grew rice on top of mass graves. Land is scarce. "What else can I do?" one man once said to me as we walked in his rice fields. He had just picked up a tooth from the ground. His plow still churned up bits of cloth and bone, remainders of the dead. A number of villagers said these lands were haunted—as were nearby village wells the Khmer Rouge had filled with corpses.

If killings took place across Cambodia during DK, Banyan was located in an area that was hit hard after the Khmer Rouge launched massive purges. The area around Banyan had been cordoned off and turned into a security center, the villagers relocated to nearby cooperatives. Over ten thousand people, and likely many thousands more, were killed at the site, located at a famous pagoda, Wat Phnom Bros, which the Khmer Rouge executioners used as their base. There were other killing fields, large and small, formal and informal, in the area as well—just as there were throughout the country.

After DK, the Banyan villagers returned home to find fields and wells filled with corpses. The stench sometimes filled the air when the wind changed direction. Many villagers had lost loved ones, although as rural villagers they had an advantage over the city dwellers who had been rusticated immediately after the revolution and were suspect from the start.

When I arrived at Banyan, I wanted to learn the villagers' stories, piece together how their local experiences tied into the larger history of the Cambodian genocide. I immediately set out to do a survey, visiting each of the families, most of whom lived in traditional wooden homes raised by piles from the ground.

It quickly became clear that, during the genocide, ethnic Vietnamese and Muslim Chams had been targeted along with "new people" from the cities, whose impure backgrounds marked them as potential counterrevolutionaries. A number of villagers told me how they had seen truckloads of people being driven to their death at the Wat Phnom Bros killing fields.

As they told me their stories, I also learned about the Khmer Rouge cadre who had terrorized them. "I didn't dare look at their faces when they passed," the villagers would often say. Many of the cadre were from different parts of Cambodia. But some were local. The villagers told me where they lived. I had heard their spectacular stories of suffering and death. Now I wanted to interview the spectacular perpetrators who figured so prominently in their stories—and to answer the question of why.

———

TONY: Before getting to the question why the Khmer Rouge killed nearly two million people, I wonder if the villagers in Banyan were affected by growing rice on mass graves and drinking water from wells that had been filled with dead bodies. Such reuse of gruesome sites is a common phenomenon. Belgian farmers at Waterloo still rake up skeletal remains from soldiers who died on the battlefield in 1815, and in 1951 Moluccan soldiers and their families who fled from Indonesia for having fought alongside the defeated Dutch colonial troops were housed in former German concentration camps in the Netherlands. Sometimes, torture centers are turned into memorial museums, as happened with the S-21 security center in Cambodia and the ESMA secret detention center in Argentina [ESMA refers to the Escuela Superior de Mecánica de la Armada, the Navy mechanics school]. More often, the infrastructure of deposed repressive regimes, such as buildings, prisons, and schools, are occupied again by the new authorities. Do such material witnesses of atrocity crimes affect people in any way?

ALEX: That's an interesting question that can be approached from a couple of directions. The first operates on the individual level. Each person has a personal history that may or may not intersect with the remains or do so to greater or lesser extents. And this is true as well of family and community histories. And then, of course, there is also the state level, which can impact how the remains are remembered and treated—and when. There is an important temporal dimension to all of this. A person, family, community, and state's relationship to remains changes over time and even during the year at moments of commemoration. Immediately after DK, for example, the new People's Republic of Kampuchea (PRK) government launched a massive effort to commemorate the genocide since the legitimacy of its government was tied significantly to having overthrown a genocidal regime. That government launched a number of what we would now call transitional justice efforts, including the creation of memorials where the remains of the dead were displayed (figs. 2 and 3). Some of these still exist today, including Choeung Ek (see fig. 13), where a large memorial has been built on the grounds of the site where many prisoners from S-21, the DK prison Duch ran, were killed. There is also one near Banyan.

State-sponsored commemorations were held at these sites a few times a year, including a national Day of Liberation and Day to Remain Tied in Anger. These days of commemoration are still observed, but they are different—and less affect-laden for most—than they were during the PRK regime. There are many twists and turns to this story, which involves

FIGURE 2. Unidentified woman speaking at a People's Republic of Kampuchea commemoration event. During the PRK regime, the government sponsored annual commemorations, including the Day to Remain Tied in Anger on May 20, which often were held at memorial sites constructed throughout the country after DK. Like the woman in this photo, victims would recount their stories of suffering under the Khmer Rouge. Courtesy DC-Cam/SRI.

FIGURE 3. The remains of victims at a genocide memorial site located in Svay Pha-Em pagoda, Svay Rieng Province, Cambodia, around 1983. Courtesy DC-Cam/SRI.

everything from education to politics to peace and reconciliation efforts. And of course, individuals have their own memories and histories that inflect their relationship to these local memorials, where, for example, some may hold ritual transactions with the spirits of the dead in accordance with Buddhist beliefs regarding karma and reincarnation. So, your question raises many issues and requires different levels of analysis to answer.

———

I sought out Khmer Rouge perpetrators with some trepidation. Yes, an aspiring anthropologist gets nervous even if Lara Croft and Indiana Jones don't. And it's OK to have emotions like fear and unease. How could it be otherwise? The key is to remain aware of emotion and how it mediates the ethnographic encounter. But that's an issue discussed later in this book as we consider how perpetrator researchers process difficult content and experiences, in part through dreams, sometimes even ones in which chimeras appear as I recount in chapter 4.

And chimeras are scary! The monsters breathe fire after all. Many of us have been watching the spectacular perpetrator for years. We read about him in books and newspapers, see him on our television or computer screens.[1] (And yes, the spectacular perpetrator is usually spotted as a "him," although we take extra notice on those rare occasions when the spectacular perpetrator is a "her" or someone nonbinary.) Osama bin Laden. Saddam Hussein. Milošević. Charles Taylor. Mao. Videla. The list is long. The spectacular perpetrator is also featured in the movies, an evil chimera to be defeated. Think Lord Voldemort of Harry Potter fame. Norman Bates from Hitchcock's *Psycho*. Sauron from *The Lord of the Rings*. Darth Vader.

The spectacular perpetrator often comes in two types. On the one hand, there is the crazed leader. Hitler is exemplary in this regard, a charismatic and fanatical leader who spoke before adoring crowds with whom he exchanged Nazi salutes. And indeed, Nazi propaganda used new technologies to create spectacular propaganda films, perhaps most famously Leni Riefenstahl's 1935 *Triumph of the Will*. On the other hand, there are the "fanatic" or "sadistic" perpetrators who implement the project of mass murder or do the mass killing—like Alfredo Astiz, the Argentine "Blond Angel," whose trial sparked the conversation that led to this book.

In popular discourse, such representations make explanation easy. The spectacular perpetrator is evil, sadistic, a hater. Chimeras are inhuman monsters after all. This explanation also sometimes informs research as scholars focus on personality and its dysfunctions. Some of the first research in perpetrator studies focused on the pathologies of Hitler, his henchmen, and even Germans in general.[2] The field of psychohistory emerged in part from this orientation.

A parallel and sometimes overlapping stream of analysis sought explanation in our evolutionary history and instincts, sometimes arguing that civilization is a veneer that suppresses innate violent tendencies.[3] Another line of analysis ranked societies in terms of their degree of civilization with violence linked to earlier states of savagery and barbarism. If Hitchcock's film *Psycho* dramatizes the focus on personality, the book *The Lord of the Flies* suggests that violence is instinctual, a regressive predisposition rooted in evolutionary history and characteristic of "primitive" society.

In the 1960s and 1970s, scholars began to supplement or oppose such explanations focused on internal psychoevolutionary factors with studies that revealed the importance of environment and social life. Hannah Arendt's study of Eichmann was a famous step in this direction. So too were Milgram's shock experiments (in which participants thought they were shocking people, sometimes to dangerous levels, in the name of science) and Zimbardo's Stanford prison experiment (in which subjects assigned to be prison guards began to abuse those assigned to be prisoners).[4]

Interactionists would seek a balance, drawing on both individual and group factors, a trend spectacularly revealed by the BBC prison experiment, which sought to update Zimbardo's study.[5] It was in this context that Christopher Browning's *Ordinary Men* was published in 1992.[6] Browning leaned toward the social, and emphasized a host of factors, ranging from peer pressure to feelings of duty, which motivated "ordinary" rank-and-file perpetrators working in small groups. The extraordinary "psycho" perpetrator had become fully banal. If this perspective still dominates, it has at moments encountered opposition, perhaps most famously in Daniel Goldhagen's 1966 *Hitler's Willing Executioners*, which garnered enormous attention, especially in Germany, for arguing that Nazi perpetrators were not just ordinary men but ordinary Germans, culturally predisposed by an extreme form of anti-Semitism that made them want to eliminate Jews.[7] Goldhagen had stepped into the domain of anthropology, drawing on the concept of culture even as he made a culturally determinist argument.[8]

In doing so, Goldhagen underscored a major gap in the anthropological literature. Anthropologists had studied and fought for indigenous groups under threat, but they had left the topic of genocide almost completely unexamined. There were only a handful of articles on the Holocaust and almost nothing on the Armenian or Ukrainian cases, among others. There were a number of reasons for this situation, including the long-standing fear of "the Nazi exception" that was in tension with anthropological notions of relativism as illustrated by the controversies surrounding the 1947 American Anthropological Association's statement on human rights.[9]

This situation was changing in the 1990s, catalyzed in part by the end of the Cold War, as I was conducting my research in Banyan. Attention would turn from a concern with authoritarianism to new sets of concerns, including peace building, humanitarianism, and human rights. There was a growing literature on the anthropology of political violence, one in which Tony was a leader as his chapters in this book illustrate.[10] The conflicts of the mid-1990s in the former Yugoslavia and Rwanda redirected attention on the issue of genocide. Meanwhile, the fields of genocide studies and transitional justice were emerging, both of which were concerned with "the perpetrator" (as well as the category to which it is opposed, "the victim") as an object of study.

At that time, fields like psychology, law, criminology, and Holocaust studies had perhaps more fully undertaken research on perpetrators, though often with a Nazi-focus and usually not from the comparative vantage of genocide and mass violence that characterizes the field of perpetrator research today. During the post–Cold War transition to this broader purview, a growing number of scholars from different fields began to conduct research on perpetrators. This was the research context in which I arrived in the field in Cambodia and set out to do perpetrator research, which was still a relatively unformed field, especially in anthropology. Little did I know, but I was about to undertake spectacular ethnography. How could it have been otherwise?

————

TONY: You went to study the Cambodian genocide loaded with knowledge about the chimeras of other genocides and mass violence. Did this help you with your fieldwork? I went to Argentina with the same baggage and discovered eventually that it hindered my understanding by asking the wrong questions and using the wrong analytical models, as I explain in chapter 3.

ALEX: That's a great question. The field of perpetrator studies is very much rooted in the study of Nazi atrocities, even as there are many other currents and streams that inform it. Freud is a good example. He thought deeply about pathology and motivation but not so much about the ideas of criminality, victimization, and violation that inform the construct of perpetration.

The Nuremberg trials, Auschwitz, and especially Eichmann trials were groundbreaking events that helped lay the ground for the study of perpetrators. This historical connection to Nazi atrocities is both a strength and a weakness of the field of perpetrator studies. It is important to recognize how the field of genocide studies is informed by the Holocaust prototype—condensed in the image of Auschwitz—that provides conceptual affordances but also blinds researchers and overly restricts the purview of the field.

The same is true of perpetrator studies. Holocaust prototypes or templates are now global and pervade a wide range of discourses—not just scholarly work but also popular culture, ethics, and the politics of memory. The horrors of the Holocaust echo discursively around much of the world, taking local form in places like Cambodia's Tuol Sleng Genocide Museum while also framed in relation to global norms, such as the "never again" and "never forget" imperatives.

It is notable that there are researchers in both genocide studies and perpetrator studies—and there is much overlap with those fields along with Holocaust studies—who are approaching perpetration with a much-needed critical lens. For me, the key is to always look for the ways in which we have become conceptually frozen or fear to look. This opens space for reimagining a field. This is why I chose my chapter title as I should probably explain now.

———

I have been using the term *spectacular* to underscore to the dramatic optics the interviewer brings to the ethnographic encounter. Derived from the Latin term *spectāculum*, the adjective *spectacular* refers to something that is spectacle-like in terms of being "striking, amazing, lavish." A spectacle is "an organized (usu. public) display or entertainment, *esp.* one on a large or splendid scale."[11]

The object of the spectacle is someone or something "of a striking or unusual character" that may be viewed with "curiosity, contempt, or admiration." Secondarily, *spectacle* may refer to "a means of seeing; something made of glass," ranging from a window or mirror to eyeglasses. In this sense, a spectacle is "a medium through which something is regarded; a point of view." Through the Latin root *spek* (to observe), the term *spectacular* is related to a cluster of words, such as *perspective* and *specter*. Here we get a foreshadowing of a specter that is the focus of chapter 6, Medusa.

What, if anything, is an interview with a perpetrator other than spectacular? It is an encounter structured around the extraordinary: the ultimate transgression, the killing of another human being. In Cambodia, as in other sites of genocide, the violence was so extensive that it pushes the limits of comprehension. If all interviews involve optics, then, interviews with perpetrators are of a spectacular sort, treading the ground of dramatic and devastating violence.

And so I arrived in Banyan with a bag of optics in hand. On the one hand, I had grown up in a milieu in which images of perpetrators circulated in films, books, and the media. I had also been raised in the United States, with its narrative of exceptionalism making the violence characteristic of faraway places like Cambodia seem distant and exotic—even as the history of US violence, ranging from slavery to the slaughter of indigenous peoples, was conveniently ignored.[12] On the other hand, I had spent several years prior to my fieldwork doing a literature review, reading everything from social theory to many of the texts on perpetrators discussed above.

I also read every survivor memoir that had been published, including *A Cambodian Odyssey*, written by Haing Ngor, a Cambodian genocide survivor and actor who won the Academy Award for Best Supporting Actor for his role in *The Killing Fields*.[13] It was through the perspective of these authors, many of whom were educated professionals who had fled Cambodia during or after the genocide, that I first glimpsed the spectacular Khmer Rouge perpetrator.

Indeed, the stories of victims (and we could speak of the spectacular victim as well) constitute a third key stream informing the optics I brought to bear in my interviews. If the spectacular perpetrator was portrayed in polished and fluid prose in memoirs like *A Cambodian Odyssey*—the chimera fully revealed and depicted in dramatic pose— those I heard about during my initial survey research in Banyan emerged in the choppier and everyday village vernacular form of casual conversation in people's homes.

But the stories were still dramatic. It wasn't distant perpetrator-architect leaders like Pol Pot or Nuon Chea who loomed largest in their accounts but instead the local cadre who terrorized their lives. There was Grandmother Yit, a cadre from southwestern Cambodia who was so fierce she was said to have killed her husband, who had fallen under suspicion, to prove her loyalty to the Khmer Rouge cause. (Grandmother Yit would later testify at the Khmer Rouge Tribunal and claim, as most perpetrators do, that she was a victim.)

Another cadre, Phat, was known to roll up her sleeves before she and her execution squad led their victims into the forest to be killed. Feared for her brutality during DK, she was beaten to death by locals when the Khmer Rouge fell from power. A mild-mannered Banyan villager recalled: "More and more people kept coming, including grandfathers and grandchildren. They really hated her because she had killed so many people. I hit her two times, too. I hated her because she had killed my husband. We wanted revenge."

If some perpetrator-facilitators were from other parts of Cambodia, the Banyan villagers had known others all their lives. One man, "Vong," recalled how, after being appointed to a leadership position, another villager named Boan, who had embraced Khmer Rouge ideology, warned there were "hidden enemies burrowing within." Boan reported dozens of people. "We were all terrified," Vong told me. "Even though I was exhausted from work, it was hard to sleep at night because I feared they would come take me away to be executed. We didn't even dare look at the faces of the big cadre. If one passed by, I would turn my face away or look down. We were so scared."

At one point, Boan arrested Vong for trying to steal two potatoes. Vong thought he would be killed but, perhaps because of his peasant background, he was released. After Boan was purged, his replacement, Saun, showed Vong that he was on a list of suspected enemies that included the names of people who had been executed. Saun erased Vong's name from the list. Life was much better under Saun's rule: only one person was killed and that was because of research done by the secret police.

As the contrast between Boan and Saun suggests, the spectacular perpetrator was hard to find in the field. Phat and Boan were dead. Grandmother Yit, like so many of the other people my informants named had disappeared immediately after DK and was rumored to be living in a distant province where remnants of the Khmer Rouge were still fighting the government. And those who were still alive, local, and available, like Saun, were often the exceptions. The exceptional suggests that which is "unusual" and deviates from the norm, sometimes with a hint of the good (say, an exceptional person).[14] And so we might speak of "the exceptional perpetrator," the spectacular perpetrator's distant kin—having a family resemblance but somewhat different.

Indeed, in interviews, perpetrators often want you to see them as exceptions, not spectacular perpetrators. (A smaller number do sometimes brag and boast of their deeds, often with a hypermasculine swagger.) This was true when I met with Saun. Playing on the exceptional theme, he stressed how he helped Vong and many other villagers during DK. There is truth to his account: other villagers confirmed Saun was relatively benign.

If some perpetrators more or less deny their involvement ("the denying perpetrator"), most fall somewhere on the spectrum between the endpoints of spectacle and exception. Better yet, we might think about their acts of perpetration as varying through time and place and therefore potentially having both spectacular and exceptional phases and moments. Primo Levi famously called this sort of deeply contextualized perspective, which considers the messiness and ambiguity of human action in contexts of mass murder, the gray zone.[15]

In interviews, perpetrators sometimes emphasize such ambiguity—along with situational constraint, obedience to authority, and justifiable cause—as they seek to convince the researcher that they are more exceptional than spectacular. This is one fulcrum around which the dynamic of ethnographic seduction, which Tony discusses in his essay in this section, plays out. Even Pol Pot, shortly before he died, argued for the righteousness of the Khmer Rouge cause while saying, "Look at me: am I a savage person?"[16]

––––––

TONY: This is very recognizable! Argentine perpetrators would generally present themselves as ordinary men. "We're not Nazis," one of them told me. Sometimes, however, perpetrators show pride in a job well done, like Astiz and Eichmann. What is this? Obedience to authority? Hypermasculinity? There seems to be a sense of pride about being skilled at what they did; the skill at making captives confess, at killing, and the ability to give a precise order.

ALEX: You have put your finger on a key point that directly bears upon interviewing perpetrators. Few people, of course, want to be identified as a spectacular perpetrator after the fact, though perhaps there are a few who relish the associated aura of power. Most want to be acknowledged as fellow human beings, and we, as researchers, may afford them that space of humanity.

As we discussed in the introduction, this acknowledgment obviously is not exculpatory. But it does create the space within which perpetration can be better understood as we cast our spectacular optics aside as best as we are able. And this space is precisely where, during interviews, former perpetrators, especially the hard-core ones, often begin to feel comfortable and reveal more. In a sense, they want you to become a bit like them and complicit as well. Perhaps this complicity is intertwined with the seduction you discuss.

Some researchers, as we note in the introduction, are confrontational in such interviews. I am more of a patient listener who allows silences to linger since important things are often said in and around a long pause. As for the pride, I think you point to something important, especially for the true believer—hypermasculinity can be part of it, but the key undercurrent is satisfaction, even inflation, for a job well done in pursuit of a larger and righteous cause. Duch, Astiz, and Eichmann all share this quality.

———

This pattern of displacing responsibility has come up frequently, in direct and indirect ways, in my interviews with perpetrators as they seek to humanize themselves and their actions while contending they are exceptions, not spectacular perpetrators. In doing so, of course, they bring their own set of spectacular optics to the encounter as they meet a foreigner, a scholar and researcher, a (relatively) well-to-do person, someone with status of a sort, a US citizen, and an author who wants to hear and include their stories in a text.

This "spectacular anthropologist" wanted to learn about their pasts. Some former perpetrators I interviewed denied their deeds. Others tried to spin the events, presenting themselves in a relatively good light. A smaller number wanted to tell the truth for different reasons ranging from Buddhist conviction to simply helping me with my research. At the onset, as part of my university's protocols for human subject protection protocols, I offered to use pseudonyms, which immediately raised questions about why I would make such an offer. Many then asked me to do so.

Each interview was distinct; many were unpredictable. I held them at pagodas, in rice fields, at people's homes, and in offices. Sometimes I felt unsafe; in other situations, I felt at ease. I brought a list of bullet points on a piece of paper to the interview, a rough guide to the topics I wanted to cover. Then I listened, trying to never interrupt (the golden rule of oral interviewing), allowing for silences and pauses, being respectful, and providing cues that I was attuned to what the person was saying while avoiding overly strong facial expressions, body movements, and tone of voice.

The interviews often went on for hours, sometimes in extreme humidity and heat. The topics we discussed were frequently awful: torture, human liver eating, imprisonment, and execution. Sometimes, the interviews felt surreal. Afterward, I'd type up notes, including key topics discussed and the details of the interview and my impressions. I met some perpetrators once; others several times. Still others I met repeatedly and have known for years. I can't call any of them friends—there's a certain distant formality involved in perpetrator interviews—but I am always respectful, courteous, and friendly, odd as it sometimes seems given the content of what we're discussing and what the interviewees did.

Each interview takes places in a context that often involves other actors, including victims whom I have also interviewed extensively. When I first arrived at Banyan in the 1990s, there was little electricity, no phones, no internet, and no phonebook. Finding perpetrators was often quite difficult in these circumstances, which is almost inconceivable in today's world of email, internet, social media, and smartphones. And indeed, almost all the Banyan villagers today have some sort of smartphone, even if many have basic subscription plans.

I found most of the perpetrators I interviewed during my initial stint of fieldwork in Cambodia through word of mouth. My Banyan survey was critical in this regard, providing historical details about what happened in the area and who the key Khmer Rouge actors were. I wanted to trace the violence that took place near Banyan, located in an area that was the focus of a major Khmer Rouge purge, back to the DK Party Center, including S-21 prison, the interrogation and torture center that operated directly under the command of the Khmer Rouge leaders.

If there was one shared characteristic of the interviews, it was their unpredictability. Almost everyone, especially those who did the physical killing, tried to downplay their involvement even when they partly acknowledged their role. A handful denied any involvement or offered one-word or one-sentence replies. Everyone wanted to be exceptional, not spectacular, although many were quite willing to tell spectacular DK perpetrator stories. Some of the stories were clearly about themselves while related in this alter-ego guise.

Each interview was informed by the optics the parties brought to the encounter and the dialogue that took place. Some former Khmer Rouge were cooperative; others remained taciturn. Some offered incisive remarks; others, quick superficial replies.

TONY: Alex, you write that the villagers in Banyan didn't dare to look at the Khmer Rouge cadre. I have heard the same from ex-disappeared in Argentina and also read this in many accounts by torture victims and political prisoners: never look them in the eye. Why do you think this is so? And how was this for you? Did you look straight at the victims, the torturers, and executioners as you were interviewing them?

ALEX: I did, though in an attentive but casual manner. There is always a dance of the eyes that mediates our human encounters, and this is certainly true of interviews with perpetrators—and survivors—given the strong emotions that circulate, including shame. So, this dance of the eyes is part of that space of humanity I mentioned before, one in which you also have to attend to the person, their personality, their ways of speaking and being in the world, and their nonverbal behaviors like eye contact. As for this dance of the eyes during the time of mass violence, fear, terror, and status were clearly involved. A host of verbal and nonverbal cues, including the gaze and movements of the eyes, expressed and asserted the relationship of dominance and subordination that is obviously central to perpetration. They could also mean the difference between life and death.

While some of the former Khmer Rouge cadre had disappeared, lived far away, moved, or died, others lived in the same place—sometimes the same house—where they had lived before DK. Suon, the official who had replaced Boan in Vong's cooperative, was among those I was able to find. We spoke at his home. He was moderately forthcoming but portrayed himself as a low-level and reluctant participant in the Khmer Rouge project. He emphasized that he would have been killed if he had turned down the offer to replace Boan and that he tried to help the villagers, erasing the names of those who had been listed as suspects. He let them steal food and said he did the same. If he had been harsh, Suon contended, the villagers "would have been furious [after DK] and I wouldn't be alive today." Vong's recollections supported Suon's story.

Many former Khmer Rouge I met made similar claims, suggesting that others had the decision-making power and did the killing. And the contrast between Boan and Suon underscores how individuals had a degree of latitude and could choose to govern in a more or less benign manner—although it is also true that Suon came to power as the main purge in the area was ending and might have acted differently if he had held power earlier.

Other villagers confirmed that Suon was less harsh than Boan. Vong called him "a good person." He did not fit the spectacular perpetrator imaginary of the hate-spewing Khmer Rouge monster. Indeed, this is the default position for former Khmer Rouge, a "perpetrator slot" into which they are automatically filled.[17] In the context of DK, the Khmer Rouge chimera has been bound up with geopolitics (the anticommunism of the Cold War), domestic politics (the post-DK Cambodian government legitimacy narratives), and everyday understandings of genocide.

Some scholars, and later defense teams at the UN-backed tribunal that was held decades later in Cambodia, have pointed out the limitations of the spectacular optic, which brings with it a set of assumptions that may occlude understanding, including assumptions about the temporal and spatial variation in the DK violence.[18] The flip side to such accounts is that they may also lay the ground for denials like those given by former Khmer Rouge leaders seeking to claim that they had no control over renegade local officials. This was the case with "Brother Number Two," Nuon Chea, the most senior living Khmer Rouge leaders tried at the Extraordinary Chambers in the Courts of Cambodia (ECCC) and someone whose denial I confronted firsthand while testifying as an expert witness at the ECCC in 2016.[19]

If Nuon Chea was widely identified as a spectacular perpetrator, villagers like Suon illustrate the limitations of the legalistic category of "perpetrator," an inflection denoting someone who commits "a crime or evil act."[20] As we note in the introduction, although it is important to have such legal categories (and not fall victim to ethnographic seduction), we also need to avoid fetishizing them and attend to the "gray zone" complexities that the spectacular perpetrator optic obscures.

––––––––

The spectacular perpetrator chimera quickly disappeared in most of my interviews, even those with Khmer Rouge who had worked at spectacular killing sites like Phnom Bros pagoda and Duch's S-21 security center. From the start of my fieldwork, I sought to learn more about what had happened at Phnom Bros, given that its killing fields edged into Banyan. The villagers recounted spectacular stories about what had happened there. They witnessed truckloads of victims entering the facility. Others recounted how, just after DK, they had found mass graves filling the pagoda grounds where they had prayed and observed Buddhist rites.

Vong recalled: "Some of the mass graves still had limbs sticking up through the dirt. The place stank." They found a lion statue where, they claimed, the executioners had sharpened their blades. But the site had been guarded and off-limits, meaning that the villagers hadn't actually witnessed the killings. The one cadre whose name some knew—Chuon, the head of the Phnom Bros security center—had committed suicide by jumping in front of a Vietnamese tank at the end of DK.

At first, it seemed unlikely I would be able to interview anyone who had worked at the site. As my ethnographic network expanded, I began to get leads. One led me to Neari. During DK, her family was targeted for elimination because her father had been a teacher and therefore was suspect as an intellectual and civil servant from the previous regime.[21] One by one, her family members were killed until just Neari and her sister remained. She survived only by agreeing to marry a Khmer Rouge soldier, Khel, who worked at Phnom Bros with Chuon. I interviewed Neari first, then Khel.

When I arrived at his home, the anticipated spectacular perpetrator met me with downcast eyes and a half smile. Then he handed me a handwritten document that detailed what had transpired while he was stationed at Phnom Bros in 1977, a year when a Khmer Rouge officer named Reap orchestrated mass executions at the site. Khel even listed the members of the Phnom Bros execution squad. Like Suon and so many other perpetrators, he positioned himself on the edges of the killings but not as directly involved, a move often made to avoid culpability and shame. Khel emphasized that Khmer Rouge cadre and soldiers like himself were also scared.

Khel said that Chuon, with whom he became close friends, would shake his head disapprovingly while the killings were being carried out and say that the executioners had "excessive hearts." Chuon, Khel said, dreamed of escape: "He would sniff the stench of the corpses and shake his head and tell me, 'I brought you to work in the land of death.'" They secretly listened to Voice of America and dreamed of going to the United States, where they would "expose what Pol Pot is doing in Cambodia." By the end of our first meeting, Khel was speaking more confidently and more often breaking into his half smile, his ethnographic seduction (to use the key term Tony takes up in the next chapter) well underway.

As with all interviews, I sought to triangulate and verify the information. I was particularly interested in Reap, who was purged after allegedly trying to start a rebellion. I figured that, given his rank, he would likely have been sent to S-21, Duch's interrogation and torture center. And so for a month I did research in Phnom Penh at the museum and archive located on the site of S-21. I eventually found his confession, which he had given after torture and interrogation. I also sought the confessions of his subordinates, one of whom mentioned in passing how his brigade had "cleaned up" enemies in the area. After producing acceptable confessions, Reap and his key subordinates were executed at S-21.

Even as I sought information about Reap, I also wanted to learn more about the perpetrators who had worked at S-21. Surely if there were a spectacular perpetrator to be found it would be there. In contrast to the present, when many former S-21 cadre have been interviewed or testified at the Khmer Rouge Tribunal, these spectacular perpetrators were difficult to find—especially given that, as I noted earlier, there weren't cell phones and roads were often difficult to traverse.

Toward the end of my doctoral fieldwork, I manage to arrange an interview with Lor, a notorious S-21 cadre.[22] A Tuol Sleng official claimed that Lor had admitted to killing four hundred people. Vann Nath, one of the few S-21 survivors, told me that Lor had actually killed more, perhaps as many as two thousand men, women, and children. Lor was, he said, "savage like an animal in the forest, like a wild dog or a tiger. I didn't dare look at his face. . . . We were terrified of him."

This spectacular perpetrator still roamed free, and I was about to meet him. I imagined Lor as a heinous person who would exude evil from head to toe. But the chimera once again quickly disappeared. Lor was a poor farmer in his thirties who greeted me politely and with a broad smile. In contrast to Khel and Suon, he moved and spoke confidently, his answers clipped, to the point, and delivered in monotone.

After exchanging initial pleasantries, I asked about his path to the revolution (he was conscripted in his rural village during the civil war) and S-21. Lor admitted he was a guard at the prison, eventually becoming responsible for transporting prisoners to a killing field located just outside of Phnom Penh. Lor said he wasn't on the execution squad but instead checked off the names of the prisoners before they were killed.

Like Khel, Lor described the method of execution in detail. One or two soldiers would lead a prisoner to a ditch in front of which he or she was ordered to kneel. A guard then struck the prisoner on the back of the neck with an iron bar and dumped their body into the mass grave. Lor didn't mention that the prisoner's necks were also slit to ensure they were dead. Years later, I would have the experience of traveling with Lor to the site, where he walked me through the entire process. He would also describe it while testifying at the Khmer Rouge Tribunal in 2009.

After DK, Lor was sentenced to a year in prison for his crimes. When interrogated by the police, Lor said he lied, thinking he would be killed anyway, and told them, "I am the killer, by myself, of one thousand people." At this point, I asked Lor, "So, during the Pol Pot period you never killed anyone?" Lor paused before he replied, "I did kill one or two people, but I did this so that others wouldn't accuse me of being unable to cut off my heart."

When I asked why he had killed "one or two people," Lor explained that Duch, the head of S-21, was present at the time and asked, "Have you ever dared to kill one or two of them, Lor?" When Lor replied that he had not, Duch said, "Like your heart isn't cut off. Go get that prisoner and try it once. Do it one time so I can see." Lor told a soldier who was about to execute a prisoner to give him the iron bar and then "struck the prisoner so they could watch me. I hit him one time with the iron bar and the prisoner fell to the ground. . . . When my boss asked me to do this, if I didn't do this—I couldn't refuse." As he spoke, I thought of Reap, the Phnom Bros executioner later executed in this same manner.

Lor was about as "spectacular" as spectacular perpetrators get. But as always, the chimera quickly slipped away, leaving behind the question of questions: Why? Labeling perpetrators like Lor "a monster"— and many people have done so—is too easy, suggesting that explanation lies in one-word answers. The first step to interviewing perpetrators is to recognize our preconceptions and set aside our spectacular optics to the best of our ability.

In anthropology, we refer to this as the methodology of cultural relativism, which is taken to an extreme when interviewing perpetrators. Many people mistakenly think this method entails moral abrogation. It doesn't. The method of cultural relativism asks that we reflect upon our assumptions and suspend judgment, as best we can, in the space of the interview and listen to another human being—with openness and full acknowledgment of their humanity. The spectacular perpetrator is a chimera; people like Lor are not. As we will see in the chapters that follow, their stories of perpetration are nevertheless hard to listen to, leaving the researcher with spectacular "baggage" and often extremely difficult experiences to process and later recast into scholarly prose. Sometimes, as we discuss in part II, they even haunt our dreams.

TWO

Seductive Perpetrators

THE LIEUTENANT ASSIGNED to my visit to the Museum of the Fight against Subversion encouraged me to enter the museum's replica of a people's prison. I hesitantly descended the wooden ladder into the dark underground space, uncertain of what I would find there. Gripping the sides of the ladder, I stepped slowly from rung to rung. The lieutenant was stooped over the opening. When my head was below ground level, he told me to crawl inside the cavity dug into the subsoil. The place was narrow, just large enough for one person to lie down on the barely visible mattress. And then everything went black. The lieutenant had covered the opening with the movable metal desk that concealed the prison. He must have wanted me to feel, if only for a few minutes, what incarcerated officers had gone through for months. Yet my thoughts didn't go out to them. In the pitch darkness, I remembered the thousands of disappeared who had been held captive at the Campo de Mayo army base. In particular, I recalled the story of one shackled inmate who had been forgotten by his interrogators, sitting hooded on the floor for fourteen hours a day during six months. His captors eventually killed him for outliving his usefulness.[1] Before I could complete my thoughts, I heard the metal desk scraping over the floor and diffuse daylight entered the opening.

The Major Juan Carlos Leonetti Museum of the Fight against Sub-version was founded in October 1978 at the Campo de Mayo army base, located northeast of Buenos Aires. In July 1976, Major Leonetti had lost his life in a fire fight with Mario Roberto Santucho, the commander in chief of the People's Revolutionary Army, also known as the ERP (Ejército Revolucionario del Pueblo). Santucho was heavily wounded. He was rushed to Campo de Mayo for interrogation but died in its hospital during surgery. The Marxist guerrilla organization fell apart and disbanded in April 1977. Argentina's other major guerrilla organization, the Montoneros, held out for a few more years despite the growing defection of combatants and their relentless pursuit by the military.

Named in honor of Major Leonetti, the museum was created when Argentina's guerrilla insurgency was largely defeated. The museum was open only to military visitors. It exhibited captured weapons and ammunition, uniforms, flags and insignia, books of revolutionary thinkers (including Herbert Marcuse), radio jammers, and a replica of a people's prison. Dressed in his blood-stained clothes, Santucho's preserved body had been put on display for several years as proof of the military victory.[2]

My visit to the museum in 1989 had been arranged by a high-ranking officer who wanted me to see the magnitude of Argentina's guerrilla insurgency and understand better what the armed forces had been up against, including the incarceration in people's prisons. I became aware of the existence of people's prisons after reading Major Julio Larrabure's diary. He had been abducted by the ERP in Córdoba in August 1974 and was moved three months later to a small windowless cell below a dry-goods store in Rosario. The 2-meter-by-1.5-meter cell contained a bed and a portable toilet. The air was refreshed by a ventilator. The asthmatic Larrabure was terrified that the ventilator would break down. He died from asphyxiation on August 19, 1975, either from hanging himself or by strangulation. His emaciated corpse was dumped in a ditch near an abandoned railway station.[3]

Did my brief confinement at the museum allow me to sense what officers had felt in a people's prison? Rather than the brief experience underground, the existence of the replica and the collection of captured weapons and revolutionary material helped me better understand why the Argentine military went on an all-out offensive against the guerrilla organizations and the political opposition movement. My knowledge of the military's counterinsurgency operations and state terrorism, and by extension perpetratorhood, was mainly achieved through interviews with officers, ex-guerrillas, torture victims, and searching relatives, as well as by reading secret military documents and battle plans, court records and truth commission testimonies, clandestine guerrilla publications, and speeches and interviews by military commanders.

Ethnographic interviewing is much more than a research method. Interviews are distinct communicative events that produce knowledge, texts, and dialogues between collaborative interlocutors.[4] How did I establish a fruitful interaction with perpetrators from the Argentine armed forces, and how could I grasp their lived experiences through interviews? Ideally, rapport is a smooth and preferably long-term research relationship in which cultural knowledge is shared freely and openly because of the trust between ethnographers and their interlocutors. However, mutual trust and the candid exchange of knowledge are often hampered with perpetrators because they don't want to incriminate themselves and often try to justify their actions.

How can reliable research be conducted without rapport between interviewers and interviewees? Mutual mistrust seems to shake the foundation of anthropological research, but I argue in this chapter that rapport and trust are not required when interviewing perpetrators. Ethnographers can put themselves in their place without having a close bond because empathy doesn't require trust.

Cognitive Empathy

Empathy is crucial for ethnographic fieldwork. A century ago, Bronislaw Malinowski stated that anthropology's mission was to grasp people's point of view in order to cast light on human nature: "Though it may be given to us for a moment to enter into the soul of a savage and through his eyes to look at the outer world and feel ourselves what it must feel to *him* to be himself—yet our final goal is to enrich and deepen our own world's vision, to understand our own nature and to make it finer, intellectually and artistically."[5] Clifford Geertz reformulated the anthropological project half a century later as "setting down the meaning particular social actions have for the actor . . . [and] what the knowledge thus attained demonstrates about the society."[6] Geertz dismissed as impossible Malinowski's aim to grasp "the native's point of view," and thus know people's "subjective states" and "typical ways of thinking and feeling."[7] Ethnographers cannot put themselves in someone's place, he argued, but understand people's perspective only by "searching out and analyzing the symbolic forms—words, images, institutions, behaviors—in terms of which, in each place, people actually represented themselves to themselves and to one another."[8] Geertz advocated an experience-distant method of gathering ethnographic knowledge, one that delineated the cultural systems underlying people's representations of the social and natural world.

Geertz misrepresented empathy. Despite his rejection of Malinowski's approach, Geertz also acquired ethnographic data through empathy, namely through cognitive empathy. He was thus able to single out the representations and layered webs of meaning that mediated people's perception of the world. Cognitive empathy refers to the process of assuming another person's mental representations of the world and observing their externalizations in discourse, social practices, material culture, and cultural institutions.[9] In the case of my research in Argentina, cognitive empathy allowed me to outline the political ideology and worldview of the Argentine military, to describe their interpretation of the country's guerrilla insurgency and leftist protest movement in the context of the Cold War, and to delineate the strategies, tactics, and operations of counterinsurgency warfare and state terrorism.

Cognitive empathy is not the only means to acquire knowledge about perpetrators and their violence. In his documentary *Shoah*, Claude Lanzmann interviewed Franz Schalling, a member of the German Order Police stationed at the Chelmno extermination camp. Lanzmann wasn't interested in Schelling's mental representation of the Holocaust, and he wasn't trying to understand the killing procedure from his subjective perspective. Instead, he was after a technical description of the gassing of Jewish inmates at Chelmno:

CLAUDE LANZMANN (CL): Describe the gas vans.

FRANZ SCHALLING (FS): They stretched, say, from here to the window. Just big trucks, like moving vans, with two rear doors.

CL: What system was used? How did they kill them?

FS: With exhaust fumes. It went like this. A Pole yelled "Gas!" Then the driver got under the van to hook up the pipe that fed the gas into the van.

CL: Yes, but how?

FS: From the motor.

CL: Yes, but through what?

FS: A pipe—a tube. He fiddled around under the truck. I'm not sure how.

CL: It was just exhaust gas?

FS: That's all.[10]

———

ALEX: Can we please pause here for a moment. Some readers may be wondering why you just used an example from the Holocaust to illustrate a nonempathic way of acquiring knowledge. This raises the broader question of how the Holocaust has influenced Argentine thinking about the military dictatorships and the enforced disappearances?

TONY: The Holocaust is the most studied genocide in the world. The vast scholarly and literary work about the Holocaust has been a source of inspiration for me to understand other forms of mass violence. Also, the Holocaust is never far away in the Netherlands. My neighbor's house was requisitioned by SS officers during the Second World War. Down the street, there was a kindergarten run by students who succeeded in saving 150 Jewish children from deportation, and during a renovation in my house a hiding place was discovered under the bathroom floor. This familiarity with the Holocaust has helped but also hindered my study of Argentina's mass violence because the Holocaust has become a universal paradigm of evil and suffering, also in Argentina.

Argentine human rights activists and some judges and scholars have drawn parallels between Nazi Germany and dictatorial Argentina by using terms such as *concentration camp* and *genocidal perpetrators* to denounce the regime's enforced disappearances. In 1981, the prominent newspaper director Jacobo Timerman published an account of his four-day disappearance. The book became an international best seller and sealed the portrayal of Argentine officers as Nazis because Timerman equated the junta's ideology with Nazism. Several Argentine scholars and most human rights activists eventually embraced this comparison to interpret the systematic disappearances as genocide—mistakenly, in my opinion. I explain their adoption of the genocide frame as a means to mourn the immense losses experienced by the victim-survivors and the bereaved relatives. They cope with their suffering by imagining the disappearances as the most extreme form of violence known to humankind: genocide. In this way, the Argentine scholars who advocate the Holocaust template enter into a moral alliance with victims and survivors.

Argentine perpetrators uniformly reject a comparison of Argentina's disappearances and the Holocaust, which according to them occurred in historically different times and involved different ideologies, rationales, organizational structures, and operating procedures. Veterans of the military dictatorship don't want to be seen as the paradigmatic example of evil, especially when they are convinced that they saved the Argentine people from a communism that caused tens of millions of dead in China and the Soviet Union and that brought on the Cambodian killing fields.

Claude Lanzmann recorded some of his interviews with Nazi perpetrators secretly, determined to document the Holocaust for posterity into its tiniest details. Such an approach would be a violation of anthropology's professional code of ethics. I openly taped the interviews and offered to return with a written transcript. This also gave me the opportunity to continue the interview.

As did Alex, I generally worked from a topic list that contained political events important to most Argentines, not just perpetrators. As an opening question, I asked some officers about the execution of General Aramburu in 1970 by the Montoneros. In other interviews, I showed a reproduction of Goya's painting *The Third of May 1808*, which depicts the execution of Spanish civilians by a French firing squad during the uprising against Napoleon's occupation of Spain. My next question depended on the answer given but was always intended to raise my cognitive empathy. Preferably, I would descend from the abstract to the concrete in an attempt to change the interview into a conversation that allowed for reflections on Argentina's armed violence and state repression in the 1970s.[11] For example, I asked General Ramón Genaro Díaz Bessone to describe his experience of the guerrilla attack by the Montoneros on the Twenty-Ninth Mounted Infantry Regiment in Formosa on October 5, 1975:

> I arrived when the hostilities had already ended, but I saw the dead and I saw the wounded. Well, the dead. The bodies of soldiers, [noncommissioned officers], and officers were lying covered in one part of the barracks. And there were mothers. I remember the mothers of the soldiers, how they were distressed from the immense pain over their dead sons. And the guerrillas were on the other side, and there was not one relative present. Why? First, because it was impossible to identify them because their fingerprints had been erased. They erased them with acid or pumice stone. Second, the documents were false. They were carrying documents that said whatever. Furthermore, some parents were ashamed and didn't even want to go and inquire; others were afraid, a silly fear because we handed over the body if they came. We never knew who the parents or relatives were. And we had to bury them all, through the intervention of judges moreover, as N.N. [no name]. These could be the disappeared.

The photograph in figure 4 appeared in the national newspaper *La Nación* the day after the attack. The caption said that a policeman was taking the fingerprints of a dead guerrilla. Maybe he was unable to do so because the fingerprints had been removed, as General Díaz Bessone suggested. The contradiction between the contemporary news report and the general's account, fifteen years later, shows the uncertainties of perpetrator research.

This description by the perpetrator-architect and perpetrator-organizer Díaz Bessone helped me discover the military's classification of friendly and enemy forces, the differential treatment of the dead, and

FIGURE 4. A dead guerrilla after the attack on the Twenty-Ninth Mounted Infantry Regiment in Formosa, Argentina, on October 5, 1975. Source: es.wikipedia.

the dehumanization of revolutionaries and their relatives. The general suggested that parents seemed somehow not to care about recovering the bodies of their children, implying that they didn't behave as loving fathers and mothers. The corpses ended up in anonymous graves and then entered the list of the disappeared. The dead soldiers, in contrast, were lamented by their grief-stricken mothers and buried with state honor.

Cognitive empathy helped me discover the framework of perpetratorhood. Argentina was organized in a grid of defense zones and combat areas to dismantle the guerrilla organizations and the heterogeneous leftist opposition movement. This framework was instituted by generals who commanded the five army corps and who coordinated the participation of the navy, air force, police, and gendarmerie. Counterinsurgency and state terrorism were implemented with the systematic practice of abduction, torture, assassination, and disappearance. Task groups composed of low-ranking officers and police operated within their combat area. They patrolled the streets, monitored public transport, and raided homes and workplaces.[12] Argentine perpetrators made it appear in interviews as if they were exclusively fighting combatants and their support troops, but they disappeared many more political opponents who were not directly involved in the insurgency but held revolutionary sympathies—such as left-leaning union representatives, human rights lawyers, grassroots workers, physicians, priests that propagated liberation theology, and especially members of youth and student organizations linked organically to the guerrilla organizations.

Repressive operations share several structural and organizational features with ordinary practices, as illustrated by the journalist and writer Vasily Grossman, who suggested that the massacre of Ukrainian Jews during the Second World War was modeled after the clearing of infected cattle: "Before slaughtering infected cattle, various preparatory measures have to be carried out: pits and trenches must be dug; the cattle must be transported to where they are to be slaughtered; instructions must be issued to qualified workers."[13] I used my knowledge of formal organizations to call forth a cognitive empathy of Argentina's repressive state apparatus. High-ranking officers designed the state terrorism, middle-ranking officers implemented the organizational framework, and low-ranking officers and noncommissioned officers commanded the operations and carried out the mass killings and disappearances. Anthropologists can understand repressive organizations—their architects, organizers, and facilitators—because of their general familiarity with formal organizations. But none of their daily experiences comes close to the actual abduction, torture, killing, and disappearing of people. How, then, can anthropologists evoke the emotions of the practitioners committing such horrendous acts?

Affective Empathy

Affective empathy refers to the process of sensing a person's emotions and feelings.[14] Ethnographers put themselves emotionally in the other's place and then imagine how that person experiences the world. They do so without identifying or merging with the other, because "empathy must be seen as an experiential engagement with the other that recognizes and preserves the self-other difference."[15] Affective empathy is not essential to ethnographic fieldwork, but my understanding of the political violence in Argentina benefited from trying to grasp the experiences of perpetrators.

In May 1990, I interviewed the retired major Ernesto Barreiro. He had been accused of being a chief interrogator at La Perla secret detention center, located near the city of Córdoba. About halfway through the interview, I asked this perpetrator-organizer and perpetrator-facilitator why torture had been used in Argentina to extract information from captives, even though scientific studies had shown that forced interrogations were unproductive. "I would say that physical violence is the enemy of good information," he responded. "I flatter myself by saying that I was one of the principal opponents of the use of physical violence."

Later I returned to the subject and asked him about the truth of the accusations raised against him. I had in mind the treatment of Graciela Geuna at La Perla on June 10, 1976. She had said: "They dragged me to the torture room. They undressed me and tied me to a bed frame. They used two electric prods, one of 220 volts to the body and another with a lower voltage to the face, eyes, lips and head. The one who was torturing me was the then Lieutenant Barreiro."[16] I didn't explicitly mention Geuna's testimony but wanted him to know that I was aware of the indictments made against him. Barreiro reacted with surprise: "The accusations made against me? Torture and homicide. Yes. Totally absurd of course. I will someday say what might be true or not, but what was stated there was a monumental absurdity, entirely without any merit." In 2016, Barreiro was convicted to a life sentence for crimes against humanity.

Barreiro denied in our interview that he had mistreated captives at La Perla. He rejected torture but understood its use on emotional grounds: "When you are in front of a person who killed the son of your comrade with a bomb or who shot a policeman with three shots in the back . . . [then] the sentiment is different, entirely different, totally different. I tell you this because I have seen really irrational attitudes because of this." He went on to tell me about the violent death of Colonel Héctor Iribarren. Iribarren was head of intelligence at the Third Army Corps, with headquarters in Córdoba. He was killed on April 5, 1973, while resisting a kidnapping attempt by the Montoneros.[17] Barreiro recalled: "I arrived at a unit weighed down by a tremendous sentiment and the unit was, let's say, fighting 99 percent objectively against the subversion, but they reserved 1 percent to find the men who had killed Colonel Iribarren."

Barreiro spoke with conviction. I sensed that he approved of the 1 percent irrational conduct, an indirect reference to torture, were it not that torture was not irrational but a systematic operating procedure in Argentina. My analytical knowledge of the organization of state terrorism made me understand how intelligence officers would torture captives to map the cell-like structure of the guerrilla organizations and track down their combatants. Barreiro's account allowed me to imagine emotionally how the intelligence officers were driven by feelings of loyalty, camaraderie, and revenge to search for Colonel Iribarren's killers.

What motivated low-ranking officers like Lieutenant Barreiro to act? Alex made a foundational contribution to the understanding of genocide with his concept of genocidal priming. His argument can be extended to other mass killings. Perpetrator-facilitators are first primed for violent action by ongoing political violence, socioeconomic tensions, a Manichaean ideology, or a perceived threat to their life and existence. These larger conditions have to be experienced by the perpetrators before they can be moved into action. Their willingness to torture and kill is then caused by a mixture of obedience to superiors, group dynamics, personal initiative, and self-realization.[18]

Affective empathy is hard to evoke when interviewing facilitators. Perpetrator researchers find great difficulty in imagining atrocious acts because they have never experienced them, although there are inmates of Nazi concentration camps and disappeared persons in Argentina who lived to write about their experiences as psychiatrists and social scientists. In a general sense, the anthropologist and psychoanalyst Douglas Hollan has stated that people can activate their emotional engagement through "an associational network of memories, images, and meanings in the empathizer's mind that are then mapped onto the experiences and perspectives of the other in an attempt to understand them."[19] Such thoughts and reflections, however, are hard to evoke in the study of perpetratorhood when the ethnographer lacks personal memories of violence and dehumanization. Still, this knowledge can be obtained by reading perpetrator confessions and victim testimonies. For example, the account by a torture victim may describe the torturer's physical conduct and his emotional reactions to the infliction of pain. The researcher might then imagine the perpetrator's subjectivity through a mirroring process that recognizes a particular emotional state, such as anger, hatred, and arousal.[20] My cognitive understanding of Argentina's state terrorism complemented this affective grasp of torture. Together, they yielded a comprehensive understanding of the perpetrator's acts and emotions.

Ethnographic Seduction

Interviews are ambiguous research practices because the interlocutors may have a selective memory and describe past events with the benefit of hindsight. Nigel Rapport has tied this partiality to the interviewee's aims and intentionality: "The interviewee is enacting an introspective, critical, usually private practice before an anthropological witness. Whatever the level of trust, one can never be certain of another's intentionality, of the purpose behind their expressions, of the meanings of their words."[21] Interviews with perpetrators are especially fraught with suspicion and mistrust, which can hinder the interviewer's cognitive and affective empathy. As Hollan and Throop have observed: "Empathic processes do not unfold in a political or moral vacuum. Rather, they are encouraged and amplified in some contexts and discouraged and suppressed in others."[22] Perpetrators may erect obstacles to empathic understanding through a detached narration or by manipulating the interview situation.

Interviews are intersubjective encounters in settings that may influence the social interaction between interviewer and interviewee. My interviews with military officers in Argentina were held at the Army Officers' Club, at a business location or in their homes. The choice of location suggested the interview's formality and entailed a particular seating arrangement. Facing one another at a desk in an office or sitting at an angle in comfortable arm chairs in a living room surrounded by personal objects has subtle effects on the social interaction.

———————

ALEX: Before you go on, I want to note that there is an interesting point of contrast between our fieldwork experiences in terms of place that raises important issues. Almost all my fieldwork, as I discussed in the previous chapter, was carried out in the countryside as opposed to urban centers and often with extremely poor farmers who were sometimes illiterate. Your interviews appear to more often be set in urban contexts and, though not exclusively of course, done with (relatively) higher-status individuals. This speaks to a contrast between the two moments of mass violence in terms of social order (upholding it versus fomenting revolution) and status (elites were immediately suspect during DK and often targeted for execution). There are many questions that emerge from such contrasts, as our readers can already tell. But I want to ask you specifically about place and position: How, in your experience, is fieldwork mediated by space and the social positioning of interviewees? How do these issues impact cognitive and affective empathy? Are there ways the researcher can be, to invoke the theme of this section of your chapter, seduced by place and position?

TONY: Thank you for pointing at research choices I made at the very beginning of my fieldwork and then never reflected on again. Influenced by *The Power Elite* of C. Wright Mills and Laura Nader's call for "studying up," I decided to conduct research on the historical protagonists of the so-called Dirty War.[23] Most of them lived in Buenos Aires, and so did many ex-disappeared, human rights leaders, and former guerrilla commanders. I must admit that initially I found it hard to reconcile the testimonies by victim-survivors about the torture and assassinations in hundreds of secret detention centers with those of the high-ranking officers I was interviewing in their comfortable offices and spacious apartments. Well versed in political thought and Cold War thinking, they sounded convincing in their analyses of Argentina's years of revolutionary fervor and violence—except with respect to their denial of the disappearances. Why had these polite and sometimes even gracious generals organized tens of thousands of disappearances? Early on, I experienced a dissonance between knowledge and feelings that had to be resolved. This is where cognitive and affective empathy became crucial. The more I learned about Argentina's political history and the more I listened to the conflicting interpretations of the country's mass violence, the better able I was to situate my interviewees in the wheelworks of repression and imagine how the officers were ideologically and emotionally invested in the dictatorship. At the same time, I began to understand the process of ethnographic seduction, which helped me to recognize and neutralize the effects of their subjectivity and the social setting of our meetings.

The interviewee is a host who may consciously try to manipulate the meeting, as Alex shows in this book's first interlude about his tense meeting with the Cambodian perpetrator Khan. I had similar experiences. I once interviewed an officer who opened the drawer of his desk and silently put a pistol on top of the table while looking at me. I asked him casually whether it had a nine-millimeter caliber. He confirmed my guess and then asked in an unexpected turn of the conversation if I was Jewish, a strange question posed to someone named Antonius, or *Antonio* in Spanish. I said no and returned the question by asking if he was Jewish. Interviewing another officer in his home, I saw several weapons in the living room, and, when I went to the bathroom, I noticed an Ithaca shotgun on a ledge above the toilet. The presence of the weapons didn't frighten me, but the knowledge that many disappeared had been killed at close range with Ithaca guns made me feel uncomfortable.

Also the lighting in a setting may be important. If possible, I would choose to sit with my back to a window. The daylight would shine on my interviewee and I would be in the shade. This positioning allowed me to see the interviewee's reactions to my questions, while he was left in the dark about my facial expressions. This may seem Machiavellian, and indeed it was, but I had discovered during my first interviews that military officers tried to force a similar seating arrangement on me.

Open interviews are social encounters in which the interlocutors actively forge and reforge their relationship. They construct and reformulate the knowledge shared, and communicate and reinterpret its meaning.[24] Open interviews try to grasp "the actor's understandings of his or her life world, his or her interpretations, meanings and narrations. It is qualitative and descriptive, seeking the nuances and particularities of the human condition in a humanist tradition."[25] My cognitive and affective empathy was shaped by the intersubjective dynamics of the interviews. These social encounters were influenced by a prevailing mistrust, because I conducted many interviews with military officers who at the time could still be prosecuted. I saw them as perpetrators, and they probably saw me as a left-leaning intellectual under the sway of the Mothers of the Plaza de Mayo.

In his classic text *Behind Many Masks*, Gerald Berreman emphasized the importance of good rapport and trustworthiness to convince informants that sensitive knowledge would always be kept confidential.[26] I therefore tried to create a friendly atmosphere in which the mutual mistrust would recede to the background. Questions and answers gave slowly and subtly way to a more personal conversation that could run its unpredictable course. This dialogue would continue until either one of us decided to take control again and revert to a more formal interview mode.

The conscious aim to evoke cognitive and affective empathy influenced the interviews. My interview style was generally nonconfrontational. The questions were mostly neutral and my comments nonjudgmental. For example, rather than asking Major Barreiro if he had tortured people or confronting him with the testimony of Graciela

Geuna, I asked: "What about the accusations raised against you?" I can only speculate here, but I believe that this approach made him willing to explain the emotional motivation of intelligence officers to use torture. Only occasionally I would remain quiet when I sensed that this would yield a more extensive answer. Unlike Alex, I usually kept the flow of the interview going because I feared that lengthy silences would make my interlocutors more conscious and therefore more measured in their replies. If the interviewee halted abruptly mid-conversation, then I would wait for him to resume. I assumed that he had reflected on his last words and was trying to navigate his response to safer ground. I would then reformulate my question to circumvent his evasion and return to the topic that made him pause. The interviews with Argentine officers, perpetrators or not, were thus subtle plays of persuasion and rarely deliberate confrontations.

Hathaway and Atkinson have proposed a "good cop, bad cop" approach to obtain sensitive information. At first, they cultivate trust by asking friendly questions. Then they take a more skeptical and confrontational attitude.[27] I tried this approach a few times but with varying success. I played the benign, open-minded researcher during my first interview with General Díaz Bessone before turning critical during the follow-up interview. I asked him what he thought of people who compared Argentina's disappearances to the Holocaust. He responded angrily: "Do you realize that comparing the Holocaust in Europe—the Jews that were turned into soap in the gas camps and whatever else—with what has happened in Argentina . . . but that is an enormous absurdity!"

With some exceptions, such as Major Barreiro, I interviewed mostly officers who occupied high- and middle-ranking positions during the dictatorship, because I was more interested in the reasoning and emotions behind the strategy and tactics of state terrorism and counterinsurgency than in the repressive operations themselves. There were many testimonies by victim-survivors about torturers, but little was known about the Argentine generals, admirals, and brigadiers who masterminded the repression. At the time of my fieldwork, these men were in their sixties and accustomed to speaking in public. They didn't ask me to keep our interviews confidential, and several were pleased that I recorded them on tape to avoid misquotation. I am therefore quite sure that they would have ended an aggressive interview immediately or would have been tight lipped during the rest of the interview.

My interview strategy was not to contest the truth of their answers frontally, even when I knew them to be wrong, but to pose my inquiries in a more roundabout way. I pretended to accept their discourse at face value and probed further into the justifications of state terrorism. This approach created a semblance of trust in their words, and by extension in their person, which helped to shield my mistrust.[28] Our courteous interaction—not to be mistaken for rapport—must have caught the senior officers by surprise because they were used to being attacked verbally by the media and the human rights movement. Now they could speak their mind, of course without revealing anything that would incriminate them.

This approach has its emotional costs. Affective empathy confronted me with the violent past of a perpetrator with whom I was having a polite conversation. I had a recurrent awareness of his dark side, a side capable of inflicting the great harm that I tried to understand. The everyday trust in our fellow human beings and the confidence in ourselves disintegrate during these brief reflections. Suppressing these thoughts out of emotional self-protection is understandable but would undo the affective empathy cultivated during an interview. Imagining oneself in such situations helps to formulate questions that would not arise otherwise, in particular about the perpetrator's personal experience and everyday life. How did you protect your family from harm? What did your wife know about your work in the armed forces? How did the kidnapping of officers by guerrilla insurgents affect your routines and emotions? How did you know whom to trust among your children's friends? What do you feel in hindsight about your role during the military dictatorship?

Interviewers may reveal emotional reactions through their body language. Rear Admiral Horacio Mayorga must have seen the look on my face when he said that he would explain how many captives of the navy came to their end: "What did they do? I tell you what happened in the navy, without any false sentiments. You will say, 'But did they . . . ?'

No, no, if not, I won't tell you anything and that's the end of it." He must have interpreted my facial expression as disbelief, but I was not showing disbelief about what he was going to tell me but that he was going to tell me at all. Mayorga continued: "Very well, they injected them and threw them in the sea. They didn't . . . He didn't even know that he was going to die, I can assure you."

At the time of this interview, there were only accounts by former captives who had seen the preparations for the death flights. Mayorga had noticed the effect of his unprecedented revelation and must have sensed that I had come to regard him as a reliable source. The uncovering of secret information gave him an opportunity to enhance his just-won credibility. He added that the captives were tortured only at the beginning of the dictatorship and that soon the information about the guerrilla organizations was so complete that torture was unnecessary. It sounded convincing at the moment, and he had seen this. He played a politics of truth on me that affected my ability to critically examine his reasoning. His rhetorical argument seemed to increase my cognitive empathy to a degree that I would clearly understand the rationale behind the state terrorism. On the way back to my apartment, I realized that Mayorga had misled me.

In addition to Mayorga's rhetorical exploitation of my empathy to construct a misguided truth, I was also susceptible to an unconscious dynamic that further weakened my reflexivity and critical detachment. Instead of sounding him out about the death flights or contesting his denial of torture, I asked him about the attack on a naval frigate by guerrilla divers in August 1975.

This sudden switch in the flow of our conversation was puzzling. Later I understood that it had been caused by my unconscious reaction to Mayorga's demeanor, known in psychoanalytic theory as counter-transference, or the displacement of unconscious affects on another person.[29] My temporary belief in his truthfulness created an unconscious projection, and even a brief merging of self and other, which I mistakenly experienced as affective empathy. I had accepted a discourse that was disguised as an authentic disclosure of sensitive information and had temporarily lost my independence as a researcher.

The combination of conscious moves and unconscious reactions can result in ethnographic seduction. The word *seduction* derives from the Latin verb *sēdūcĕre*, which means "to lead aside or away." One of the wider meanings of *seduce* is "to lead (a person) astray in conduct or belief."[30] Perpetrators may succeed in diverting ethnographers from their line of questioning by responding to their reactions. The conversation is redirected to protect a positive self-image, avoid compromising issues, and make ethnographers accept their discourse as the truth. I found the same process at work in my interviews with former guerrillas, ex-disappeared, human rights leaders, and bishops. They all had personal and political stakes in having their version of the past accepted as the only truth.

The crux of ethnographic seduction is that it makes the ethnographer accept the interviewee's shallow discourse at face value. The interviewer's questions follow the logic of this discourse instead of probing further. Ethnographic seduction sidesteps and disables the dialectic of empathy and detachment that is characteristic of fieldwork. The ethnographer is completely absorbed by a manifest discourse and doesn't intervene with questions that can discover a deeper and perhaps more truthful discourse.[31] An awareness of ethnographic seduction is therefore important to improve the quality of interviews.

How can ethnographic seduction be recognized? A good surface feeling, and a personal like or dislike of the interviewee, indicates that the ethnographer is emotionally vulnerable to manipulation. A reflexive examination of the unconscious emotional dynamics—manifested in feelings of congeniality, abrupt silences, a meeting of minds, the absence of a critical detachment, and nightmares—can help the researcher overcome ethnographic seduction. Some signs can be recognized and corrected during the interview. I already mentioned the sudden switch in topic of an ongoing conversation with Mayorga, which I would have avoided if I had understood ethnographic seduction at that time, but there can also be slips of the tongue, blank silences, jokes, and a mental blockage as to how to continue the interview. In the days after the interview, moments of depression and compulsive thoughts and dreams about the interlocutor may occur. Once the process of ethnographic seduction is discovered, interviewers can avoid its distorting effects.[32] They will then be on guard in follow-up interviews and succeed in controlling the emotional stirrings and countering any intentional manipulations.

ALEX: Your discussion of seductive perpetrators and ethnographic seduction is so important for researchers. As I think about the introduction where, for example, we discuss researchers who have used unorthodox strategies, and the previous chapter, when I mentioned the spectacular anthropologist, I wonder if we might speak of seductive researchers. It seems to me that this is an undercurrent of all fieldwork, where for the most part the researcher occupies a relatively high-status position, youth notwithstanding, and has to engage in a bit of enticement (perhaps indirect pressure as well) to procure the agreement of informants to talk and then, during the interview, to speak to the points of their research concerns. Perpetrator research is particularly fraught in this regard as we talk about throughout this book. Do you think we need to also address the issue of ethnographic seduction on the part of the researcher? Should we also be talking about the seductive researcher, the seductive anthropologist, or even research seduction? Is there a potentially unseemly side of research that too often gets buried and needs to be considered throughout the researcher process?

TONY: What a fascinating question, Alex! To be honest, I never thought about seductive researchers. I believe that subjectivity is crucial here. As you note, fieldworkers can be in a higher position of power and status than their research participants. Think here of European anthropologists who conducted ethnographic research during colonial times and consciously used their status to extract knowledge from their informants. There exists also an unconscious side to seductive research in the case of ethnographers working among the poor and the displaced. In these situations, a fieldworker may project unconscious affects on research participants who may develop countertransferential reactions that result in socially desirable answers. In retrospect, I recognize this unconscious dynamic in my earlier fieldwork in Brazil, where my hierarchical relationship with poor raft fishermen resulted in different ethnographic encounters than with large landowners. In Argentina, I noticed that a few middle-ranking officers who had rebelled against their superiors in the mid-1980s, and were therefore convicted and forced into retirement, responded to my questions in an unusually modest manner because they were eager to convince me of their nationalist ideas and the injustice done to them.

I can only acknowledge your observation about the potentially unseemly side of perpetrator research, hence the term *pornography of violence*. I guess that your metaphor of Medusa's gaze, which you explain in its complex relation to perpetrator research, is spot on. Perpetratorhood and violence can seduce, petrify, and mesmerize researchers, as it does war correspondents and people in general. People are repelled by the images of death and destruction they see on their television screens, but they still can't take their eyes off them. Just think of 9/11. How many times have we seen the planes crashing into the World Trade Center and kept watching? Our doubts in choosing an appropriate literary style to describe mass violence indicates our struggle with these emotions, as you show in chapter 6.

Empathy without Compassion

Ethnographers can understand perpetrators by imagining themselves in their hierarchical positions in repressive organizations through cognitive empathy and grasping the accompanying emotions through affective empathy. Empathy should not be confused with compassion. Members of Argentina's military regarded themselves as victims of revolutionary violence and entitled to carry out their legal mandate as the state's armed defenders. They felt that they were sacrificing their lives to protect Argentina's Western culture and its Christian religion and values.

Compassion for victims makes all the sense in the world, but how can I have compassion for Navy Captain Adolfo Scilingo, who participated in two death flights in 1977, dropping sedated captives from a plane over sea, and then tried to erase his troubling memories? "I think about them and I repress them," Scilingo said in an interview. "They were undressed while being unconscious and when the flight commander gave the order, depending on the location of the plane, the hatch was opened and they were thrown out naked, one by one."[33]

Scilingo didn't lack a historical awareness or moral reflection when he and Lieutenant Vaca were about to throw captives to their death: "I saw the thirteen naked persons, half sitting and sleeping, leaning against one another, on the left side of the plane. Similar to a scene from a concentration camp in the Second World War. If telepathy exists then it was at this moment. Vaca broke the silence and while looking at me said: 'It seems like a Nazi photo.' The silence became more intense. I will never forget this image."[34] Scilingo's confession consisted of gruesome details mixed with bouts of self-pity. He suffered from recurrent nightmares and felt victimized by the superior officers who had ordered the death flights. Scilingo may have been traumatized by his horrendous acts, but should I feel compassion for him?

If compassion means to suffer together with someone, then what did Argentine perpetrators suffer from? They were mourning comrades and family members killed during guerrilla attacks, feared a communist revolution that would radically change Argentina's way of life, and were emotionally affected by their own repressive practices. As one junior officer complained about his superiors: "They ordered us to fight against the subversion, saying that we were defending society against the enemy . . . We were not prepared for that type of a fight and they made us do things that we never dreamed of as military men. They said it was for our families."[35] This sacrifice was necessary according to Lieutenant General Videla, because "nothing more and nothing less than the national being was at stake."[36] The guerrilla insurgency and the broad opposition movement of workers, students, and political activists were seen as an existential and personal threat that had to be eliminated at any cost.

Acting violently against human beings takes a toll, especially when the victims are subdued combatants and defenseless civilians. Perpetrators break their own moral codes and violate a social trust that was nurtured during childhood. Yet once moral boundaries are crossed, often by dehumanizing victims, then perpetrators forfeit my compassion. Humanly, I cannot have compassion for persons who designed repressive structures and cruel operating procedures, intentionally harming helpless human beings or willfully deceiving them as they were slowly led to their death. Still, professionally I have an interest in human beings, and how individuals are conditioned, constrained, and enabled by others, including perpetrators, whom I try to understand through cognitive and affective empathy.

INTERLUDES

The Perpetrator and the Witness

"CAMBODIA'S KILLERS LIVE ON IN quiet infamy," the newspaper head-line read. The short article described how a man known as Grandfather Khan continued to live unpunished among the villagers he had terror-ized during the years of Democratic Kampuchea, the period of Khmer Rouge rule in Cambodia.[1]

Khan, the article explained, had killed hundreds of people in the prison camp he commanded and in the area surrounding it. Survivors reported that some of his victims were strung up by their feet and evis-cerated, internal organs left to dangle before their faces as they died. He also allegedly consumed the liver and bile of his victims in the belief that doing so would allow him to absorb their vitality.

It's difficult to write these sentences, which can never fully capture the atrocities they are supposed to describe. As I discussed in chapter 1, I have been trying to understand such horrors since I was a graduate student. I still seek answers. Why does genocide occur? What motivates a perpetrator to kill? How does a person like Khan bring himself to not just murder another human being but to do so in the cruelest of ways?

In the summer of 2000, I returned to Cambodia to conduct fol-low-up research for a book. I decided to try to find Khan and ask him, "Why did you do it?" "Ming," the journalist who had written the story, agreed to travel with me to Khan's home district. As we drove there,

Ming told me about her suffering while living under Khan's authority. At one point, Ming and a friend peered through the window of the local pagoda and saw a prisoner who had just been eviscerated by Khan's men. We also discussed the reasons some Khmer Rouge consumed human liver and bile, a practice I consider in detail in *Why Did They Kill? Cambodia in the Shadow of Genocide.*

After a couple of hours of driving, we arrived at the subdistrict office located by the pagoda where Ming had witnessed the evisceration. A modest building with latticed windows, the subdistrict office had been constructed out of clean, bare wooden planks. Rough-hewn posts held up the roof. The current head of the subdistrict, Luong, was perhaps sixty and had close-cropped gray hair. He greeted us with a friendly smile and spoke to me in a mixture of Khmer, broken English, and French.

When he heard that we were planning to see Khan, he frowned for a moment. He suggested that we send a moped taxi to see if Khan was at home and to ask if he would meet us at the subdistrict office. Ming's glance told me that she thought this was a much better and safer way to encounter Khan. We thanked Luong for his suggestion and sent the moped taxi off.

I sat down on a hard wooden bench in front of the office. It had become a hot, humid morning. I had no idea if Khan would appear. He might not be home or, if he was, might not come.

Over the years, I have interviewed many perpetrators. Few admit to committing the atrocities others accuse them of. Often, however, they are willing to talk in detail if asked why other perpetrators performed genocidal deeds. This indirect method of questioning allows them to save face and uncovers a great deal about the mind of facilitators. Some perpetrators downplay their involvement.

Two days earlier, I had interviewed a notorious prison guard said to have executed hundreds of people. He denied this allegation but admitted he had killed "one or two." Clearly, this vague answer suggested he had killed many more.

Reflecting on Khan's serious and renowned crimes, I began to doubt he would come. Then gravel sputtered in the dirt as a moped pulled up to the office.

"He's here," Luong said in a low voice. Ming shifted uneasily on the bench. We all turned to look.

The first thing I noticed were Khan's eyes, sunk into the crevice between high cheekbones and a low brow. He stared at us, which is considered rude and aggressive in Cambodia. His chin stuck out defiantly and the skin between his eyebrows was deeply creased, giving him a fearsome look. He had likely put on his best clothing to meet us: a white shirt with only three buttons and fastened at the top, a pair of black pants that didn't zip up, and a red-and-white checkered *krama* that gave his eyes a red tint.

Khan was once a poor peasant farmer, precisely the type of person the Khmer Rouge would appoint to positions of power because of their "pure" class background. He looked to be in his sixties and was unlike any other perpetrator I had ever met. When I stood to greet him, he responded but without any of the outward friendliness I usually encounter when meeting Cambodians, even former perpetrators.

Luong offered us the use of a small "office" that contained dirty laundry, gasoline drums, dining utensils, and a desk. We sat on blue plastic chairs, Khan opposite Ming and me, perhaps three or four feet away. The only light came from an open door and the cracks between the wooden planks of the wall. Silhouetted against the light, Khan looked even more menacing.

I explained to Khan that I was a professor conducting research for a book on Democratic Kampuchea, then told him I was examining Cambodian cultural understandings and the psychology of the Khmer Rouge in particular. When I asked him if he was willing to be interviewed, he looked at me as if my question were silly and muttered, "Yes, yes."

When interviewing perpetrators, I always ask general questions first and then move toward my central concern, which is why people kill.

"Before you joined the Khmer Rouge, what did you do?"

"Farmer."

"When did you join the Khmer Rouge?"

"Nineteen seventy."

"In what capacity?"

"Soldier."

"What type of political education were you given at that time?"

"None."

Unlike Ming's story, which had started with a cascade of words, Khan's began with monosyllables. I took a deep breath and wiped the sweat from my face.

After fifteen minutes of questioning, I managed to find out that he had served as a Khmer Rouge soldier from 1970 to 1973, fighting Lon Nol forces in Takeo Province. In 1973, he went to work at the subdistrict office. Eventually, he acknowledged that he had attended political education meetings at which he heard about such concepts as class contradiction, building a proper revolutionary consciousness, and defeating the enemy. When I asked him if he had ever discussed Marxist-Leninist philosophy with anyone, he said no, then added that he was illiterate and didn't understand such things.

I began to move my line of questioning toward my goal: understanding why he had participated in the genocide.

"When did the prison open?"

"What prison?"

"The one that was located here, by the subdistrict office."

"There wasn't a prison here," he replied matter-of-factly. Ming's eyes widened.

Khan's words hung in the air. No one said anything for a long time.

Uncertain of how to respond, I looked at Khan, who glared back, his face braced against the light leaking through the walls.

The enormity of what he was doing slowly began to sink in. Most perpetrators will claim that they had a lesser or different position, were just following orders, or had never actually killed anyone. But no perpetrator I had interviewed had ever tried to deny the very existence of a prison or execution center. Maybe this is why he had come to talk to me: to erase history.

Ming suddenly asked me in English, "Do you want me to tell him what I saw?"

"Only if that's what you want to do," I replied. She returned to her silence.

This man linked to the suffering of so many people, including her mother, had just denied one of her most powerful memories.

I decided to question Khan from a different angle. Because I hadn't contradicted him, he seemed more at ease. His answers grew more lengthy, and he even acknowledged that he had been the head of the subdistrict militia.

When I asked him about the line of command, he offered the names of his superiors without hesitation. Grandfather Kee ran the subdistrict office, and San, a relative of Ta Mok, a notorious Khmer Rouge general, was the district head.

When I returned to the topic of killing, however, he reverted to monosyllables.

"At the subdistrict level, how were people's backgrounds investigated?" I asked.

"In the normal manner," he replied vaguely.

Addressing Khan, Ming said, "Others have told us that people were killed in a savage manner in this area."

Immediately, he responded, speaking with a confident, self-satisfied air.

"No. In this subdistrict, there wasn't any killing. They killed in neighboring subdistricts. In this subdistrict there was no killing. That is the truth. People just like to say such things."

Ming started, "But the people in the subdistrict said—"

Khan cut her off. "No, nobody was killed in this area."

Ming laughed in disbelief. In English she announced, "He's a liar."

She looked at the dirt floor. Maybe the sight of him had become unbearable. Without looking up, she addressed him in Khmer. "Many people have told me about the things you did."

Scowling at her, he repeated his denial: "No one was killed in this subdistrict. People say such things, but I didn't do anything. It's unjust. There isn't any evidence. Where is the prison? Where is the proof?"

At this point I broke in. "I'm a professor. I've read many books on the Pol Pot period, and I'm writing one myself. I've interviewed hundreds of people all over Cambodia, including individuals who, like yourself, were heads of the subdistrict militia. In all of these books and interviews, I never heard of a subdistrict where not a single person died. Never."

Now it was Khan's turn to pause. Our eyes locked together. Eventually he broke off his stare, perhaps uncertain of what I knew: "Not here, not here. There's no proof."

I continued, "In most subdistricts, including this one, people wrote to the government and described the horrors they witnessed, including the deaths of their family and friends."

Khan shifted in his chair. He said: "No one was killed here. Not a single person. If we arrested people, they would later be set free. You can't believe what you hear. Nobody saw anything. If anyone was killed, it was people from the district security office who came and did it."

Ming cut in, saying: "I'm going to tell you the truth. During the Pol Pot period, I lived here also. I saw them kill a man in the pagoda."

Khan leaned forward and gave her the full force of his scowl. His voice rising, he repeated: "No one was killed here, not even one person. There's no evidence."

"You're a liar," she said angrily.

Khan glared at her, a small bead of perspiration trickling down his forehead.

Finally, he murmured: "The prison was just a holding center. None of the prisoners was killed there. The district people came and took them away. I don't know what they did with them." He said this in a matter-of-fact tone, as if trying to gloss over the fact that he had just radically altered his story.

Ming laughed and, in English, announced, "So, now he admits it."

When I asked Khan about conditions in the prison, his replies came more quickly. The area around the prison had been sealed off, he explained, and security officers from the district came to take the prisoners away. He again denied that people were executed at the prison and told us that, like everyone else, he feared for his life, particularly when people from the district security office appeared.

At the end of the Pol Pot period, he said, an angry mob had chased him into the jungle, and he was later imprisoned for a year by the Vietnam-backed government that had overthrown the Khmer Rouge regime.

When I asked why the mob had chased him, he replied: "I don't know why. They must have made a mistake."

A piece of paper slipped out of my notebook and floated to the ground beside Khan's chair. It was my list of questions and interview topics. Without hesitation, he picked up the sheet and extended it to me. When I reached out to receive it, our hands met. For an instant, I felt his skin, calloused from years of labor, and the line between perpetrator and person blurred. He could have been almost any other Cambodian farmer.

"How would you respond if one of the prisoners whom you arrested and who died came back to life?" I asked.

For once, he didn't offer an immediate denial. He was perspiring a great deal now and seemed tired. "That would make me really happy. I would bow down and ask for forgiveness," he said.

"You'd say you were sorry?"

"Yes," he replied. Was he finally acknowledging his brutal deeds? Or had he simply not understood that my question implied he was guilty?

We had been talking for well over an hour, and the interview was drawing to a close. But Ming was not ready to let Khan go. "Do you think there should be a tribunal?" she asked him. At the time of this meeting, the United Nations and the Cambodian government were in negotiations to bring high-ranking Khmer Rouge cadre to trial. Many former Khmer Rouge were therefore worried about being indicted, although various officials had promised that only the top leaders would be tried.

Khan responded: "Sure, why not? I'm not afraid. Since I didn't do anything, I don't have anything to be afraid of. I just followed the orders of the leaders." Still, he looked uneasy. Maybe frightening him was Ming's way of getting back at him.

Angrily, she responded: "But you were a leader, the head of the sub-district militia. You commanded people."

"I just followed orders."

"Everyone was afraid of you back then. I heard people say that if you stared at a person, even for a moment, that person would disappear the next day."

"No. They just say things like that about me, that I was savage. It's not true. I helped the people. If they were hungry, I would try to get food for them."

A man slipped into the room to retrieve some dishes. Khan looked at him, then back at us, indicating that it was time for him to return home.

I had saved one last set of questions for him. "How many people worked for you in the militia?" I asked.

"Forty or so."

"What were some of their names?"

"None of them is still alive," he said, spitting on the floor. He realized that I wanted to talk to other people and ask them about the prison.

"But what are their names?"

Khan named a few people who, he assured us, were dead. I pressed him.

"Surely out of the forty, someone must still be alive?"

"They're either dead or moved away. I don't know where they went."

"All of them?" I asked.

Khan paused for a moment, then said, "There's one man, Samrong, who worked with me in the militia. He lives in my village."

Ming abruptly addressed Khan: "Who arrested Sopha Lim?"

"Sopha Lim." Khan repeated the name, seeming to recognize it. "She wasn't arrested."

Ming was clearly irritated. "That's my mother. My mother. She was led to a grave and told it was hers."

"No," Khan said, erasing the past with one word.

Ming raised her voice. "Stop lying to me."

"I'm not lying."

"I'm angry now because you're trying to tell me that my mother was never arrested. It's my mother you're talking about. I was there. I know."

"No," Khan repeated, adding: "It's time for me to eat. I'm supposed to meet some people."

The interview was over. We all stood up and walked outside. We arranged for Khan to be driven back to his village by a moped taxi driver. The driver revved his engine, and Khan climbed on the back. As the wheels churned up the earth where the bodies of his prisoners lay, Khan glanced back at us, scowling. The roar of the moped faded in the distance, becoming a hum, then silence.

"They Were No More. None of Them. They Had Become Disappeared."

A Creative Nonfiction Testimony

WHEN THE MILITARY TOOK OVER Argentina in March 1976, I, Matilde Herrera, expected that people would be arrested and assassinated, but I never, ever imagined that the repression would be so brutal and perfectly planned.[1] Nobody imagined this. My children, José, Martín, and Valeria, had joined the revolutionary movement in the early 1970s. They wanted to end poverty in Argentina. No violence is worse than poverty. Poverty kills children from hunger and lack of medical care. Poverty deprives them of schooling. I'm very proud of my children. They had everything: food, clothing, holidays in Europe, and the best schools. They could have done whatever they wanted in life but they chose to sacrifice themselves for the future of others. Injustice was more intolerable to them than fear.

In 1959, I separated from my first husband Rafa (Rafael José Beláustegui). We had grown apart, and I decided to raise the three children by myself. The military coup by General Onganía in 1966 was a blow to the spirit of rebellion that was blossoming in Argentina. Films were censored, and miniskirts and bikinis were forbidden. In an attempt to

95

stop students from radicalizing, any political activity at the university was declared illegal. This suffocating climate also affected my children. José, my eldest son, was sent to the haircutter three days in a row because his hair continued to be too long. He was greatly influenced by Che Guevara who had fought for the liberation of humankind until his death in 1967. José started reading the works of Lenin and Mao, and became involved in the Maoist Revolutionary Communist Party in 1968 when he was thirteen, fourteen years old. His elder sister by two years, Valeria, joined the National Liberation Movement.

The killing of Juan José Cabral by the police during a student protest in the city of Corrientes in May 1969 left a deep impression on José and Valeria and made them even more committed to the revolutionary struggle. The widespread anger at the violent repression of student protests in Corrientes and other cities came to a climax on May 29, 1969, in the city of Córdoba. Tens of thousands of students and workers united in a massive protest march to the city center. It was tremendous. The police tried to repress the protesters with tear gas and bullets. The crowd turned violent when the autoworker Máximo Mena was killed. And then the army arrived. Students sealed off two neighborhoods with hundreds of barricades, and a few guerrilla snipers held off the soldiers. The army took the city at the cost of dozens of dead protesters. There was a general belief in leftist circles that the time was ripe for a social revolution. In July 1970, the People's Revolutionary Army (ERP, or Ejército Revolucionario del Pueblo) was founded. Mario Roberto Santucho became the commander in chief. The ERP started an armed insurgency, together with the Montoneros and other small guerrilla organizations.

My son José continued his political activism, and in 1971 he helped create a clandestine high school student organization that opposed Argentina's authoritarian educational system. The organization had close ties to the guerrilla insurgency and sought to forge links between the student protests and the worker protests. I didn't know then that José and Valeria had joined the Argentine Liberation Front (Fuerzas Armadas de Liberación) in 1972 or that Martín had also become politically active. Perhaps they took this step after the navy massacred sixteen guerrillas in August 1972 who were held prisoner at the naval air base in Trelew. It was around this time that José decided not to enroll in the university. He wanted to become a carpenter to be close to the working class. At the carpentry shop, he fell in love with Electra, the owner's daughter.

Under the weight of the guerrilla attacks and the incessant street protests, the dictatorship of Lieutenant General Lanusse was forced to call for general elections in 1973. Juan Domingo Perón became Argentina's president after spending eighteen years in exile. The Montoneros laid down their arms because their goal of overthrowing Lanusse and returning Perón to power had been achieved, but the Marxist ERP continued to attack the armed forces until they could reach a final victory.

One evening in April 1974, José came home for dinner. "Mother, I have something important to tell you," he said. "I have decided to join the People's Revolutionary Army." I looked at him but couldn't say anything. I felt as if I was drowning. I saw his entire life pass before my eyes.

"I don't want to know," I said. "They're going to kill you!"

"Mother, I can't live with my back to injustice."

"José, I don't want to know anything. What if they follow me or detain me? Will I be able to hold my tongue if they torture me? Why are you telling me this?"

"Mother, the party thinks it's best that some parents know. It's the best way to protect us."

We sat down. I didn't want to argue with him. The worst I could have done was to leave him unprotected, to make him feel that his mother had abandoned him. "And Valeria and Martín?" I asked.

"Not yet," he said with a smile.

The next day I awoke crying. I didn't say anything to Bobby (Roberto Aizenberg), my second husband, because I needed to calm down first. But every day I became more anxious. I couldn't stop crying; in the street, in the bus. I started wearing sun glasses because I was afraid to draw attention when tears welled up and ran down my face.

Rafa took this photo around this time (fig. 5). Did he fear that the political activism of our children would end in disaster? Did he sense

FIGURE 5. Matilde Herrera and her children, José, Martín, and Valeria. Photo by Rafael José Beláustegui. Source: faustomarecelo.blogspot.com. Reproduced with permission from Tania Luján Waisberg.

that this might be our last family reunion? The children look resolute. Were they aware of the sacrifices they had to make to achieve the social revolution they desired so much? For me, now, fifteen years later, the photo shows the tragedy of it all, and the losses that I, we, and the Argentine people have suffered.

José and his wife, Electra, were living in a working-class neighborhood on the outskirts of Buenos Aires. They narrowly escaped when the police raided their home in September 1974. The pressure was mounting. They had to move underground. José didn't lose faith. In a letter from January 14, 1975, he wrote: "Things are going well and the party is growing fast. If we stick to our strategy, then we will pass to a stage of generalized war and strengthen our indestructible Revolution." By April 1975, Valeria and her husband, Ricardo, and Martín and his wife,

María Cristina, had also entered the People's Revolutionary Army. All my children were now living in illegality.

The military stepped up the repression in February 1975 because the ERP had started a rural guerrilla company to create a liberated zone in northwest Argentina. The Montoneros had also picked up arms again after Perón died in July 1974. In September 1975, José and Electra had a son, our grandson Antonio. This happiness was soon overshadowed. On December 23, 1975, hundreds of ERP combatants attacked a military base south of Buenos Aires. Many died that day. We spent a sad Christmas Eve together. "Enough," I said. "Please. The enemy is too strong."

"You don't understand, mother. We have to put trust in the popular support. Mistakes are made but we cannot fail the people in the struggle that accompanies this one: the struggle for social justice."

"They're going to kill you all."

"For every fallen comrade, others will stand up."

On February 6, 1976, Valeria gave birth to Tania, our granddaughter. The armed forces overthrew the government on March 24, 1976 and suspended all constitutional rights. More and more people were disappearing. And then it was our turn. Martín and María Cristina were abducted on July 26, 1976, by ten armed men dressed as civilians. Martín was to turn twenty the next day. María Cristina was two months pregnant. Five days after their disappearance, I met José and Valeria in a café. I didn't know that this was going to be the last time I would see Valeria.

I began the search for Martín and María Cristina. I called my first husband, Rafa, who was in Brazil, to return to Argentina and help me. We presented a habeas corpus request to the court and contacted officers and bishops, who sometimes spoke in cryptic sentences, such as "Your children have embarked on a long journey from which they may not return." I sought information wherever I could, walking the streets under the winter rains. I fell seriously ill. Pneumonia. Slowly, I began to recover and started thinking about a stay in Paris that had been arranged by Bobby before Martín and María Cristina disappeared. José and Valeria encouraged me to go to France because Rafa would continue the search in Argentina.

Bobby and I arrived in Paris in September 1976. I wrote José and Valeria once or twice a week and received their letters in return. I walked for hours through a Paris I did not see. Bobby and I were thinking of returning to Buenos Aires by the end of October. However, the military repression was getting worse, making it impossible to see the children. We decided to postpone our departure. Just before Christmas, with our bags packed, I received a message: "Someone said that if Matilde Herrera returns, they will kill her." Who had said this? What did it mean? Friends confirmed the rumor and warned that I might be detained when stepping off the plane. My return would only endanger the children.

Months passed. In May 1977, Bobby received an alarming letter from José: Valeria and Ricardo had disappeared on May 13. Their daughter, Tania, was safe with Ricardo's mother, who had been called by the police to pick her up. Rafa was doing everything possible to find Valeria and Ricardo, and he urged José and Electra to leave the country. On May 30, on José's twenty-third birthday, he and Electra were abducted from the apartment of friends in the posh Recoleta neighborhood of Buenos Aires. I heard later that José hadn't lost his irony. "Do you have a cyanide capsule?" one of the assailants asked, because some guerrillas concealed a suicide capsule in their mouth. "No," responded José, "but I have a bitter taste in my mouth." José and Electra were hooded and pistol-whipped into a Ford Falcon car. After a short ride, they arrived at an unknown place. They were undressed, soaked with ice-cold water, and left for hours on the bare floor. More than a month later, Electra's parents received a phone call that they should come and fetch their grandson Antonio.

They were no more. None of them. They had become disappeared. Where did their young lives go? I couldn't cry. I continued to eat, sleep, and talk to friends, but I knew that if I gave in to my pain, I would have been unable to continue living. I didn't cry, because I sensed that if I would sit down and cry, I would never ever be able to get back on my feet again. Still living in Paris, I heard that José and Electra had been seen alive five months after their abduction. There was no sign of Valeria or Ricardo. I also learned that Valeria had been two months pregnant when she was abducted. She was taken to the secret maternity ward of the Campo de Mayo army base and gave birth to a baby boy in December 1977, according to a nurse from the Military Hospital. I never knew what happened to Martín and María Cristina, or if she ever delivered her baby. I returned to Argentina in 1983 and have been searching for my missing grandchildren ever since.

Part II

DREAMING

THREE

The Night Stalkers

I'm standing in a small bar. People are having drinks at the counter. There is a barkeeper dressed in white with a cap on his head, as in an American soda shop from the 1950s. Two women sit in a corner. I walk to the public telephone in the bar and make a call to the Foundation of the Search for the Disappeared. Speaking in Portuguese, I pretend to have a twenty-two-year-old younger brother who has disappeared. I ask if they can help me locate him. I receive no answer. I repeat my question, but again no answer, only a mumble. I add that I can't say anything else over the phone and want to talk to them in person. Again no answer. I wake up.

ON THE SURFACE, THIS DREAM from September 1990 during my fieldwork in Buenos Aires seemed obvious: it referred to my ongoing research into Argentina's disappearances during the last military dictatorship. But why this particular dream? According to Freud, dreams often contain ambivalent day residues, traces of problems that trouble the dreamer during the day and then appear in a veiled form at night. Had I been worrying about the progress of my research or the denials and silences of the Argentine officers I was interviewing?

What complicated my self-analysis was that Freud's classic work *The Interpretation of Dreams* argued that a day residue should not be taken literally, that it is only a vehicle to express an unconscious wish.

Freud stated, "The daytime thought, which was not in itself a wish but on the contrary a worry, was obliged to find a connection in some way or other with an infantile wish which was now unconscious and suppressed . . . there was no necessity for there being any connection whatever between the content of the wish and that of the worry."[1] Dreams thus serve to fulfill unconscious wishes. What could this unconscious wish be? Fortunately, professional help was at hand.

In the 1950s, psychoanalysis developed a growing appeal among Argentina's middle class. During the turbulent 1970s, even the Argentine military adopted some of the field's vocabulary to explain the country's ills. For instance, Brigadier General Agosti, a member of the military junta, stated in 1978 that the guerrilla insurgency had been caused by a national identity crisis: "We no longer knew who we were, where we had come from, where we were, at what we aspired and in what we believed; that is to say, we did not know our self."[2]

The coup d'état of 1976 had been a necessary cure in the opinion of the armed forces. The coup would restore the country's Western, Christian culture after its infiltration by alien ideas. Despite their psychological interpretation of the political situation, the military believed that psychoanalysis had corrupted Argentina. Freud was regarded as subversive of the family because he emphasized the importance of sex instead of religious faith and patriarchy. The armed forces went after psychotherapists who provided counseling to guerrilla combatants or worked in state hospitals that serviced working-class neighborhoods.[3] A triumphant General Vilas concluded, "If the military would have allowed the proliferation of disintegrative elements—psychoanalysts, psychiatrists, Freudians, et cetera—who stirred up the consciences and put doubt on our national and family roots, then we would have been defeated."[4] However, state terrorism could not eliminate the cultural insertion of psychoanalysis in Argentina's society or the demand for psychotherapy after the military fell from power in 1983.

––––––

ALEX: Interesting. In both the Argentine and Cambodian cases, the perpetrators waged a sort of war against the mind. Consciousness was absolutely critical to the Khmer Rouge. Everyone was required to forge a pure revolutionary consciousness, which meant constantly working to excise counterrevolutionary thoughts and tendencies. Those who faltered in this task were often targeted for execution. Some were said to suffer from "memory sickness." For the Khmer Rouge, consciousness was linked to politics and organization—the triad of their party line.

Just how central was the battle over the mind for the military junta? Was it as elaborately formulated as it was for the Khmer Rouge? And was there the same sort of emphasis on purity of mind, society, and body politic and a related battle against contamination (of mind and society).

TONY: The mind was very central to the Argentine military. They emphasized for instance that ideologues were more dangerous than armed guerrillas because they infected people's minds with subversive ideas and created revolutionary selves. All captives were given a number upon entry in a secret detention center and their danger to society was assessed. Irremediable inmates were given a death sentence, but some disappeared were considered potentially useful to society. The conquest of their minds was achieved through a process of social dismantlement. Extensive torture and lengthy confinement in tiny cells— hooded, naked, and shackled—could transform them from subversives into "citizens." One sign on the way to recuperation was to remain unmoved when hearing someone being tortured. The officers disapproved of showing compassion toward torture victims, and crying was seen as an indication of weakness. The navy had a rehabilitation program at the officers' mess in Buenos Aires where captives had to prove they had been "reborn" by the treatment. If so, then they were rewarded with their reappearance in society or their exile abroad.

Publications about the ESMA secret detention center are generally accompanied by a photograph of a neoclassical building with Escuela de Mecánica de la Armada (Navy Mechanics School) written on the architrave. This building has become synonymous with the navy's torture center in Buenos Aires. However, the disappeared were kept, tortured, and assassinated in a nearby building, namely the officers' mess (fig. 6).

The Argentine military blamed parents for not properly raising their disappeared children. The Argentine people, and especially the working

FIGURE 6. Officers' Mess at the Navy Mechanics School (ESMA), Buenos Aires. Photo by Antonius Robben.

class and the student generation, had to be reeducated. Improper dress, such as miniskirts, was forbidden, and literature, films, and music were censored. Schools and universities had military overseers, and the labor unions and political parties were outlawed. As I explained in my book *Political Violence and Trauma in Argentina*, the military was fighting a cultural war against the guerrilla insurgency and a heterogeneous opposition movement. In this so-called clash of cultures, it tried to impose their cultural project on the Argentine people. Steeped in Thomism, the military believed in a divine social hierarchy—unlike the revolutionary's utopia of social equality—paternal authority, private property, the nuclear family, patriotism, and Christian values. The Khmer Rouge and the Argentine military were thus ideological opposites, but they both used extreme violence to force their vision onto society.

Although a skeptic about psychoanalysis after reading the work of Claude Lévi-Strauss (I will say more about that later), I had entered analysis in Buenos Aires in May 1989 to understand its significance to Argentine culture. I could thus share my dream of September 1990 with my analyst. She suggested that it showed several identifications with my father and his deceased younger brother, Johannes "Jo" Petrus, with whom he had been very close and who was twenty-two years old when German troops invaded the Netherlands in May 1940. Different stories circulated in my family. I will relate his story as I heard it through the years and add the contradictory archival information about his death.

Jo had been arrested in 1943 by the Gestapo (German Secret State Police) for smuggling food-ration coupons to Jews hiding in Amsterdam. He was interrogated in the notorious Scheveningen prison and then incarcerated in the Dutch concentration camps of Vught and Amersfoort. In May 1944, he was transported to Dachau. On July 2, 1944, Jo wrote a censored letter in German to his parents, brothers, and sisters in which he told them about "the beautiful Alps of Tyrol. Everything is so lovely with the high mountains in snow. I'm in good health and hope you are too." Nevertheless, he asked them repeatedly to send him bread and soap. From Dachau, he was taken in July to Gross-Rosen, and in November to Auschwitz. Evacuated from Auschwitz in January 1945 on a death march to the labor camp Geppersdorf, he developed a serious infection in his left arm and was sent to the sick barracks of Dörnhau, a subcamp of Gross-Rosen. Inmates called Dörnhau the "cold crematorium" because of the absence of medical care and the high death rate.[5] Jo died on April 29, 1945, at Dörnhau, eight days before the camp's liberation by Soviet troops. He might also have died at the hospital in Wüstegiersdorf, a village near Dörnhau. His body was cremated or dumped in a mass grave.

The letter from Dachau, reproduced in figure 7, is the only material trace left of my uncle. The letter's front contains my grandfather's address and detailed instructions about correspondence with inmates. Prisoners could send two letters per month and receive money orders, packages, and two letters per month. The instructions emphasized fur-

FIGURE 7. Letter by Jo Robben from Dachau concentration camp, dated July 2, 1944. Photo by Antonius Robben.

ther that "requests for release directed at the camp authorities are useless," and "visits to the concentration camp are categorically forbidden."

My uncle's relatives were desperate for news when the war in Europe ended in May 1945, especially after several concentration camp survivors still dressed in striped prisoner clothing told my grandparents that Jo was still alive in a Russian camp. They asked for money to bring their missing son home, but my grandfather didn't trust them. Months later, the Red Cross notified that Jo had died from blood poisoning or typhoid fever in Dörnhau or Wüstegiersdorf.

According to my analyst, "L," the dream expressed a transferential displacement of my father's wish to find his missing brother to my unconscious desire to fulfill his wish by way of Argentina's disappeared.[6] I was in my father's place and from this position searched for "my" missing brother Jo among the disappeared of Argentina. Her surprising observation made me realize how the research agendas of anthropologists may be connected to their inner lives. She also remarked that the dream account revealed that my father had been looking for his brother in me.

I think she was right. My father had wanted to baptize me Johannes, a potentially lifelong burden that my mother opposed. My parents finally agreed on calling me by my father's first name, Antonius, and thus unintentionally reinforced our mutual identification and shaped my internalized model of paternal authority. This unconscious model, with its accompanying ambivalence of love and hostility, became projected onto other figures of authority later in life and influenced the way I related to perpetrators. Fieldwork requires due attention to the impact of such psychodynamic influences on ethnographic research because, as Jennifer Hunt has said, "much thought and activity takes place outside of conscious awareness . . . [and] the unconscious meanings which mediate everyday life are linked to complex webs of significance which can ultimately be traced to childhood experiences."[7]

The figures of authority in Argentina also included L, my guide to the unconscious. I therefore reproduce her analytic interventions in my dream accounts. In particular, I focus on the reflection of the fieldwork relations and anxieties in my dreams and show how her psychoanalytic interpretations clarified the encounters with perpetrators and ultimately improved my ethnographic analysis.[8]

Authority Figures as Research Collaborators

Ethnographic knowledge emerges from the interpersonal dynamics and verbal exchanges of the field encounter. Barbara Meyerhoff regarded this dialogic construction as a "third voice, which is neither the voice of the informant nor the voice of the interviewer, but the voice of their collaboration."[9] This understanding is valuable for underscoring the cocreative nature of interviews and to emphasize that a dialogue cannot be reduced to the voices of the interlocutors. Still, dialogues are not limited to the dynamics of the field encounter but are also influenced by the unconscious. The third voice contains the echoes of the parental voices internalized by ethnographers and interviewees. Vincent Crapanzano has argued that the ethnographic relation between self and other is interposed by a Third. This Third is what Jacques Lacan called the "third personage," or father, who mediates the relation between mother and child.[10] This third is not the real flesh-and-blood father but the symbolic father. This father is "the symbolic matrix for a series of other symbols (such as authority, law, and God, as Freud noted, and language, culture, and convention)."[11]

The symbolic paternal authority is psychologically involved in the field relations with research participants. The symbolic father is the proto-authority, the original form onto which other male figures of authority are grafted, at least in male-dominated societies. The importance of the father—real or symbolic—should not be taken literally, especially in a time of divorce and single motherhood. Yet "despite the physical and emotional absence of a real father, there is always some kind of internal picture or representation."[12] The single mother's inner father, in other words, is reproduced in the relationship with her children. Of course, the internal symbolic father is not determinative. People's self-knowledge, changing gender relations, and ideological convictions about power and authority are of transformative value. This is not to say that the psychodynamics of paternal authority loses all significance. My internalized paternal authority entered ethnographic encounters in a disguised form when it was transposed onto male perpetrators in Argentina, resulting in a correspondence between paternal and political authority that had been explicitly reinforced during periods of military domination.

The interviewee's unconscious processes are generally inaccessible, especially in the case of perpetrators, but a study of a society's gendered authority model can provide some insight. The dictatorship that ousted President Perón in 1955 reintroduced the *patria potestas* in Argentina's National Constitution. This Roman law established the father's authority over his wife and children as the head of family and household. The military later bemoaned its weakening by what they saw as the decadence of the 1960s and the corrosion of authority by the revolutionary fervor of the 1970s. As a former guerrilla of the Montoneros wrote about this turbulent period, the successful rebellion against the military during the early 1970s "was transferred to, for example, the relation between parents and children, teachers and students, managers and employees: any type of authoritarianism was demolished from one day to the next, and transgression became the norm."[13] The military junta of 1976 wanted to resurrect Argentina's traditional family values and people's respect for political authority. John Borneman has observed that in most repressive regimes of the twentieth century, "the authority of the father and of the leader became closely intertwined," as the dictator "appropriates for himself all forms of paternal authority; all authority is exercised in his name."[14]

––––––

ALEX: There are some interesting points of contrast with the Cambodia case here. During DK, the Khmer Rouge sought to erase gender in a number of ways, ranging from taking away gendered social roles (for example, by introducing communal eating) to standardizing appearance and dress (for example, by having everyone dress in black and women crop their hair short). It was as if they were seeking to create a society of uniform, equal, minimally gendered revolutionaries—a society of "comrades." Gender differences remained, to be sure, but they were minimized and often manifest in indirect and less visible ways.

That is very different from the situation you are describing. And of course, hypermasculinity, ultranationalism, fetishization of tradition, a call for renewal, and scapegoating have all been linked to fascism. Do you regard the military junta in Argentina as fascist? I don't think you mention that term in this entire book, so I assume not. Does the term have any analytical purchase for you and why?

TONY: With respect to gender, the Argentine dictatorship was exactly the opposite of the Khmer Rouge. It very much tried to emphasize a hierarchical gender differentiation. Women should dress in skirts, be feminine and subservient to men, and take care of the home and the children. This is why the military were at a loss about how to respond to the street protests of the Mothers of the Plaza de Mayo. The women violated but also affirmed the traditional gender roles. They acted as protective mothers—and therefore symbolized this status by using cloth diapers as headscarves—but did so in a male public domain that was the realm of politics. Hence, the military called them the "crazy women." It is interesting that the guerrilla organizations wanted to abolish gender inequality, but that in reality women were generally assigned to noncombat duties and had to carry out domestic chores such as cooking, washing, and cleaning. This didn't help them in the torture rooms because male and female guerrillas were considered equally dangerous.

Was the Argentine junta fascist? This is a complicated question whose answer depends on what you mean by fascism. There are historians who define fascism as a unique political movement that arose in Italy, Germany, and Spain during the interbellum and cannot be transferred to other times and places. The regimes of Hitler and Mussolini were defeated in the Second World War, while Franco slowly released his grip on the Spanish people primarily for economic reasons. European fascism was antidemocratic and virulently anticommunist, which was also the case for Argentina's junta. In a broader sense, fascism was a mass movement that emphasized nationalism under the aegis of a strong charismatic, authoritarian leader who drew large popular crowds that legitimized his absolute rule. Instead, the junta forbid crowd gatherings other than the public celebration of football victories. Mass mobilizations were seen as a seed bed of revolutionary change and reminded the junta of the populist leader Juan Domingo Perón, who rallied his supporters at the Plaza de Mayo to support his government. I therefore don't think that the Argentine junta can be called fascist in a historical or political sense, but its right-wing authoritarian rule and repressive practices did resemble those of Europe's fascist states.

————

Images of perpetrators and the mothers may not be what they seem to show. The picture in figure 8 went global in October 1982. The police

FIGURE 8. Deputy Chief Carlos Enrique Gallone, of Argentina's Federal Police, holds Susana de Leguía at the Plaza de Mayo, October 5, 1982. Photo by Marcelo Ranea. Source: Wikimedia Commons.

officer's embrace was interpreted as a comforting gesture toward a distraught mother protesting her son's disappearance. The photographer explained years later that in fact the deputy chief of the Federal Police, Carlos Enrique Gallone, was restraining her. She was angrily confronting him for not allowing the Mothers of the Plaza de Mayo to hand a petition to President Bignone, the head of the military government. In July 2008, Gallone was convicted and sentenced to life in prison for the execution of thirty disappeared persons in the town of Fátima on August 20, 1976, and for destruction of their corpses with dynamite as revenge for the assassination of General Omar Actis the day before. Gallone showed the photo during his defense in court. To prove his good relationship with Argentina's human rights organizations, he claimed that the woman was thanking him.[15]

———

My internalized paternal authority shaped the relationships with Argentine perpetrators and officers who were consciously and unconsciously imbued with feelings of male superiority. They had either occupied commanding posts in the military regime or had ruled over their victims as torturers and executioners. Although retired at the time of the interviews, many had retained an overbearing demeanor and used their secret knowledge about the enforced disappearances to retain a continuing grip on Argentine society. The ambivalent emotional affinities and conflicts toward my father were thus transferred to my professional encounters with Argentine officers and became manifest in fieldwork anxieties.

A decade before reflexive anthropology initiated the self-scrutiny of fieldworkers, George Devereux had already stated that all ethnographers are troubled by fieldwork anxieties. These anxieties might be caused by the researcher's personality or a confrontation with emotionally troubling cultural beliefs and practices. Devereux explained that fieldworkers tend to defend themselves by using objectifying theories and methodologies while disregarding their personal disturbances.[16] My predominant fieldwork anxieties consisted of conscious feelings of professional inadequacy about interviewing perpetrators, an unconscious ambivalence toward male figures of authority, and the conscious awareness of conflicting emotions when facing perpetrators who were courteous and helpful but had been described in victim testimonies as cruel and violent.

Fieldwork Anxieties and Perpetrators

My first contact with an Argentine officer accused of crimes against humanity was arranged by the director of the military library in Buenos Aires.[17] General Díaz Bessone had been commander of the Second Army Corps in 1975 and 1976, and minister of planning between November 1976 and December 1977. A prolific writer, he was regarded as an ideologue of the dictatorship. The general was under indictment when we met in June 1989 at the Army Officers' Club (Círculo Militar) located in Palacio Paz, a nineteenth-century city palace that had seen better days. Díaz Bessone was a large man of sixty-four years old with a firm baritone voice and a demanding look. Thinning gray hair covered his head, and his face was marked by a small brown mole under the corner of his right eye. That night I had the following dream:

> *I'm standing in the living room of my childhood home in the*
> *Netherlands. My father is also there. The curtains are drawn,*
> *and the room is sparsely furnished. On the mantel, there hangs a*
> *painting. My father says, "I think that our neighbor will like this*
> *painting." He opens the door and General Díaz Bessone steps in. He*
> *says that he likes the painting and leaves.*

The next day I went to analysis. I narrated my dream and said that I had felt uneasy before interviewing with the general. I had worried: How should I greet him? How should I open the conversation? What should I tell him about my research? What if he rejected the project or would become angry when I mentioned Argentina's disappeared? Would I be able to foster good rapport or even have another interview?

L remained silent. I continued with a hesitant explanation of the dream, trying to identify existing worries through introspection. The living room in the dream was a day residue because it resembled the rather morose room where I had met the general. The closed curtains suggested the dim light and the ambiguity of our yet undefined relationship. I added that this first encounter had been marked by suspicion and mutual reserve. The cause of my anxiety seemed a concern about establishing rapport, as I had experienced before while conducting fieldwork in Brazil. Following Freud's classic interpretation, I also ventured to explain the dream as wish fulfillment. I was latently desiring my father's approval in a manifest wish for the general's approval.

"Emotions are authoritarian," L began. "Emotions impose themselves on people and may therefore destabilize them." My anxiety dream had arisen from feelings of powerlessness, she said, from being stuck in a dead end during an emergency, namely facing a general accused of ordering the torture and disappearance of defenseless women, children, and men. This anxiety placed me in an emotional state of surrender, even though I had suggested that our meeting had been characterized by mutual mistrust. According to L, the anxiety dream, my free associations, and the attempt at self-analysis revealed how I tried to master the emotional impact of authority figures like General Díaz Bessone.

The photo of General Díaz Bessone was published in November 1976 in the popular Argentine magazine *Panorama*, just after he had been appointed minister of planning in the military government of Lieutenant General Videla (fig. 9). The picture was a presentation of what

FIGURE 9. General Ramón Genaro Díaz Bessone, of Argentina. Source: Wikimedia Commons.

he must have seen as his ideal self: a general dedicated to defend his country against leftist revolutionaries and determined to create the so-called new republic based on family, religion, and the nation. The photo continued to portray the man of vision he still regarded himself when I interviewed him thirteen years later.

I had several more anxiety dreams in the following weeks as I continued to interview Díaz Bessone, but analysis increased my self-confidence. We settled on a courteous mode of exchange, which also had a calming effect on my relationships with other Argentine officers and perpetrators. The success in overcoming this fieldwork anxiety became apparent when in December 1989 I succeeded in arranging two lengthy interviews with Argentina's highest military judges, the Supreme Council of the Armed Forces, and asked questions that I would not have dared to raise several months earlier.

Arriving punctually at the seat of Argentina's military supreme court, I was welcomed by the doorman. We walked up the stairway, and he left me in a small office. After a few minutes I was greeted by Brigadier Carlos Ramón Echegoyen. He explained the meeting's procedure. The vice president would ask me two things: a short autobiography and a summary of my current investigation. The brigadier led me through a labyrinth of corridors until we reached the conference room, an enclosed space with dark wooden paneling and a large rectangular table with a violet tablecloth. I went around the table to shake the hands of the generals, admirals, and brigadiers, and was shown my place at the table's short end, opposite the vice president, General Virgilio Górriz.

After the vice president and I finished our brief introductions, Rear Admiral Juan Carlos Frías asked permission to explain the political developments that had led to the coup d'état of March 1976. Despite the mild objection of several judges, he continued to hold the floor for nearly an hour. Then it was my turn to ask a first question. I paused for a moment, looked around the table, and dropped a bombshell: "Why did the armed forces not execute the guerrillas publicly?"

The officers were taken aback. Somehow, one general did not grasp my question and began to explain that the armed forces had never executed guerrillas publicly. He was interrupted politely and told that I had asked why the guerrillas had *not* been executed openly. Rear Admiral Eduardo Davion replied: "If one would have done what you are asking, the reason why, then there would have been immediate revenge, not only on the executioner or those who presided over the trial but also on their families. That is to say, the terror had also infused terror among the armed forces, and they responded with terror. This is the tremendous problem, the tremendous tragedy of this war."

Brigadier Carlos Echeverria Martínez completely agreed when we continued our conversation the next day. "One can only fight terror by instilling a greater terror in the enemy," he said. "And here we probably had to embark on that uncommon course that hurt and disgusted us all. If we wouldn't have more or less taken this road then Argentina would have been a bastion of Marxism at this moment."

I had deliberately provoked the men into revealing the military strategy behind the disappearance of tens of thousands of Argentines. In addition, they disclosed the underlying emotions. My assertive, almost defiant posture was enabled by the understanding and dissolution of my early fieldwork anxiety. L's analytic interventions, and especially her dream interpretations, allowed me to be aware of the intersubjective dynamics of ethnographic encounters with high-ranking officers and perpetrators.

Analytical Authority and the Way to the Unconscious

And what about my analyst? Wasn't she an authority figure in her own right? How did L influence my research? Our relationship became the subject of analysis two days after I had seen the film *Stalker* by the Russian director Andrei Tarkovsky. Here is a summary of how I narrated the plot during the analytic hour. I retain the factual errors caused by my selective memory of the dream after waking up:

> *Stalker portrays the perilous journey of three men into a forbidden Zone affected by a meteorite. The Zone became hermetically sealed off by armed guards when strange things started happening there: flowers bloomed without smell and birds were heard singing but not seen. The three men—identified as Stalker, Professor, and*

Writer—enter the Zone to find the Room where all desires are realized. Stalker is an insignificant man who has done nothing worthy in life but has the talent to lead others through the Zone's traps and illusions. The three men travel by motorized trolley across an abandoned railroad track and continue on foot once they are close to their destination. Stalker leads the way by throwing metal nuts to chart the trek to the Room through a surreal landscape of decaying tanks and buildings. The journey is full of danger: a black dog appears, a telephone rings, Stalker's hair turns gray. Writer is the ever skeptic who doesn't believe in the spiritual, only in matter and hard facts, but is eventually shaken by the supernatural events that surround the journey. Resting near a well, Writer is confronted with ugly, negative thoughts. He remembers that as a child he had seen someone kill himself. This death turned on him and became an anguish that gnawed at his self during his entire life. Professor is full of faith and wants to find the Room of hidden desires to destroy it with a bomb, afraid that a dictator will use it for evil ends. However, when the three men arrive at the Room of Desire, they do not enter. Are they afraid of their unknown deepest wish, a desire that propels their entire existence? Or is that wish the desire to die, to rush toward death? Stalker seems to suggest that hope is life's only driving force. Does hope prolong life and outmaneuver death?

Figure 10 is a still from Tarkovsky's film *Stalker*. Writer lingers in the front after having taken a wrong turn, as if hesitant to approach the Room of Desire. Stalker and Professor are in the background, waiting for him to join them to their journey's destination. The picture represents my skepticism about psychoanalysis as well as the tension of entering an analytic session, unknowing as to what to find there.

Tarkovsky defined a stalker "as one who crosses the borders and penetrates a forbidden Zone with a specific objective."[18] I interpreted the film *Stalker* as an allegory of psychoanalytic practice. Stalker resembled my analyst. Constantly on guard, she guided me to the unconscious. The film's long trolley ride symbolizes the slow analytic process of reaching this hidden zone. The metal nuts are a metaphor for the an-

FIGURE 10. Writer, Stalker, and Professor in the Zone. Still from the film *Stalker* by Andrei Tarkovsky. Reproduced with permission from FSUE Mosfilm Cinema Concern.

alyst's interventions. Attentive to the free associations, slips of tongue, and dreams, L was steering me around obstacles and pitfalls through pointed questions. This roundabout way was also taken by Stalker, who insisted that a straight approach to the Room of Desire was dangerous. Writer and Professor stood for the two sides of my ethnographic struggle. Writer represented my search for meaning as an interpretive scholar from a humanist tradition. Professor represented my search for the hidden facts about the disappearances, a search that was a defense against psychologically intolerable truths.

L observed that my cinematographic rendition of *Stalker* distinguished three stages. First, there is the long road full of obstacles and barriers. Like Stalker who was throwing metal nuts to test whether the passageway was safe, I saw the analyst as raising questions whose answers would eventually lead to the unconscious. Next, I described the scene near the well where Writer realized how he had witnessed a suicide that nestled in his unconscious. If one can pass through this severe emotional test, L observed, then one can continue to the final stage: entering the Room of Desire. Like Stalker, who watched over his two travel companions, I imagined that she was helping me to recognize, understand, and liberate myself from certain obstacles in life, and resolve my unconscious conflicts.

L was indeed my stalker, the authority to whose skills I surrendered and who I paid a fee to navigate me safely through my inner world. Alex calls this process in the next chapter the excavation of the unconscious. Excavation is a perceptive metaphor because it points at the dangers and the rewards of digging in unknown terrain. My analyst was able to guide me through this subsoil by interpreting her emotional reactions (countertransference) to the reactions (transferences) of my unresolved inner conflicts to her. These unconscious feelings were in fact intended for "significant persons of early childhood, unconsciously displaced on to persons in the present," which in my case was L.[19] She was thus able to analyze my dreams by examining her countertransferential reactions. In this sense, psychoanalysts are like reflexive anthropologists who use themselves as hermeneutic tools to understand the relationships with their interlocutors through self-reflection and introspection, but with the caveat that fieldworkers are generally unaware of countertransference and can therefore become subject to ethnographic seduction.

L was also an authority figure, and I, the anthropologist. Our ethnographic relationship had the usual complications of language and intercultural misunderstanding that beset any fieldworker. She knew of course much about Argentina and the years of state terrorism but had a limited grasp of my cultural upbringing. I had to verbalize a background knowledge that could have remained unspoken for a Dutch psychoanalyst.

Like in the case of the Indian psychoanalyst Sudhir Kakar, who was trained in Germany, our different cultural backgrounds began to matter less as the analytic process continued. We were communicating in her native language, and I increasingly adopted L's analytic vocabulary, trying to please her with a generous offer of dream accounts.[20] My situation was also comparable to that of Michael Jackson in Sierra Leone. He sought the assistance of a diviner to help him cope with his fieldwork troubles. The diviner interpreted Jackson's anxiety dreams in local cultural terms, which gave Jackson valuable insight into himself, the culture under study, and the human condition.[21] In this sense, L was my Argentine diviner. Like Jackson's dream expert, she provided a vocabulary to interpret my waking experiences and unconscious processes.

Lévi-Strauss noticed a similar parallel between psychoanalysis and shamanism. "In both cases," he wrote, "the purpose is to bring to a conscious level conflicts and resistances which have remained unconscious."[22] He even argued that the unconscious is empty, a mere receptor that receives and reworks people's emotions and memories.[23] These insights had made me a skeptic of psychoanalysis in graduate school. Again, the film *Stalker* offered some insight. Did the Zone and the Room of Desire really exist according the film's script? Tarkovsky commented: "I don't know. In a way, it's a product of the Stalker's imagination. We thought about it this way: he was the one who created that place, to bring people and show them around, to convince them of the reality of his creation."[24]

Likewise, Freud had done much to conceptualize the unconscious, and L had been trained as a stalker. She was taught a cultural terminology attuned to the Western societies in which it had taken root, especially in Argentina. My skepticism lessened as I continued the analysis in Buenos Aires and slowly adopted her analytic perspective on fundamental internalizations and ongoing identifications that create our subjecthood as human beings. More broadly, L's interventions helped my research.

ALEX: Before you move on to the next section, I'd like to follow up on how, during graduate school, you became a skeptic of psychoanalysis and eventually overcame that skepticism. In anthropology, as well as other fields, there is a bias against texts that draw on Freud and psychoanalysis. Part of this, of course, is linked to the early dominance of the culture and personality school in anthropology and related national character studies. The bias persists to this day, and texts that draw on Freud are sometimes reflexively dismissed as reductive. It is odd given that some scholars who would never cite Freud are happy to draw on theorists, often French, who are deeply informed by Freud. Lacan, Derrida, Deleuze, and Guattari are just a few examples. I don't want to bog down the flow of your essay, but I wonder if you could say more about this issue in general and in relationship to your own research.

TONY: This is a hard question, Alex. I'm of two minds about psychoanalysis, or better, three. On the one hand, psychoanalytic theory is reductionist because of its belief in a unified theory of the unconscious. I find this unconvincing. There are too many intervening forces on the relation between the unconscious and the complex, multilayered reality in which people live and act. I'm therefore more drawn to object-relations theory (Fairbairn, Bowlby, Winnicott), which concentrates on people's relational constitution, than to classic Freudian theory which focuses on a psychic energy directed at pleasure-seeking and the avoidance of pain and suffering. On the other hand, psychoanalytic thinking raises fertile questions and encourages researchers to explore new and surprising areas of investigation without having to do so from a psychoanalytic mold. And then there's psychoanalytic practice, which I found very stimulating because it allowed for a fruitful self-examination that made me more conscious of my scholarly work. The benefits continued after leaving Argentina. I remained attentive to my biases, and this helped me during the writing stage.

You're right that anthropology's rejection of, if not hostility to, psychoanalytic theory is curious considering the infatuation with French thinkers inspired by Freud. The easy answer is that certain Freudian concepts have become incorporated in our vocabulary and thought, so there's no need to spell them out. My alternative answer is that the work of these French scholars can be interpreted in multiple ways because of their level of abstraction. This allows anthropologists to select those concepts that resonate with their ethnographic data without having to buy into the entire theoretical framework.

The Anxiety of Historical Situations

I'm standing in a park in my place of birth in the Netherlands. Its old trees cast a solemn, cathedral-like shadow. There are decaying leaves on the ground. The large, heavy branches form a green canopy that protects me from the strong sunlight. I am in Germany, walking with a childhood friend through the park. We see a conglomeration of buildings from the sixteenth or seventeenth century. It seems a convent with a small chapel attached. We enter the chapel with its rows of beautiful oak benches and a sober-looking altar. There is only one long bench in the chapel, and it prevents us from approaching the altar. We leave the chapel by the rear entrance and arrive at an elevator. Someone tells us to go up to the third or fourth floor to view the complex of old buildings. Somehow, I press two buttons at the same time, and the elevator stops between the second and third floor. To our surprise, a door slides open and we step into a large room. The curtains are almost drawn and the natural light, already filtered by the trees, gives the room a laden, almost solemn, atmosphere. A large, heavy wooden table has been set for a dinner with eight to ten guests. As we are slowly walking through the room, an elderly lady with some authority, probably the head of housekeeping, looks at us sternly and asks what we are doing there. She tells us that the room is completely off-limits. I step forward and explain that the elevator brought us there by accident. She orders us to leave. I take a right-hand turn and see an alcove with an old man sitting in a dark leather chair. I cannot see his face because he sits turned away from the room's entrance at a sixty-degree angle. His head is tilted forward as if he has dozed off while waiting for dinner to be served. His lower arms are on the chair's armrests. The moment I see this old man in the somber light—the dark alcove is only lit by a dim reflection from the dining room—I realize it is Adolf Hitler. Although

old and defenseless, he emanates an evil aura that impresses me
tremendously. He has lived his life in his way, without remorse or
guilt feelings. His evilness is natural, as if he had no choice. Now, in
his old age, his worldly power has been spent but his spiritual power
is still present. Germany has recovered from the war, old wounds
have healed, and Hitler has survived unbeknownst to the world. The
woman is aware of Hitler's presence but is uncertain whether I have
seen him. Again, she orders us to leave. We take the elevator to the
ground floor, and then find ourselves being chased by Wehrmacht
soldiers who apparently suspect our discovery. We run through the
chapel and arrive in the park. I wake up.

I immediately thought that this dream of June 1989 was referring to my
ongoing struggle to analyze Argentina's periodic outbursts of political
violence. I was weighing two interpretations. On the one hand, I saw a
parallel between the genocide of Patagonia's indigenous population by
the Argentine military during the 1870s and the state terrorism against
Argentina's revolutionary movement in the 1970s. On the other hand, I
perceived several correspondences between the German and Argentine
dictatorial regimes. Both believed to be fighting a decisive battle against
communism and depicted the fight as a total war of the armed forces
and the people against a common enemy. Both regimes also dehuman-
ized and disappeared their captives. At the time I was torn between
these two comparative analyses, and I speculated that this conflict was
displaced on a dream about Adolf Hitler.

Hitler personified Nazi Germany's devastating impact on the Netherlands. On a population of nearly 9 million, the five years of war and
German occupation had caused 250,000 dead, including 102,000 Jews.
Also, more than 600,000 Dutch men and women had been forced to work
in Germany. Growing up in the Netherlands after the war, one could not
escape its presence in books, films, monuments, memorials, museums,
sites of memory, commemorations, and the visible reminders of wartime
destruction and postwar reconstruction. Hitler's imposing appearance in
my dream obstructed a self-reflexive access to the unconscious, a bar-
rier that was reinforced by the oneiric aura of his evil nature. This dream

image was hard to relinquish during the analytic hour and hindered the free association of seemingly disconnected thoughts that could reveal any unconscious conflicts to the psychoanalyst.

"Why do you compare Argentina to Nazi Germany?" L asked perceptively, even though I had kept my two hypothetical models from her. My answer was academic: I emphasized the heuristic value of comparing two historical realities. It was important to step out of the strictures of a particular context and discover which ideologies, structures, and practices were common in authoritarian regimes other than Argentina. She responded that historical situations are always self-contained and therefore hard to cope with emotionally. My dream was an anxiety dream that searched for other realities whose symbolic value was to highlight that which is hidden in pure description. The torture and disappearance of Argentine civilians and the kidnapping of babies born from blindfolded and later assassinated mothers were incomprehensible and emotionally hard to accept. A comparison with Nazi Germany removed the uniqueness from Argentina. In fact, some Argentine scholars, judges, lawyers, and many human rights activists have denounced the forced disappearances as genocide, not unlike the Holocaust. Instead, I think that the disappearances are so incomprehensible to them that only the term *genocide* is compatible with the sociocultural trauma suffered by the Argentine people. Genocide and trauma are on a par for them, and their commensurability contributes to the mourning of Argentina's losses.[25]

A comparison of Argentina and Nazi Germany had temporarily enabled an emotional and cognitive integration of my knowledge of Argentina's political violence into a wider understanding of authoritarian regimes, but it had also blinded me to the distinctiveness of Argentine history. L's dream analysis freed me from my preoccupation with the Second World War and made me aware of the emotional conflicts that were entwined with my family's wartime history. Now, I could study Argentina's uniqueness in its own historical context and without the burden of my father's lifelong preoccupation with his missing brother.

These psychoanalytic insights showed that fieldworkers should take their upbringing and personal development into account when

conducting research. They themselves are after all the tools of investigation because empirical data emerge as much from intersubjective
relationships with research participants as from direct observations.
The anthropological enterprise is therefore also, often unknowingly, a
personal journey to the fieldworker's subjectivity. Yet anthropologists
are trained to separate the personal from the professional. They try
to influence the fieldwork relations and the data gathering process by
consciously cultivating rapport while ignoring the deep emotions that
dwell inside them and that have an effect on their ethnographic encounters. This disengagement of the personal and the professional is reinforced by the expository objective-like prose that became questioned
during the reflexive and literary turn of the 1980s.

I have examined the influence of fieldwork anxieties and unconscious processes on my ethnographic research among Argentine
perpetrators and showed the merits of a psychoanalytic mapping of
emotional conflicts through dream analysis. My experience of entering
psychoanalysis during fieldwork was probably unique in anthropology.
I therefore don't want suggest that other fieldworkers should follow suit,
but this experience allows me to emphasize the importance of understanding one's dreams and emotions in the field. Insight can also be
achieved without psychoanalysis, as Alex shows in the next chapter,
through an ethnographic analysis of the day residues or recent everyday worries that are thinly disguised in nightdreams and daydreams.[26]

Day residues are not simply decoys of unconscious conflicts, as
Freud assumed, but indicate events and lived experiences that have an
emotional value for the dreamer. Dreaming and conducting research
are communicating realities. The scholarly importance of interpreting
emotionally laden dreams is not restricted to the excavation of unconscious processes originating in early childhood but bears on the
ongoing social interaction in the field. Anthropologists who conduct
perpetrator research have to be attentive to the connections between
nocturnal dreams and waking experiences, between daydreams and
worries about fieldwork, the psychodynamics that influences the interaction with perpetrators, and emotional reactions to the often evasive
accounts of violence and terror.

FOUR

Ruin

February 3, 2012 (Night)
Charcoal gray, the old fortress stands alone, a perfect square of stone rising from the barren landscape.[1] No plant cracks the hard dirt that surrounds the structure. Nothing living can be seen or heard. The air is still. No light breaks through the clouds. It is neither day nor night.

Suddenly, someone is here with me, a presence familiar yet strange, perhaps friendly, but clearly dangerous. This person lingers on the border of shadow and light, compels me to go into one of the square stone turrets placed on each corner of the unadorned fortress walls.

I stand on the ground floor of one of the windowless turrets. In the center, a narrow staircase encased by light spirals steeply into the shadows. The stairs and walls are etched with spiderwebs.

"Go," the faceless man demands.

Slowly, I ascend the steps. I worry that the man will attack me from behind, try to shove me over the handrail. I can no longer see the ground, just the beam of light surrounding the stairwell that blurs and gradually fades into the darkness above and below.

I finally reach the top. The staircase leads to a dead end, where thick and impenetrable concrete forbids access to where I want to go above, onto ramparts set against a moonless sky. Blocked, I turn to go back down.

"Why don't you go first?" I ask the man, who I never clearly see.
"No," he replies sharply. "Proceed."
One by one, I climb the stairwells inside the fortress turrets. They
look the same. Each has an identical blocked end.
As I mount the last stairwell, I am completely alone. I want to
flee, run back as fast as I can. I press on. My fear and anxiety build.
The light fades. Ahead, I can only see dense cobweb tangles and
handwriting on a wall, the print too faint to read.

I WAKE WITH A START, disoriented, then certain I had dreamed of S-21.

Yesterday, the Supreme Court Chamber (SCC) at the Khmer Rouge Tribunal had ruled on various appeals in the trial of Duch, the commandant of S-21 security center, where more than twelve thousand people were interrogated, tortured, and killed. Duch contends he should be released. This morning, I am supposed to meet S-21 survivor Bou Meng at the Tuol Sleng Genocide Museum, which now stands on the grounds of S-21, to discuss the SCC's decision.

If the details of the dream, at first clear, begin to fade, I still feel its emotional pull as I depart for Tuol Sleng. I know I must revisit the exhibition room in which hangs a defaced photograph of Duch, one I want to use as the cover of the book I need to start writing about his trial. How will I see the image now that Duch's long trial is over?

Over the course of the week, as I try to understand Duch, the prison he ran, and the path I might take to write about his trial, I return to Tuol Sleng again and again.

———

Now, looking back at this dream , and my initial thoughts about it, as I was doing fieldwork on the Khmer Rouge Tribunal, *ruin* is the first word that comes to mind. I often begin to process fieldwork—and start writing as I am doing now—through this sort of free association, using words, text, images, idioms, and field notes as the first pieces of clay from which to start molding ethnography.

When a word like this comes to mind, I turn to etymology and the *Oxford English Dictionary*. The word *ruin* is interesting in this regard.[2]

Its Latin root, *ruĕre*, means "to fall," an idea that is captured by the different senses of *ruin* as "collapse" or "downfall." We speak of ruins as the remainders of a greater (and more whole) state in the past.

So, too, may a person fall into ruin, ranging from gendered connotations of a "ruined" woman to "a person reduced to abject poverty." The verb form underscores the term's connotation of destruction, decay, and decline. To ruin someone or something suggests reduction into "a state of decay, collapse, or disintegration" or inflicting "great and irretrievable damage, loss, or disaster," including deprivation of "social and moral standing."

Ruins are spectacular—to invoke the trope of my earlier chapter. They suggest optics, something striking and remarkable, if uncanny. We want to glimpse ruins, which suggest an excess—"something more" that remains as a trace—that captivates us, drawing our attention even if we fear to make it the direct object of our gaze. As a result, ruins are seen obliquely, adding to their mystique, which sometimes edges into fetish.

This mystique, coupled with the project of excavation that ruins afford, is part of the reason so many scholars have drawn on the metaphor of ruin in one way or another to consider their objects of study. Examples range from the philosophical (Foucault's "archaeology of knowledge") to the literary (W. G. Sebald's *Austerlitz*). But perhaps the most famous use of the ruin metaphor is Freud's model of the mind linking mental health to excavations of the unconscious.[3]

While acknowledging and selectively drawing on such scholarship, this chapter uses the metaphor of ruin to consider the dream I had while conducting fieldwork in Cambodia in 2012—an anthropology of ruin if you will. If in "The Night Stalkers," Tony examines how ongoing dream analysis can augment perpetrator research, I situate a single dream in the context of my field site ("the dig") before considering it in terms of abjection (the psychological impact of perpetrator research) and excavation (the ethnographic excavation of ruins, including the way these excavations are inflected by desire). This discussion flows from the first section of this book on interviewing and anticipates the third on writing about perpetrators, which deals with curation (the objectification, sublimation, and commodification of ruins into ethnographic form).

TONY: There's a long scholarly tradition in studying ruins as meta-phors of decay, temporality, and the destructive forces of history and nature. What has received little attention is that ruins can also serve as metonyms. Metonyms substitute a name of something for the name of a related thing, such as a "professional killer" who is called a "trigger." In archival research about the bombing of Rotterdam during the Second World War, I discovered that Dutch newspapers, which were censored by the occupying German authorities, didn't mention the corpses lying in the ruins and rubble but only wrote about the material destruction. The ruins stood metonymically for the dead. These metonyms created contiguous relationships between the ruins and the corpses, express-ing the joint destruction of buildings and inhabitants during the hun-dreds of German and Allied bombardments.[4]

I wonder if such semantic contiguity is also at play in your association of the word *ruin* with your dream. Was the damaged S-21 security center, later renovated into the Tuol Sleng memorial museum, a metonym of the torture and killings that took place there? Did not only the dream but also the waking association sublimate your existential anxiety about the horrors of S-21 as a form of self-protection?

ALEX: That's a fascinating pair of interlocking questions. Let me answer the last one first with a quick yes. There is no doubt that working in the ruins for me and for the perpetrator researcher more broadly taps into existential anxiety and is something that must be processed and worked out. And your chapter on dreams illustrates the importance of psychoanalysis in this regard as well in addition to serving as a research tool.

With regard to your second question about S-21, I think metonymy is definitely at play with Tuol Sleng standing—as Auschwitz does for the Holocaust—for the broader mass violence that took place during DK. But Tuol Sleng is also interesting because it was mobilized by the PRK gov-ernment to serve in this sort of metonymical position. In this case, as op-posed to censoring the bodily deaths as was the case with the Rotterdam bombings, the bodily remains were foregrounded at the museum from start to finish, including very graphic photographs of those imprisoned and executed. Your question raises the larger issue of what such sites foreground and background, what I speak of articulation and redaction in the book I wrote on Duch and as I discuss later in this chapter and in chapter 6.

The Dig

When I had the aforementioned dream, I was well into my fieldwork research on the Khmer Rouge Tribunal. This hybrid court, the outcome of a long negotiation between the United Nations and the Cambodian government, commenced operation in 2006, the year after *Why Did They Kill? Cambodia in the Shadow of Genocide*, the book that emerged from my dissertation fieldwork, was published.

My new research project on the tribunal marked a reorientation of my research from a focus on the genocidal process and perpetrator motivation to the aftermaths of genocide and the meaning of global justice. If Khmer Rouge perpetrators, ranging from the senior Khmer Rouge leaders on trial to the mid- and lower-level soldiers and cadre who served as witnesses, figured prominently in this new study, it was supposed to inflect more broadly and consider issues like victim and civil party participation in the proceedings.

That was the plan. Then the project was hijacked by Duch. Or at least that's how I sometimes think of how I soon found myself writing a book focused on the commandant of the S-21 security center, which operated directly under the control of the Khmer Rouge leadership in Phnom Penh. By this time, Pol Pot had died and the Case 002 trial of "Brother Number Two," Nuon Chea, and three other senior leaders was on a slow track and wouldn't commence until late 2011, just months before my dream.

Duch was the first defendant to go on trial (Case 001), with the main proceedings taking place in 2009 and the verdict delivered in 2010 (fig. 11). It was a spectacular case focused on a spectacular perpetrator and defendant. Not only was Duch the first former Khmer Rouge figure to be tried, but he ostensibly was a cooperative witness who admitted guilt and took responsibility—even if many civil parties contended that

FIGURE 11. Duch (Kaing Guek Eav), former head of S-21, at an initial hearing, Extraordinary Chambers in the Courts of Cambodia courtroom, Phnom Penh, February 17, 2009. Duch was the first person to be tried at the Khmer Rouge Tribunal in ECCC Case 001. He was convicted of crimes against humanity and other crimes on July 26, 2010. Courtesy ECCC by ECCC/Pool/Adrees Latif.

he was only doing so selectively when the evidence against him was clear. A former math teacher, Duch took the stand and, in proceedings that were often the focus of national attention, spoke at length about what had transpired during Democratic Kampuchea (DK). The teacher-turned-torturer sometimes seemed to be acting like Cambodia's historian of the Khmer Rouge past.

Duch's trial was also spectacular because it focused on S-21, Cambodia's "Auschwitz." After DK, the Peoples' Republic of Kampuchea (PRK), which had toppled the Khmer Rouge in January 1979 with massive military support from Vietnam, had established the Tuol Sleng Genocide Museum on the grounds of S-21. It became the national memorial on Khmer Rouge crimes and a focus on PRK propaganda, which staked the legitimacy of this new regime—one that included many former Khmer Rouge cadre whose factions had been purged—on having overthrown what it described as a Hitler-like and diabolical faction led by Pol Pot.

Built quickly in 1979 with the help of Vietnamese advisers, Tuol Sleng was meant to shock, upset, and give visitors a direct look at the atrocities that had taken place during "the Pol Pot period," as the DK regime had begun to be called in keeping with PRK politics.[5] Most museum visitors, for example, were first taken to a series of barren cells that included black-and-white photographs of the corpses of prisoners who had been executed in their beds as the Khmer Rouge regime collapsed. Bloodstains were left on the tiled floors.

The new PRK government immediately began to bring foreign delegations and domestic constituencies to Tuol Sleng, which it offered as proof of the atrocities committed by Pol Pot and his loyalists. While the museum has changed over time, especially in recent years with the introduction of a slick audio tour, it is still shocking to visitors, including the many tourists for whom it is a "must see" part of their visit to Cambodia. Indeed, Tuol Sleng and the Choeung Ek killing fields, where many of the S-21 prisoners were executed, stand near the top of the lists of "things to do in Phnom Penh" on websites like TripAdvisor.

Given that Pol Pot was dead, Duch's trial was all the more spectacular because he was the notorious commandant of this infamous prison that the Cambodian government made symbolic of DK atrocity crimes. Indeed, for the Cambodian government, the Khmer Rouge Tribunal was important not just to hold former Khmer Rouge leaders accountable but also to burnish its legitimacy.

This backdrop is necessary to situate my fieldwork dream of February 2, 2012. As noted above, I had arrived in Cambodia just the morning before to attend the Supreme Court Chamber's (SCC) final decision on Duch's case, which all sides had appealed after his 2010 trial chamber conviction. While I was already doing data analysis, I had been waiting for this symbolic and procedural conclusion to Duch's trial before starting to write. So beyond being momentous as a legal decision, the SCC's judgment on the Duch case, given on the morning of February 3, had significance for my research.

I had hit the ground running upon my arrival in Cambodia since there were a number of outreach events related to the SCC's final decision on Duch's case. In the early afternoon, I attended a forum at Tuol Sleng where Case 001 civil parties voiced their concerns. Chum Mey, one of the handful of S-21 survivors, spoke of how he couldn't accept Duch's apology, which he viewed as insincere, and wanted Duch sentenced to life in prison as opposed to the Trial Chamber's sentence of thirty-five years less mitigation and time served (which effectively reduced Duch's sentence to nineteen years). Another civil party began to sob as Chum Mey spoke, whereupon a mental health professional gently consoled her.

After the forum, I went to a late afternoon event at the Documentation Center of Cambodia, a local nongovernmental organization with which I have worked for years. It had brought together participants from some of its projects to mark the occasion of the final decision in Duch's case. The ten participants, who were sitting around a square wooden table, included two former S-21 torturers, the daughter of a S-21 victim (Chan Kim Srun) whose photo is prominently displayed at Tuol Sleng, and an educator who, not knowing Duch's identity, had worked with Duch in the 1990s. The group had just finished watching a film, *Mass Grave at Pagoda*, which depicts an encounter between a former perpetrator and victim. It begins with the question "Is forgiveness possible?" It was a question I considered at the DC-Cam table where former S-21 perpetrators sat by family members of victims. In my journal, I scribbled "could start book with [this] DC-Cam event."

Early the next morning, I traveled to the court with the group to hear the SCC's judgment. The court was packed with villagers, monks, students, activists, journalists, officials, and foreigners like me. We listened as the SCC reversed portions of the trial chamber verdict, including the sentence, which it changed to life imprisonment. Duch, who had been fidgeting during the proceedings, looked stunned. Afterward Chum Mey told journalists, "It is the absolute justice that I had hoped for more than three decades." He added, "I'm very at ease now" (fig. 12). Meanwhile, some people complained that the switch to the life sentence was due to Cambodian government pressure and was another example of how the court was politically compromised.

Afterward, I went to the Choeung Ek killing fields (fig. 13), where the civil parties had gathered to celebrate the decision and remember the spirits of the dead. The DC-Cam group, in turn, had gone to Tuol Sleng where, Sek Say, the daughter of the prisoner depicted in the photograph, broke down and sobbed (fig. 14). Meanwhile, I had arranged to meet the next morning at Tuol Sleng with Chum Mey and another S-21 survivor, Bou Meng, who, like Chum Mey, had been tortured at the prison.

———

TONY: The Tuol Sleng Genocide Museum is regarded as Cambodia's Auschwitz, a place that condenses the atrocities of the Khmer Rouge regime in one prominent site of memory. It seems similar to the secret detention center located in the Officers' Mess at the Navy Mechanics School (ESMA) in Buenos Aires, which was also turned into a memorial

FIGURE 12. (*Left to right*) S-21 survivors Bou Meng, Chum Mey, and Vann Nath holding the Case 001 verdict in Duch's trial, August 12, 2010. During Duch's trial, all three men testified about their experience of being tortured and imprisoned at S-21. Bou Meng and Chum Mey also served as civil parties in Case 001. Courtesy ECCC.

FIGURE 13. Choeung Ek Memorial Stupa, March 2, 2013. In 1977, Duch turned Choeung Ek, a former Chinese cemetery located fifteen miles southwest of Phnom Penh, into an extermination center where thousands of S-21 prisoners were trucked to and killed. The grounds were covered with as many as 129 mass graves. The bones of some of the dead, which began to be exhumed in 1980, are displayed behind the glass windows in the towering stupa, which is a centerpiece of the Choeung Ek Genocide Center that is now located on the site. Photo by Alex Hinton.

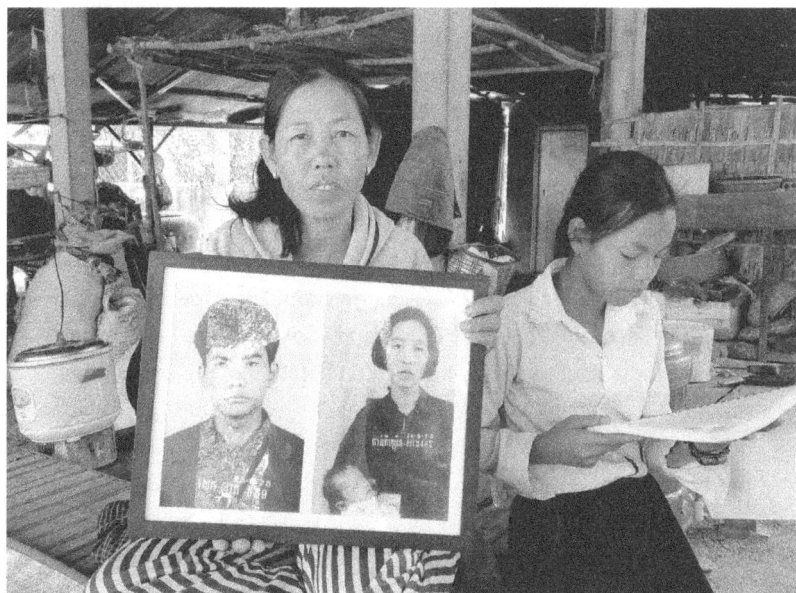

FIGURE 14. Sek Say, who participated in the DC-Cam outreach session, holding S-21 mug shots of her father (*left*), a former Khmer Rouge cadre, and her mother (Chan Kim Srun), who cradles one of Sek Sey's siblings. All three were killed at the prison. Courtesy DC-Cam/SRI.

museum. Tourists from around the globe visit these museums to get a sense of painful histories that had stirred the world. How does the comparison with Nazi extermination camps influence people's experience of these places? I once visited the ESMA in the company of a German tourist. We strolled through the park-like grounds of the large complex of buildings when the tour guide halted before a sign at the Officers' Mess that read (in Spanish) "Clandestine Detention, Torture and Extermination Center." When we entered the building where around four thousand captives had been held and tortured between 1976 and 1983, the German tourist blurted out in disbelief: "This is all?" She had visited Auschwitz as part of the school curriculum and was surprised that the notorious navy torture center consisted of only one building. Considering that Cambodia's S-21 security center is not much larger, I wonder how the comparison with Auschwitz influences the foreign visitors of Tuol Sleng, and how did it influence you when you visited Auschwitz?

ALEX: Tuol Sleng is an interesting point of contrast. The PRK regime, which constructed the genocide museum in 1979, was strongly aligned with Vietnam, and through it the Soviet bloc. Through this connection, Soviet bloc memorialization efforts, including the Auschwitz Museum, influenced the creation of Tuol Sleng. The genocide museum, for example, has a display of victims' clothing, a direct echo of a famous Auschwitz exhibition. I think international tourists more readily make the connection between Cambodia and Nazi Germany, one that is further strengthened by the inclusion of Cambodia in the genocide studies canon and also by the focus on numbers of dead. These are all points of contrast between ESMA and Tuol Sleng, perhaps, particularly given the later use and ongoing contestation of the application of the term *genocide* to the Argentinean case—something you mention briefly in chapter 2. Where all three memorials intersect is through notions like "never again" and "never forget," which are linked to the global circulation of Holocaust memory. Indeed, tourists fill the visitor books at Tuol Sleng with such phrases, which no doubt help them, like the perpetrator researcher excavating the ruins of mass death, cope with the feelings of existential anxiety, dread, and abjection that your second question underscores. Maybe I should say more about these emotions.

Abjection

This, then, was the immediate backdrop of my dream. It was a critical juncture for my research, which was transitioning from analysis to writing. Since arriving in Cambodia a day and a half earlier, I had listened to civil parties at a genocide museum, sat at a table with perpetrators and victims, attended an event at a site of mass graves, and watched Duch's face darken as he was given a life sentence by the SCC. Now, after several years of research on the court, I had to write a book about him, a daunting task.

I also knew I would be returning the next morning to Tuol Sleng to meet two S-21 survivors, both of whom had been severely tortured. I have visited the museum dozens of times. I always do so with dread. It is a place of ruin in many ways beginning with the victims whose lives were ruined in a horrible manner. Tuol Sleng is curated to underscore this point: blood on the floor, prisoner mug shots, a display of torture instruments, paintings depicting in vivid detail the atrocities that occurred at S-21, and so forth (figs. 15 and 16).

While the museum grounds have recently been somewhat beautified, the Tuol Sleng landscape remains bleak. Four chipped, grayish-white buildings, former classrooms turned into a security center by the former teacher and then prison commandant, stand at its core. Until recently, the Tuol Sleng grounds seemed parched and barren, with hard concrete benches, where visitors sometimes sob. Visitor notebooks record the effect on visitors, who search for ways to respond to the horrors they have seen. Some offer clipped responses—"unbelievable," "beyond words," "evil"—and others turn to Holocaust-related phrases like "never again" and "never forget."

Having focused much of my scholarship on genocide and political violence, I deal with this sort of material all the time. It's hard—Tuol Sleng especially so. Returning to the idea of ruin, it is a place where people "fell" hard and fast during DK. Many visitors "collapse" at the

FIGURE 15. Victim memorial, Tuol Sleng Genocide Museum interior courtyard, Phnom Penh, February 22, 2013. Built in early 1979 on the central grounds of S-21, the Tuol Sleng museum served both as a memorial and as evidence of the horrific crimes committed by the DK regime. The courtyard victim memorial is one of the first displays visitors see before entering Building A, which features the cells where the corpses of prisoners were discovered immediately after DK. Photo by Alex Hinton.

enormity of the site today. After going there, the visitor feels "ruined" in the sense of feeling morally stained, eroded, and decayed. When directly confronted, the site is existentially terrifying, a place where death lingers, like the spirits of the dead who are said to still haunt the grounds, and dying is depicted in the most horrible of ways.

In this respect, Tuol Sleng epitomizes the devastating impact of doing research on perpetration. It ruins you. The anthropology of perpetrators renders the researcher abject. If the word *abject* suggests rejection (being "cast out") and diminishment, it shares with *ruin* the notion of a collapse of boundaries and order—*disorder*, if you will. Julia Kristeva's discussions of abjection capture much in this regard as she explores how horror is linked to the threatened disintegration of the

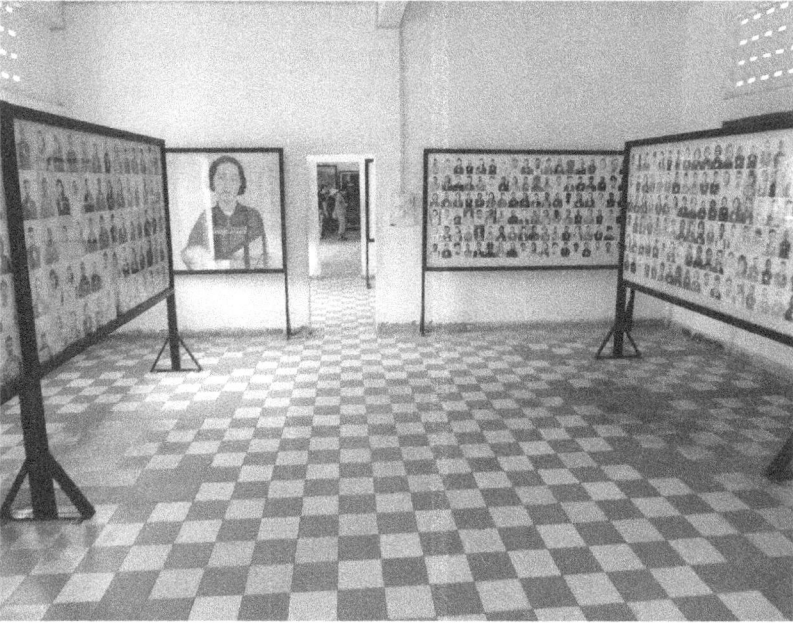

FIGURE 16. Exhibition of S-21 photographs, Building B, Tuol Sleng Genocide Museum, Phnom Penh, February 22, 2013. Many of the exhibitions in Building B feature checkerboard displays of black-and-white prisoner mug shots and other photographs discovered at S-21. Some of the detainees in the photos are bruised. In accordance with the DK revolutionary style, most prisoners are dressed in black, and the women have cropped hair. Photo by Alex Hinton.

boundary of our being, ranging from the imagined separation of self and other to the sense of wholeness and purity versus fragmentation and contamination. She has described the melancholy and depression that may accompany this sense of fragmentation through the metaphor of a black sun, an image that resonates with the landscape and context of my dream.[6] At the same time, and as Tony also demonstrated in the previous chapter, such dreams also have a creative and productive dimension, providing signposts for boundary crossing, reintegration, and new ways of knowing.

Kristeva's ideas synergize with those of Mary Douglas in interesting ways, even as Douglas focuses more on social boundaries.[7] To borrow

Douglas's term, we might say that studying perpetrators not just ruins you and makes you abject but also make you "dirty" in the sense of being socially stained. Indeed, I think many people working in this area are a bit embarrassed, perhaps even shamed when this dirtiness is publicly exposed—such as when audiences ask, "How can you?" or "What made you want to study *that*?" It makes you feel stained, even deviant.

I don't mean to engage in a self-pitying exercise. I have never written about these issues and never considered doing so until Tony suggested we co-write this book and include a section on dreaming. But it is something that needs to be acknowledged. There is a psychological cost to studying the ruins of perpetration. It leads to a direct confrontation with death and horror. It dirties you and makes you abject. Perpetrator research invites the "black sun."

The flip side of this "downfall," of course, is that it also enables growth. For, by walking among these ruins, realizing that to be human is in part to be abject, and confronting existential anxiety head-on, one may perhaps live more fully and self-aware. There are many paths to such growth, ranging from reading poetry to having psychoanalysis, but the study of "the dark side" of life offers this possibility as well, even if, as in all these journeys, it is by no means guaranteed. Dreaming may also help the dreamer process emotion and difficult experiences, as Tony recounts in vivid detail in the previous chapter.

Such growth, of course, is something that must be achieved anew each day. Many Cambodian Buddhists would refer to it as an awareness of impermanence and precarity that is part of enlightenment. My own path to the study of perpetrators was indirect, emerging only after I first went to Cambodia, as I discuss in the first part of this book, but perhaps is in part enabled by having grown up in a family of psychiatrists where discussion of "the shadow" was a frequent topic of conversation.

Existential anxiety is also related to the idea of "the banality of everyday thought" that underpins the book I ended up writing about Duch's trial, *Man or Monster? Trial of a Khmer Rouge Torturer.* The path to that book, however, was anything but direct. And indeed, I wrote a first draft of 250,000 words that I later drastically shortened and revised, a process I discuss in chapter 6. While I am pushing the metaphor and anticipating the next topic of this book, we might also liken the writing process to the exploration of ruins and subsequent renewal as the ethnographer curates fieldwork "data."

Looking back, the dream I had the night after the SCC's final decision on the Duch case condenses many of these aspects of ruin and abjection as they relate both to my ongoing research and related processing of the emotions and experiences I was having in the field at a moment in time.

When I woke up, I immediately wrote down the details of the dream in my journal, with the entry heading noting that it was a dream about a "Tuol Sleng–like white building." The second sentence reads "Someone is no longer there," underscoring the loss and absence connected to the site. While the suffering and loss of life associated with S-21 and Tuol Sleng is an obvious way to read the manifest content of the dream, it also suggests a more abstract absence, perhaps the gap of meaning with which our explanations must grapple, my lack of a clear vision of how to write a book about Duch's trial, and the abject loss I experienced as a researcher and person through my ongoing research on genocide, Duch, S-21, and Tuol Sleng—including torture and interrogation, which were central to Duch's case.

Along these lines, the figure who is present is intangible, ambiguous, and shifting, heard but not seen, at first somewhat friendly (my journal records the initial presence as "like an older brother," a term used by Khmer Rouge cadre to refer to their superiors), then increasingly full of menace. Indeed, the entire dream is infused with the uncanny, mixing the familiar with the strange before building toward a crescendo of fear, anxiety, and terror.

Among its referents, the "older brother" figure likely signifies Duch, who was sometimes addressed in this manner by subordinates. I immediately made the association. The figure orders me to act, and I comply with the threat of violence lingering (my journal entry notes: "worry I will be attacked from behind or pushed" off the stairwell). I'm also unable to exit this situation as I reach dead ends and remain stuck in the frightening and bleak fortress. Remarkably, when I awoke in the early morning and immediately turned on my computer to write down the details of the dream, the browser opened with a story on a "forgotten island of New York" that featured a photograph of a swivel stairwell amid the ruins of an abandoned hospital on North Brother Island near Manhattan.[8]

The sight of this stairwell was an uncanny punctuation to an uncanny dream I had before traveling to an uncanny site, Tuol Sleng, to meet Bou Meng (fig. 17) for what would be an uncanny interview. Later that day, as he told me about his suffering at S-21 and civil party experience at the ECCC, Bou Meng showed me a painting he had made of his former wife being killed at the Choeung Ek killing fields. In a mass grave, a soldier cuts his wife's neck, the blood pooling on the ground. "Who is the soldier?" I ask. "Lor," he matter-of-factly replied, naming the S-21 cadre who had told me that he killed "one or two people" at the site. At the end of the interview, Bou Meng gave me a print reproduction of painting. It was just one of a number of the uncanny moments that filled the day.

Another occurred while I had waited for Bou Meng. I had gone to

FIGURE 17. S-21 survivor and civil party Bou Meng attending the Supreme Court Chamber's final decision in Case 001, when Duch was sentenced to life imprisonment. Duch died in prison on September 2, 2020, after spending more than two decades detained or in jail. ECCC courtroom, February 3, 2012. Courtesy ECCC.

look at the Tuol Sleng photograph of the mother of the woman who had participated in the DC-Cam outreach program (fig. 18). Her mother cradles an infant, the outreach participant's baby sister, who she never met, in her arms. A tour guide brought a group to the photo, telling them: "This picture is important. It is the wife of one of the biggest [Khmer

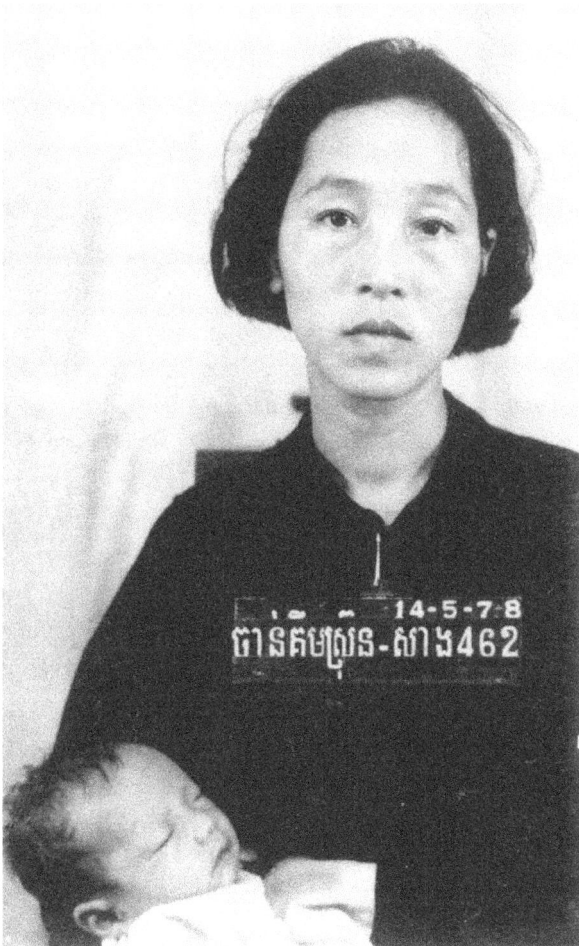

FIGURE 18. S-21 photograph of Chan Kim Srun with infant; her daughter, Sek Sey, is discussed in figure 14 (see figure 16 for an example of how this photograph is displayed at Tuol Sleng). Both Chan Kim Srun and her infant were executed. Courtesy DC-Cam/SRI.

Rouge] cadre. You can see the mother here. Her eyes look like she is crying." He pointed to her infant child. "With child at her bosom." After they left, I took a photograph of this S-21 mug shot that is a "key stop" in the genocide museum. When I looked at photograph I had taken, I noticed that it included a reflection of me taking the photograph.

———

TONY: Julia Kristeva has written that strangers provoke feelings of uncanniness because they are the incarnation of our hidden selves: "The other is my unconscious."[9] You write that anxiety dreams and conducting research on perpetration can ruin and stain the fieldworker. The perpetrator is also a stranger, "the other," on whom ethnographers project the dark side of their selves. Fieldwork with perpetrators shakes the faith in ourselves and our fellow human beings. This alienation is troubling. Everyday practices, such as eating, drinking, and sleeping, and taken for granted conventions of social interaction, such as respect, civility, privacy, and empathy, become unsettled through the harrowing narratives of violence and the dreams that rework them. As far as I see it, these uncanny feelings, strange yet familiar, are so eerie and can provoke existential anxiety because they touch on our common humanity.

ALEX: That's right. And I would just add briefly that the spectacular perpetrator, the chimera, is uncanny for precisely this reason. This is why it is all the more important to create the shared space of humanity for perpetrator research—though not always easy, and some researchers refuse this position—to work through such feelings. It isn't therapy, but entering into a space of shared humanity with former perpetrators, the many other issues like ethnographic seduction aside, can have somewhat of a therapeutic effect in the sense of forcing the perpetrator researcher to grapple with their projections and existential anxieties. Some forms of therapy, including, I might add, that practiced by my father,[10] who is a Jungian psychiatrist, are predicated upon becoming aware of and learning to live with such emotions and the sense of fragmentation with which they are linked. This perspective is very Buddhist and Lacanian as well—and, to bring us full circle to the start of your question, directly informs Kristeva's views.

Excavation

Perpetrator research can take a toll. It somehow feels unseemly to talk about it (or write about it, as I am doing now) given the enormous suffering, past and present, experienced by the victims and relatives of the victims—like the DC-Cam outreach event participant or Bou Meng. While acknowledging their much greater psychosocial burden, researchers also need to recognize their own abjection and process their ruin as they pass through the ruins of perpetration. Dreams provide one way to do so.

The processing, of course, takes place within a much larger backdrop, an intermeshing of the field site and the researcher's background, field of study, ambitions, desires, concerns, and institutional grounding. My dream was obviously situated in such a context, one I began discussing in the previous section, "The Dig." Along these lines, and continuing with the theme of ruin, we might consider this backdrop through the metaphor of excavation—perpetrator research as an archaeology of ruins. Nietzsche, Foucault, and others have provided a rich philosophical basis for undertaking such archaeologies. I want to proceed more modestly through etymology and the prism of excavation—in the sense that an archaeologist excavates ruins in an attempt to analyze and understand them.[11]

To excavate something is to "make (a hole or channel) by digging" such as by "carefully removing earth from (an area) in order to find buried remains." The Latin root of the term, *excavāre*, means "to hollow out."[12] This underlying attempt at assemblage—and the associated ways of ordering and classifying reality—involves a "hollowing" that resonates with the idea of articulation and redaction I discuss in *Man or Monster?* as well as the graphic narrative "grammar" of frames and gutters.

The excavation is also predicated upon authorization. There is, on the one hand, the "permit" that legitimates the endeavor, an approval or sanction linked to structures of power. But there is also "authorization" as that which gives "authority," such as the set of conceptual principles that legitimate the study, including the way the excavation is undertaken. This authorization, which sanctions "the author," has a sort of "fire," or force, that drives the project forward.

If the metaphor of fire is linked to violence broadly, it also suggests the motivation or "drive" (that which "compels" or "propels or carries along by force"[13]) of "the author" to carry out excavation in the first place, in particular sorts of ways, and in response to ongoing experiences in the field—including, as discussed earlier, those with content that is difficult to contain, that renders the researcher abject, and that creates traumatic gaps of meaning that must be "filled in."[14] In response, we articulate, redact, project, repress, displace, sublimate, cathect, and so forth. Among other things, dreams help us process and contain the difficult content and experiences that emerge when we do research on violence and perpetration.

The "drive" of the "author" may be passionate (propelled not just by "the fire" of libidinal or fetishistic desire, but more broadly by intensely felt emotions and even the passion to understand) or structural, such as the "fever" that emerges from the instability of authorization since it requires replication and a doubling that is never identical to the original.[15] Even if it comes from the same "authority," each dig is distinct, yields a different truth.

In comics and graphic narratives, an author creates a series of sequential frames.[16] Each is separated by a gap. As each frame is "read," a different interpretation ensues as the reader "fills in" the gap, assembles a meaning—just as the archaeologist excavates and renders a meaning from the material remains that are found. In the end, all these activities are predicated upon a gap, the cavity that is "hollowed out," the articulation that redacts.

Critical inquiry in general, and perpetrator research particularly in the context of the "drive" of this essay, is directly linked to archaeology in the sense I have described. Academic scholarship of any sort involves an archaeology that must be unpacked. This task is all the more fraught in the ruins of perpetrator research.

Such an unpacking involves an analysis of the sort of excavation being undertaking, the authorization for "the dig," and the "fire" that drives it forward. In doing so, the critical researcher of perpetrators remains concerned not just with the content of the frame but also with the "gaps" that stand outside and between them, largely unnoticed and unseen—that which has been redacted, edited, pushed out of sight. If they help us contain difficult materials, dreams are a critical tool in helping us think through our analysis and begin to "curate" and write about perpetrators, the focus of the third part of this book. As we proceed and move toward writing about perpetrators, we must continually ask: What authorizes and drives our excavations? What have we hollowed out? And how have we been affected by ruin? Dreams provide clues to the answers and help the researcher process difficult content and experiences and what often ensues: abjection.

INTERLUDES

"For the Sake of the Fatherland"

A Creative Nonfiction Testimony

ARGENTINA'S REVOLUTIONARY WAR began in September 1955 after a military uprising had forced the increasingly dictatorial president Juan Domingo Perón out of office and into exile.[1] Soon thereafter, the so-called Peronist resistance committed terrorist acts against the military government of General Aramburu, and Perón encouraged the creation of armed groups to attack military installations and sabotage Argentina's public utilities. The violence abated in the early 1960s but resurged in 1970 with the assassination of General Aramburu by the Montoneros. He was the first victim of the revived revolutionary war. The military government of Lieutenant General Lanusse went on the offensive against the guerrilla insurgency and at the same time promised a return to democracy. The successful repression of the guerrilla organizations ended on May 25, 1973, when Héctor Cámpora was sworn in as president of Argentina after winning the general elections earlier that year. Cámpora's first act in office was to release the hundreds of incarcerated guerrillas. Within days, Argentina's Congress granted them amnesty and dissolved the Federal Penal Chamber that had tried and convicted the guerrillas during the government of Lieutenant General Lanusse.

The election of the Peronist candidate Héctor Cámpora, and his cession of the presidency to Juan Domingo Perón later that year, failed to stop the aggression against the armed forces. The Montoneros put down their weapons because they had succeeded in returning Perón to power, but the People's Revolutionary Army (ERP) continued the armed violence. In September 1973, the ERP attacked an army base in Buenos Aires Province with the help of two soldiers recruited by the guerrilla organization. The military endured one death after another but remained in the barracks. When Perón died in July 1974, and his widow, Isabel Martínez de Perón, became president of Argentina, the Montoneros joined the armed struggle.

In 1974, I, General Ramón Genaro Díaz Bessone, was chief of operations of the army's general staff in Buenos Aires, and almost weekly we had to bury someone. Also, the presence of rural guerrillas in the province of Tucumán became so alarming that the Peronist government passed in February 1975 a secret decree ordering the armed forces to annihilate these subversives. But the revolutionary war was not confined to Tucumán. Many towns and cities in Argentina were affected by a strong urban guerrilla movement. There were assassinations, kidnappings, and attacks on police stations and military bases throughout Argentina. In October 1975, the government gave the order to annihilate the insurgency in the entire country.

I became commander of the Second Army Corps in Rosario in September 1975. I was placed under the permanent protection of bodyguards because one of my predecessors, General Sánchez, had been assassinated by the ERP in 1972. I traveled frequently to my family in Buenos Aires and always held a hand on my pistol, because the conscript soldier driving the car could be a guerrilla. Every day my family's apartment was checked for explosives, and also the roof was inspected because enemy combatants might lower themselves from there. It was very difficult to live under these circumstances.

My strongest experience of the revolutionary war was the attack on the Mounted Infantry Regiment of Formosa in October 1975. The Montoneros were able to enter the garrison because a soldier had opened the gate. They attacked the armory to steal weapons, but by that time the officers had organized a successful counterattack. I arrived at the base when the hostilities had already ceased, but I saw the dead and the wounded. There were some with their head blown off. Sixteen guerrillas and twelve of our men had died. The following day, the government signed the secret decree that authorized the armed forces to annihilate the subversion in Argentina.

The revolutionaries were the ones who started the aggression. If I am attacked, then I have the right to defend myself. This natural right leads to the doctrine of just war. The Argentine government asked us in 1975 to annihilate the enemy, and that's what we did. We did not repress the subversion, as is often said, but we waged war. *Repression* means to restrain, to contain. Repression is the task of the police and the security forces. The police are ordered to detain a person who is then tried by a judge. One doesn't order the security forces or the police to annihilate a criminal. One only orders the military to annihilate. Annihilation means war. The Allied forces bombed German cities, and nuclear bombs were dropped on Hiroshima and Nagasaki. Many innocent people died there. These people had nothing to do with the war. The justification was that a lesser harm was done to prevent a greater harm, namely a prolonged war that would cost the lives of many American soldiers. This is why every time Argentines talk about repression, we say: there was no repression, there was war. Until 1975, only the police was involved, not the armed forces.

Our just war was waged against an enemy that tried to impose an alien ideology on Argentina and do away with our freedom. All total-itarianisms are abominable: fascism and communism. The values of Marxism are incompatible with Argentina's Western values and Catholic faith. This was an ideological conflict, and that's why war was inevitable. They wanted to establish a socialist fatherland, a Marxist-Leninist fatherland, like in Cuba. There is no freedom there. Revolutionary justice rules there. There is no equality before the law, no economic freedom like in Argentina. The Argentine guerrillas also wanted to do away with private property. We had to stop them.

We faced a ferocious enemy. There were guerrillas who became pregnant to protect themselves because they assumed that the armed forces would show them special consideration. Often they used their own children as shields. But when I enter into war, I have to be willing to kill my enemy, even children. If I have an arrow but the other has a machine gun, then I have to find a cannon. War is a human phenomenon in which I try to impose my will on the enemy through the exercise of violence. The German military thinker Von Clausewitz said that he who employs violence without any regard for others will have an advantage. War conventions are for the nocturnal meditations of legal scholars. Revolutionaries don't respect any law or moral value. Nations don't respect war conventions. Nuclear bombs were thrown on Japan, but who was going to stop President Truman? Who was going to take him to the Nuremberg tribunal? Nobody, because he won the war. That's why the distinction between licit and illicit acts of war is absurd to me. To what extremes does this violence go? Until the objective of war is achieved. They tell me that it's forbidden in a war to torture prisoners. Was this respected by the North Vietnamese, the North Koreans, the Germans, and the Allies? And surely here in Argentina there was also torture. That's war.

There were around thirty thousand guerrillas in 1975, of which five thousand were armed combatants, and twenty-five thousand were sympathizers who provided logistic support, food, false documents, weapons, cars, and safe houses. They were fighting sixty thousand troops, assisted by the police and the security forces. In total, there were around one hundred thousand Argentines participating in this war, and there were twenty-nine million Argentines who did not. They were afraid of the guerrillas. Many families left the country. They were afraid to send their children to school because they didn't know what would happen. There were bombs in the street. Sometimes there was a shootout with the police, and someone innocent was killed.

An absolute majority of the Argentine people rejected the guerrillas. In Rosario, there are slums where very poor people live in precarious housing without sanitary facilities. The guerrillas tried to insert themselves there. These humble people could have reacted favorably to their social sermons, but they denounced the guerrillas and asked us to get them out. This war was won because the people were supporting the armed forces. If the people would have taken the side of the guerrillas, then the armed forces would have never won the war. The guerrilla organizations were defeated in 1978, but they continued their fight abroad with slander campaigns against Argentina about disappearances and so-called illegal detention centers. These detention centers were legal according to the conventions of war. The capture of guerrillas was kept secret for reasons of intelligence, and their whereabouts was kept secret for reasons of security. I am a soldier who fought a foggy war but always acted honorably and did my best for the sake of the fatherland. I therefore feel a profound injustice for being accused of wrongs that I never committed.

The revolutionary war was one problem, but there was another problem: the country's economic and political situation. We could have continued our war against the subversion without taking over the country. We were not eager to form a government, but we saw that Argentina was on the brink of disaster. There was a runaway inflation, poverty among the people, and an overall disintegration of the state, the national government, the judiciary, Congress, and at the provincial and local administrative levels. The coup d'état of March 24, 1976, was necessary not to fight the guerrilla organizations but to save the nation and create the conditions for a stable democracy.

What made the military intervention in this revolutionary war so terrible was that there was no frontier between the enemies, unlike in a war between two countries. I have to live with my former enemies. I have to go to the hospital, and drink tea in a café on a public square. There is no border that separates me from them. There remains hatred and rancor: "That's the one who killed my sister. That's the one who killed my uncle. That's the one who wears a uniform." This is the tremendous damage done to Argentina by the revolutionary war. The subversion introduced hatred into our society that maintains an open wound. We therefore have to stop talking about the war and lower the curtain, because otherwise the wound will continue to bleed. We need to look toward the future. The war is over.

Interrogation

Comrade Duch's Abecedarian[1]

*A*pology.

*B*lack ink.

*C*onfession. Conversion. Christianity.

*D*uch. Eldest son. Star student. Loner. Math teacher. Meticulous.
Khmer Rouge Revolutionary. Patriot. Party Member. Dutiful.
Prison commandant. Brute. Eyes and ears of the Party.
Obedient. Gave orders. Stoic. Fanatic. Torturer. Father. Cog in
the machine. Believer. Mass murderer. Prisoner imprisoned. The
Accused. Defendant. Criminal. Convict.

*E*nemies. Attacking from without. Burrowing from within.

*F*irst, extract their information. Next, assemble many points
for pressuring them so they cannot move. 3. Propagandize and
pressure them politically. 4. Pressure and interrogate by cursing.
5. Torture. 6. Examine and analyze the responses for further
interrogation. 7. Examine and analyze the responses to make the
document. 8. Guard them closely, prevent them from dying. Don't
let them hear one another. 9. Maintain secrecy.

*G*hosts. *Suspended between lives. Watching. Awaiting justice. Karma. An offering to the dead. Merit. Rebirth.*

(Cannot) *H*esitate *and have ideological doubts that hinder our task, even if that person is our brother or sister or someone whom we trusted.*

*I*nterrogation *note to Duch: "The Situation of Interrogating Ke Kim Huot alias Sot." "On the morning of July 21, 1977, we pounded him another round. Electrical wire and shit. This time he cursed those who hit him very much, [and said] Go ahead and beat me to death. Had him eat two or three spoonfuls of shit. . . . [B]y nightfall, we went at him again with electric wires, this time pretty seriously. He became delirious. He was all right. Later he confessed a bit as reported above . . . Sot said he had nothing to answer to send to Angkar, and since he did not, he did not know what to say, that now he just waits for death, and he can close his eyes and die easily because he has sacrificed and was loyal to the party. . . . My operative line is to continue torture with mastery, because the enemy is breaking emotionally and is at a dead end. Along with this, I ask for opinion and guidance from Angkar in carrying out this task."*

*J*oined *the revolution to liberate the country.*

*K*e *Kim Huot alias Sot. Duch's teacher, mentor, comrade, prisoner. Dim Saroun. Ke Kim Huot's wife. Also a teacher. Interrogated. Tortured. Sexually abused.*

The *L*ine. *Party line determining politics, ideology, organization, arrest, imprisonment, interrogation, torture, execution. "The crimes came from the Party line of the Communist Party of Kampuchea." Anyone considered an enemy was to be smashed.*

*M*an *or Monster? Mathematical calculation. "Make them think of their wives and children." Mastery.*

Numbers. The S-21 statistics list. 90% of the people are strong and firmly believe in the Party, the collective, and defend the Party. 10% are weak. 1% very weak. 1% are enemies. Therefore . . . Screen out the enemies no matter what."

*The **O**bjective of torturing is to get their answers. It is not done for fun. Therefore we must make them feel pain so that they will respond quickly. Another objective is to make them afraid. It is not done by individual anger to let off steam. Therefore, beat them to make them scared, but absolutely not to let them die. When torturing, it is imperative to check their health in advance and to inspect the whip. Do not get greedy and want to be quick; that leads to death and loss of a document.*

Psychological functioning: Obsessive, low self-esteem, depression, traumatic organization, disempathy, splitting, willing participant, need for mentors and strong belief, avoidance, narcissistic self-depreciation, negation, projection, repression, displacement, inhibited dream activity, reaction formation, somatization, avoidance, rationalization, denial.

Qualifications for joining the Party. 18 years or older. Already tested. Follows Party line, ideological and organizational stances of the Party. Good class pedigree. Clean morals and politics. Never involved with enemy. Clean personal history.

Revolution. Return. Revenge.

Smash. To crush or reduce to nothing. A Scream. Silence.

Torture by hand, rod, club, whip, electrical current, waterboarding, suffocation by plastic bag, pliers pulling out toe- and thumbnails, pouring salty water on wounds, eating feces, drinking urine, rape, exposure, poisonous insects, paying homage to the image of a dog.

Ugly habits. Talking to other groups. Not maintaining typewriters. Must be vigilant. It is careless, taking a pregnant woman to put in a new house. She cuts her belly open. When we get sleepy, put the enemy back.

Voice. Victim. Voiceless.

Wheel of history. Samsara. Wheel of life.

No eXit. Hostage and Actor. Caught in the gears of the revolutionary machine.

You must be vigilant: First, rough work—careless work → conflict with the collective. Second, morality with females.

Zero. Empty. No enemies. Uncontaminated.

Part III

WRITING

FIVE

Nearing the Paradox

"WHAT IS A BOOK on Argentine history going to say in the year 2020 about this period?"

In 1989, I asked General Díaz Bessone this question as we were discussing the political violence of the 1970s in an office at the Army Officers' Club in Buenos Aires. "Look," he replied: "I believe that a good historian is a person who tries to be respectful of the truth. But let's not forget one thing: the truth means describing the events as they have been, and clearly the truth cannot be gathered in full because it exists in the testimonies of people who have their own values and write the truth accordingly. But the historian in turn has his values. You who come from another country have your values. Thus, when you judge this situation here you will do so on the basis of your values; you are not neutral either." Unknowingly, General Díaz Bessone was touching on the vulnerabilities of authorship that were then being hotly debated in anthropology.

He also hit on another raw nerve. In the first months of my fieldwork, I was still bewildered by the conflicting testimonies I was recording without, however, doubting the tens of thousands of disappearances denied by General Díaz Bessone and most other officers I was interviewing. The interviews with retired officers, ex-guerrillas, survivors of torture and disappearance, bishops, politicians, and mothers of disappeared and assassinated children were tossing me from one ardently argued viewpoint to another.

Not that I hadn't been warned. The historian Robert Potash, who had written a monumental trilogy about Argentina's armed forces, urged me to limit my research to the military, adding that he didn't have the stomach to talk to the generation of officers guilty of horrendous crimes. I didn't follow his advice. I needed other testimonies to place their self-serving accounts of counterinsurgency operations and military rule in a larger perspective. I therefore introduced myself as a scholar who wanted "to hear the other side of the story," instead of talking exclusively with human rights activists, as most researchers did at the time.

My neutral positioning didn't come easy. It had to be maintained despite my personal emotions in the presence of perpetrators and the ethnographic seduction played on me during our interviews. What the armed forces and police had done to their captives and the Argentine people, in particular the torture and disappearance of tens of thousands of people and the abduction and forced adoption of hundreds of babies, was unacceptable by any standard—human, ethical, moral, political, and military. I had to keep this to myself as I was listening to denials and explanations I knew were untrue, because I wanted to uncover the military's reasoning and emotions behind the counterinsurgency operations and state terrorism.

This approach opened many doors to the military but raised the surprise and sometimes disapproval of victim-survivors and human rights leaders. What was the use of speaking with perpetrators who would tell me lies anyway? Had the truth commission report of 1984 and the trial against nine junta commanders in 1985 not provided conclusive evidence of their crimes? And how could I even talk to these people? Hebe de Bonafini of the Mothers of the Plaza de Mayo asked me in disbelief.

My last interview with General Díaz Bessone took place in November 1989, six weeks after President Menem had pardoned him and hundreds of officers and former guerrillas in an attempt to bring Argentine society together. Several months earlier the general had come to one of our interviews with congealed blood on his face. He had been attacked by "two leftists" that morning but had beaten them off with his expandable steel baton. So much for reconciliation and the closing of wounds. For our final interview, we met as usual in the Army Officers' Club. His answers were short, almost casual. I told him that I found him more relaxed and less defensive than during our previous interviews. He laughed. He had been in the middle of a political battle back then, he said. Now, everything was different. How was I to interpret our earlier interviews and incorporate in my writing the evidence that was accumulating about his responsibility for the disappearances in northeastern Argentina?

The collection of ethnographic knowledge does not cease when anthropologists leave the field. In the case of Argentina, witnesses came forward with revelations that shed a different light on earlier testimonies. Journalists, lawyers, and scholars continued with their investigations, and ongoing trials yielded new evidence about criminal acts. Officers who had denied any wrongdoing at the time of my fieldwork admitted one decade later that many excesses had taken place and confessed after two decades that the torture and disappearance of captives was a standard operating procedure.

General Díaz Bessone had never admitted to Argentina's massive disappearances during our interviews in 1989, but he did so indirectly in 2003 during an unintentionally recorded conversation with a French journalist. "Do you think that one can execute seven thousand people?" he said. "If we would have executed three persons, then the pope would have come down on us like he did with Franco [who was asked in 1975 not to execute five members of the Basque nationalist group ETA]. The entire world would have come down on us. What could we have done? Put them in prison? And later when the constitutional government would come, they would be freed and would have started anew."[1] The off-camera remarks would cost him dearly. Díaz Bessone had been indicted in 1985 for human rights violations committed in the city of Paraná but benefited from the amnesty laws and presidential pardons of the late 1980s. These laws were repealed by Argentina's Congress in 2003. New criminal trials were initiated. Díaz Bessone was indicted in 2004 and again in 2005, in part based on his remarks in 2003. He

was handed a life sentence in March 2012 for crimes against humanity, which included the illegal detention of forty-seven people and the
death of seven, but he saw himself as a victim of political persecution
for having fought a just war against a revolutionary insurgency. General
Díaz Bessone died in June 2017 under house arrest.

This chapter shows my struggle in portraying convicted perpetrators who saw themselves as saviors of the nation and were called patriots and political prisoners by their comrades and sympathizers.[2] I am
avoiding their conviction in court as my guiding representation. Such
an approach confines these complex figures to narrow legal parameters.
Instead, I try to describe and analyze perpetrators as paradoxical and
contradictory protagonists of political violence, as did Alex in his bril-
liant book *Man or Monster? The Trial of a Khmer Rouge Torturer*. First, I
draw on the novel *The Stranger* by Albert Camus as a literary example of
how to suspend the choice between guilt and innocence, and then I give
a polyphonic rendition of the massacre of sixteen Argentine guerrillas
in 1972 by the Argentine Navy.

———

ALEX: Your chapter is raising critical issues for researchers. On the one
hand, we have the complexities and ambiguities of those who commit
acts of violence. On the other hand, we have belief in causes but also
framings of the past to valorize that cause while sometimes admitting
"unfortunate excesses" in the midst of a struggle for the country. Duch
was certainly like that, and, as I discuss elsewhere in this book, I sought
to represent and foreground that ambiguity in various ways from the
use of poetic forms to the title of *Man or Monster?*

But there are also ways in which the assertion of ambiguity can further
denial, which is premised on mixing truth, lies, and uncertainty, among
other things. Nuon Chea was certainly like this. His entire defense at the
Khmer Rouge Tribunal was premised on genocide denial strategies that
the Khmer Rouge had been deploying for decades. In writing about Nuon
Chea, particularly given that I was an expert witness in his trial, I had to
directly confront this issue both in terms of the framing of *The Anthropological Witness* and in the literary strategies I deployed.

You mention this issue here and have touched on it elsewhere in this book (and your other writings), but talk more about how you navigate the issue of denial, especially in light of the ambiguities and "just cause" arguments you take up in this chapter. Can accounts of the complexities and ambiguities of perpetration be co-opted by those seeking to deny their crimes? Do they, to invoke the theme of your previous chapter, want to "seduce" the ethnographer to this end?

TONY: Indirectly you address the precariousness of perpetrator research, Alex, especially when it takes place shortly after the mass violence. Researchers are continuously overtaken by new developments. An archive is discovered here, a perpetrator confesses there, and a court reaches an unprecedented verdict that opens the way to hundreds of indictments. The less is known, the greater the denial by perpetrators. Ethnographers must therefore cultivate a field attitude of suspicion that allows them to turn concealment and seduction into opportunities of insight. I knew that the Argentine military were lying when they told me that they didn't know about the disappearances. Their denial offered me the chance to probe into the rationale behind their counterinsurgency and state terrorism by asking them about the causes and consequences of Argentina's political violence. They felt comfortable talking about this larger context because I generally didn't contest their denials. They didn't realize that their openness allowed me to understand their repressive decisions better. This approach neutralizes the politics of denial and invalidates self-serving justifications. This doesn't mean that perpetrators lose their ambiguity once their denials are disproved and they are convicted in court. As you show so well in *Man or Monster?* Duch continued to be an ambiguous figure. The life sentence didn't reduce him to a one-dimensional perpetrator because we can only understand his conduct as commander of the S-21 security center by knowing the many sides of his personality and persona.

Unexpected revelations repeatedly intervene in the writing process. There is a permanent feeling of uncertainty that the same person who denied in every register that he was not involved in human rights violations would later admit to them. My approach has been to describe and analyze the conflicting voices to the best of my ability by seeking out the principal actors involved, as I show below in the case of the massacre of sixteen Argentine guerrillas in 1972. The juxtaposition of the various accounts allows me to weigh their credibility and prevent perpetrators from using my portrayal of their ambiguity as support for their denials. Furthermore, this polyphonic representation helps us to understand better the conduct of the protagonists whose different motives, convictions, and rationalizations collided in indisputable violent events.

The Stranger's Enigma

Emotionally and morally, people tend to choose the side of victims, not that of perpetrators, because they are social beings who care for vulnerable others. Why, then, not write from the perspective of Argentine victims whose testimonies were confirmed in court and by a truth commission? But which victims? And victims according to which criteria? One thinks obviously of the disappeared, were it not that Argentines disagree on who counts as a true victim of state terrorism. Former disappeared have been accused by human rights leaders of owing their survival to collaboration with the military and by betraying their comrades, albeit under torture.

Writing from the perspective of one particular human rights organization, such as the Mothers of the Plaza de Mayo, is equally complicated. Such texts will immediately be discredited in Argentina by other human rights organizations as a partisan and false representation of reality. And how about perpetrators? How should researchers write about officers denounced as perpetrators by the human rights movement but who were never convicted? And what to do with persecuted guerrilla commanders who sent their combatants on hopeless missions? Or abducted Argentine officers who were tormented by their revolutionary captors and Khmer Rouge torturers who were arrested and assassinated by Duch? How should scholars write about such paradoxical figures? Should they maintain the paradox, as Alex suggests in the next chapter?

The French Algerian writer Albert Camus wrestled with these questions in his book *The Stranger*. The novel is about a violent death narrated by the killer whose contradictory behavior is left in the dark. The facts seem clear. The French Algerian Meursault killed an Arab Alge-

rian man who threatened him with a knife, hours after a brawl earlier
that day. The first fight had been between Meursault's friend Raymond
and the brother of Raymond's former mistress. Raymond had physically
abused her, and the brother had wanted to obtain redress. Raymond
had landed the first blow. The girl's brother then slashed Raymond with
a knife in retaliation.

Later that day Meursault and Raymond met the brother at the
beach. Raymond wanted to provoke the man so that he could take revenge. Meursault warned him: "But if he doesn't draw his knife, you
can't shoot."[3] Meursault took Raymond's gun in precaution to prevent
him from acting impulsively. "It was then that I realized that you could
either shoot or not shoot."[4] Nothing happened. Raymond and Meursault decided to take a bus home, but at the last moment Meursault
returned to the beach. There he saw the Arab Algerian man again.
Meursault took a few steps toward him, the man flashed his knife, and
Meursault shot him with Raymond's gun. He could have walked away
but decided to shoot.

Another reading of The Stranger turns Meursault into a person without will or intention. The violent death of the Arab Algerian man was
caused by the circumstances and the forces of nature. Overcome by the
oppressive heat at the beach and the sweat dripping into his eyes, perhaps suffering from sun stroke, Meursault clutched his gun as he saw
the man brandishing his knife: "My whole being tensed and I squeezed
my hand around the revolver. The trigger gave . . ."[5] Meursault's body
had acted by itself under the scorching sun.

The novel's tension between conscious motive and blind circumstance is uncomfortable for the reader. Was it murder or involuntary
manslaughter? Was Meursault guilty or innocent? The French philosophical anthropologist René Girard could see Meursault only in terms
of good or evil, innocence or guilt, a lone wolf or a victim of society.
Girard regarded the ambiguity of The Stranger, which portrays Meursault as victim and victimizer, as the novel's structural weakness.[6]

I believe that this ambiguity is deliberate. Camus used this literary
device to portray Meursault as a paradoxical figure, impossible to judge,
as is clear from the narration of the shooting. "My whole being tensed

and I squeezed my hand around the revolver. The trigger gave. . . . Then I fired four more times at the motionless body where the bullets lodged without leaving a trace."[7] Camus heightened the novel's tension by contrasting the accidental first shot with the calculated additional shots and by describing the killing in Meursault's detached narrative as if he was a bystander.

Meursault's indifference toward life and death became even more bewildering to the court by a shocking discovery. His mother had died only days before the killing. Meursault had not shed a tear at her funeral and had gone the next day to the cinema to see a comedy. Devoid of any feeling, remorse or soul, moral society disintegrates in the presence of the coldhearted Meursault. "We cannot complain that he lacks what it was not in his power to acquire," argued the prosecutor. "But here in this court the wholly negative virtue of tolerance must give way to the sterner but loftier virtue of justice. Especially when the emptiness of a man's heart becomes, as we find it in this man, an abyss threatening to swallow up society."[8]

The Stranger forces its readers to contemplate life's contradictions. Camus remarked that Meursault represents the point from which we must all start if we don't want to surrender ourselves to corrupting prejudices.[9] The persona of Meursault precedes moral classifications and his actions preclude any judgment. According to his lawyer, the trial showed that "everything is true and nothing is true!"[10] Camus portrays Meursault as amoral, rather than immoral. He is a stranger to society. In Meursault's own words, he is the "odd man out, a kind of intruder," whereas for the prosecutor he is "a monster, a man without morals."[11] *The Stranger* manifests different perspectives and serves as an example of how a literary text can maintain the tensions between victimhood, perpetratorhood, and personal character.

The Algerian writer Kamel Daoud criticized Camus for ignoring the victim's perspective and denying him an identity. Daoud called the victim Musa in his novel *The Meursault Investigation*. The novel relates the story of Harun, whose life was overshadowed by the death of his brother Musa and whose mother searched tirelessly for her son's body that had probably been carried off by the sea. Harun didn't consider himself an Arab but a Muslim. He eventually became an accidental killer, like Meursault, when he confronted a Frenchman who had entered his courtyard on a moonlit night: "I took a few steps forward, feeling my body stiffen with refusal. I wanted to fight through that resistance, and I took one more step."[12]

The confrontation took place when the Algerian independence war had nearly ended but the French OAS (Secret Armed Organization), which consisted of former French officers, continued to assassinate Algerians. "I squeezed the trigger and fired twice," Harun says. "Two bullets. One in the belly, and the other in the neck."[13] Harun and his mother buried the body in the courtyard. Five days later, Harun was detained. The colonel in charge of the investigation suspected Harun of murder but was more interested in knowing why Harun had not enlisted in the National Liberation Front during its fight against the French colonizers.

Like Camus's Meursault, Harun is neither passive nor active and neither good nor evil. Instead, Daoud portrays Harun as amoral, a position illustrated by Harun's not having joined the anticolonial war. "I didn't collaborate with the colonists and everyone in the village knew it," Harun states, "but I wasn't a mujahid either, and it bothered a great many people that I was sitting there in the middle, in that intermediary state, as if I was taking a nap under a rock on the beach."[14]

Kamel Daoud makes in *The Meursault Investigation* explicit what remains tacit in *The Stranger*. Figure 19 illustrates the colonial surveillance during the Algerian War of Independence. The photo was taken in the poor district of Belcourt in Algiers during a police operation to check more than three thousand residents. Behind the stoic demeanor of the Arab Algerian men squatting against the wall, there must be a subdued anger about their treatment but also the awareness that the French military in Vietnam had been defeated in 1954 by nationalist insurgents, and that a similar fate was possible in Algeria.

Officers like General Díaz Bessone were not amoral but ideologically and morally convinced of the use of extreme violence against enemy

FIGURE 19. French policemen control inhabitants of Algiers, April 4, 1956. Photo by Pierre Bonnin. Reproduced with permission from ANP, the Netherlands.

combatants and political opponents. Yet in my eyes and in the eyes of many Argentines, the military was responsible for a boundless violence that was unjustified by the political circumstances and the moral standards of most Argentines.

Ethnographers must portray these multiple perspectives, as Camus did in *The Stranger* and Daoud in *The Meursault Investigation*, to depict the complexity of perpetrators. However, unlike Camus and Daoud, ethnographers should not shy away from reflecting on the moral implications of the atrocities committed. I illustrate this position with the polyphonic description of a mass killing that took place in Argentina in August 1972 during the dictatorship of Lieutenant General Lanusse.

ALEX: Tony, there are so many interesting things and levels of analysis at work in this chapter. Since I first started reading it, I have wanted to ask you about the thought process that led you to write the essay in this way—your *curation* to use a term I will speak about in the next chapter. And if you had decided to curate it in a different manner, how would your representation of the polysemy and ambiguity have changed? For example, what if you had begun this essay with a dialogue between you and General Díaz Bessone? Your remarkable ethnographic perpetrator research affords so many possible curations. So unpacking your choices, including what other literary strategies you considered, as a sort of metacommentary will be useful for perpetrator researchers as they mull the possibilities and make their own choices.

TONY: Alex, your innovative semantic combination of *curation* with the writing process got me thinking. You explain the meaning of *curation* by its Latin etymological root *cūrāre*, which implies healing and curing. Yet we know that what cures us may also kill us, as in the case of radiation therapy. This thought made me associate *curation* with *curare*, because *cūrāre* and *curare* are homophones, identical sounding words with different meanings. The English word *curare* is derived from an indigenous name given by the Macushi to a poison used for hunting in the Amazon rain forest. However, *curare* is also a muscle relaxant used in Western medicine during surgery. *Curare* is what Derrida called "an undecidable," a word that captures contradictory meanings, just as the English word *drug* refers both to a medicine and to a narcotic, dependent on the syntactical context.

This chapter's "curation" consisted of writing a text that would capture the contradictory meanings of Argentine military perpetrators—beneficial to Argentina's conservative interests and harmful to the opponents. Searching for a suitable example, I remembered *The Stranger* by Albert Camus, whose main character Meursault personifies Derrida's concept of the undecidable. Meursault is a contradictory figure. He is an undecidable. He threatens but is also threatened by the social order. Of course, perpetrators are not undecidables because they do make moral choices, but *The Stranger* provided me with a literary form to express the ambiguities of perpetrators and the paradox of perpetratorhood: good for some and evil for others.

Aside from *curation*, your term the *redactic* is inspiring for writing about perpetrators. How do we frame violence and perpetratorhood?

What do we erase and what do we include? I have been experimenting with a text that suggests rather than explicitly describes acts of violence. One source of inspiration has been the Australian novelist Tim Winton. In books such as *Cloudstreet* and *Dirt Music*, Winton doesn't narrate the gradations of domestic abuse inflicted on his main characters, but he evokes an atmosphere that makes the reader intuit what happened.[15] The context supersedes the event in this literary style. Such narrative would tell the massacre of the guerrillas at an Argentine air base in 1972 from a perspective that pays less attention to the conflicting accounts of the protagonists, as I do in the following polyphonic narrative constructed out of dialogues with several protagonists.

Counterpoints of a Massacre

Argentina's guerrilla insurgency originated in the resistance movement against the military regime of General Pedro Aramburu that had ousted Juan Domingo Perón from the presidency in 1955. This resistance was suppressed by the Argentine armed forces until the Cuban Revolution of 1959 provided new inspiration. An opposition movement of students and workers culminated by 1969 in major strikes and street protests that were interpreted by fledging Argentine guerrilla groups as signs of revolutionary change.

The guerrilla organization Montoneros gave the symbolic start to the armed insurgency on May 29, 1970, by kidnapping and executing General Aramburu. The Marxist People's Revolutionary Army or Ejército Revolucionario del Pueblo (ERP) and other small guerrilla organizations joined the Montoneros with assassinations, bombings, kidnappings, bank robberies, and attacks on police stations. Lieutenant General Lanusse, Argentina's president, also sensed the change of times and initiated talks with the exiled Perón about a possible return to the country and the promise of general elections in 1973. At the same time, the police and military went after an estimated six hundred guerrillas. The campaign was successful. Many combatants had been captured by mid-1972. Hundreds were incarcerated in the prison of Rawson, a town about nine hundred miles south of Buenos Aires. They were eager to escape and restart the insurgency.

Mario Roberto Santucho, the captured ERP commander, came to lead the breakout from Rawson prison. The operation began around 6:15 p.m. on August 15, 1972. Thanks to a guard who had been bribed to smuggle in weapons, the inmates took quickly control of the prison. The only obstacle to freedom was the prison's front gate. Its guard, Juan Gregorio Valenzuela, was shot dead and another severely wounded. The gun shots alarmed the comrades who were waiting outside the prison to take the escapees in four vehicles to Rawson airport. Already skeptical about the escape plan, they thought that the operation had failed. Three trucks fled, but one passenger car stayed behind.[16]

Santucho decided that the six highest-ranking guerrilla commanders, including himself and Fernando Vaca Narvaja of the Montoneros, would depart for the airport and wait there for the others. The six men arrived at 7:15 p.m. at Rawson airport and boarded a plane that had been hijacked by several comrades. Meanwhile, the guerrillas who were still at Rawson prison ordered four taxis. Nineteen guerrillas left for the airport. Afraid that government troops would attack the hijacked plane, the six commanders decided at 7:30 p.m. to take off for Chile, leaving behind their comrades, among whom were Santucho's pregnant wife and Vaca Narvaja's partner.[17]

When the nineteen escaped guerrillas reached Rawson airport at 7:45 p.m. and discovered the plane had left, they took control of the terminal. The building was quickly surrounded by the marine infantry, commanded by Captain Luis Emilio Sosa. After four hours of negotiations, the guerrillas surrendered after a physician had confirmed that they were in good health. This medical examination was requested by the escaped prisoners as a precaution against torture. The photo in figure 20 was taken after they put down their weapons. Rather than bowing their heads in defeat, they look defiant. The woman on the right even seems to mock the soldiers with a triumphant smile.

The fourteen men and five women were transported to the Almirante Zar naval air base near Trelew because the prison in Rawson was still in the hands of the inmates.[18] At Trelew, the recaptured prisoners were held in eight cells, three on one side and five on the other, with a narrow corridor in between.[19] One week later, on August 22 at 3:30 a.m.,

FIGURE 20. Surrender of escaped political prisoners at Rawson Airport, August 15, 1972. Photo by Emilser Pereira. Courtesy Archivo de la Memoria, Argentina.

they were ordered out of their cells for an inspection. A few minutes later, thirteen prisoners were dead and six badly injured, three of whom would die within hours.

This summary of events was shared by all parties involved, but they disagreed about what had happened during the fateful minutes of the shooting. In 1990, I interviewed three key figures: former Montonero commander Fernando Vaca Narvaja, former Argentine President Lieutenant General Alejandro Lanusse, and retired Rear Admiral Horacio Mayorga.

According to the contradictory official communiqués in the days after the shooting, Navy Captain Luis Emilio Sosa had ordered the nineteen guerrillas at 3:30 a.m. to form one or two rows outside their cells for a general inspection. When he ended his round, Mariano Pujadas attacked him from behind, took his submachine gun and, according to one communiqué, wounded him. Two guards opened fire when Captain Sosa dropped to the floor to protect himself. Pujadas fired two or three times at the guards while the other guerrillas launched themselves forward. The two guards emptied their weapons on the rebelling prisoners. They killed thirteen guerrillas and wounded the remaining six. The injured prisoners received immediate medical attention, according to official sources, but only María Antonia Berger, Alberto Camps and René Haidar survived. Navy personnel had donated blood to save them.[20] On September 5, 1972, Captain Horacio Mayorga commented that some people accused the navy of carrying out a massacre, while others approved of the death of the dangerous combatants. Both were wrong, said Mayorga: "The Navy doesn't assassinate. It never did, and it never will," even though he added that those killed were "worth less, on a human scale, than the prison guard Valenzuela."[21]

The three surviving guerrillas were moved to Puerto Belgrano naval base for further medical treatment. Eventually, they were taken to the Villa Devoto prison near Buenos Aires, where they were interviewed extensively by their fellow prisoner Francisco Urondo on the eve of their release on May 25, 1973.[22] They were eventually abducted and disappeared by the Argentine Navy during the military dictatorship.

The account of events by Alberto Camps, one of the three survivors, differed from the official version. On the night of August 22, 1972, the prisoners were awoken by blows against their cell doors and screaming guards. Camps heard Captain Sosa say, "They will see what it means to pick a fight with the Navy." Shortly afterward Navy Lieutenant Bravo remarked, "Now they will see what antiguerrilla terror means," and "One fights terror with terror."[23]

The prisoners were told to stand in two lines in front of their cells and lower their heads. Suddenly, they were fired upon with two submachine guns. "When they stop," said Alberto Camps, "one hears the moans, the death rattles of the comrades, even curses. And then isolated shots begin to sound. I realize that they are finishing them off. Someone even says: 'This one is still alive,' and immediately afterwards one hears a shot."[24]

Lieutenant Bravo shot Camps in the stomach. Another officer shot Haidar in the chest and María Antonia Berger in the face. They and their three gravely wounded comrades played dead. Paramedics arrived after half an hour and provided first aid. The most seriously wounded prisoners were left to die at Trelew without receiving proper medical treatment. The three surviving wounded were only attended professionally ten hours later after having been flown to the Puerto Belgrano naval base located near the city of Bahía Blanca.

The navy had now executed sixteen guerrillas who, according to the revolutionary left, had sacrificed their lives for the well-being of the Argentine people and had shown extraordinary resolve to restart the insurgency by escaping from the prison at Rawson. The mass killing was just one episode in a long historical struggle toward a radical transformation of Argentina that would free the people from capitalist exploitation, either through a communist revolution or a national revolution that would bring the social justice promised by the exiled Juan Domingo Perón. The guerrillas had been eliminated for their legitimate resistance against a repressive regime.

The revolutionary left regarded the armed forces as the praetorian guard of Argentina's oligarchy and vassals of American imperialism. The armed forces protected the vested economic interests with military coups, the disenfranchisement of workers and students, and the violent repression of any form of public protest.[25] This larger political context and the ideological faith of the guerrillas made the account of the Trelew mass killing by Alberto Camps credible to many Argentines.

Fernando Vaca Narvaja, who had successfully escaped to Chile with five other guerrilla commanders, told me seventeen years later why the official account of the massacre was false. As in previous prison breaks, incarcerated guerrillas would always carefully study the local circumstances, because "trying to escape from a military base at which they arrived at night, without knowing the watch, the building, the features, is madness. We never committed those kinds of follies." It didn't make sense to try a reckless escape after the prisoners had surrendered themselves at Rawson airport in the presence of the media, judges, and lawyers as a guarantee for their safety.

The military did not kill all nineteen prisoners or stage a mock escape, according to Vaca Narvaja, because there were hundreds of conscript soldiers at the naval base who would have been undesirable witnesses. Furthermore, the navy eventually disappeared the three surviving prisoners because they were living witnesses to the massacre. According to Vaca Narvaja in 1990, the prisoners were assassinated to take revenge for the escape in Rawson and to kill the most experienced combatants as part of a counterinsurgency war.

In 1990, I also interviewed retired rear admiral Horacio Mayorga about the events in Rawson and Trelew. Mayorga was Argentina's commander of naval aviation in 1972 and in that capacity the superior of the Almirante Zar naval air base commander. Because the Trelew base did not have a prison but a brig to discipline soldiers, Mayorga instructed the guards to shoot if any hostages were taken by the recaptured guerrillas.

On August 22, 1972, the naval guards ordered the detainees into the passageway between the guardrooms because they believed that the inmates were hiding weapons. "They begin to search everything," Mayorga recalled, "searching for weapons, but they don't find any because they don't have weapons. More military arrive at this moment. They ask, 'What's happening?' And in the middle of the shouting and everything, [one officer says] 'I was looking for weapons,' which the others understand as, 'He has weapons,' with the result that they plant themselves in front of those [prisoners] arranged into two rows. The fire fight takes place when Pujadas and the entire group rush forward. He [Mariano Pujadas] takes the pistol from the commanding officer, and shoots at the guards."

It took two and a half hours for Mayorga to arrive in Trelew from Puerto Belgrano. "My shoes were sticking to the blood in the passageway," Mayorga recalled. "The people were still in a cataleptic state. There was a smell of gunpowder in everything." If they had really wanted to, Mayorga concluded, the naval officers could have easily killed everyone, but instead they saved the lives of Camps, Berger, and Haidar by unselfish blood donations.

Mayorga's recollection of the Trelew killings was very much intertwined with the direct consequences for him and his family. "You are talking to an ordinary admiral," he told me. "They tried to kidnap my daughter. They came looking for her at her high school. They shot my guard here at the watch, and they let me know from Puerto Belgrano that an ERP guerrilla had picked up my maid at a catechism class in the church next door, so that she would place a bomb [under my bed]. . . . The Navy made me change destinations every fifteen days when I retired, from Puerto Belgrano I went to Salta, to Ushuaia, to Rio Gallegos and so on. And this may all seem very amusing, but there comes a moment when it uproots you from everything, and it makes you afraid, it makes you afraid. This is what happens." The feeling of threat was not imaginary. Rear Admirals Emilio Berisso and Hermes Quijada were assassinated in 1972 and 1973 in revenge for the Trelew massacre.[26]

The former Argentine president Lanusse corroborated Mayorga's account during our conversation in 1990. He had been against housing the guerrillas at Trelew because it was unfit as a prison: "And precisely what I feared happened. A clumsy episode, clumsiness by one, clumsiness by the others and, well, the reaction was to spend all bullets, all the cartridges that were in the weapons. But one thing was very clear, namely that they didn't try, didn't want to kill everybody, because it would have cost nothing to kill them all. Nevertheless, three were wounded, they were alive, and everything possible was done. They succeeded in saving their lives. They took them to a hospital in Bahía Blanca and everything."

Mayorga and Lanusse stuck to the official account of the Trelew killings and their remarks about the fate of the nineteen prisoners resonated with their ideological convictions. At the height of the Cold War, with communist threats in Asia, Africa, and Latin America, and a rebellious political climate in Europe and the United States, they were determined to prevent Argentina from falling into the hands of Cuba-backed Marxist and leftist Peronist guerrillas.

The Argentine armed forces had been attacked by the insurgents, and former president Aramburu had been executed. Lanusse and Mayorga argued that the military had been entrusted by the National Constitution with the defense of the state, the country, and its people. They were protecting Argentina's Western, Christian culture against an enemy with a radically different worldview that aimed to erase religion, ban private property, and stamp out the nuclear family and paternal authority as bourgeois institutions. The counterinsurgency efforts were therefore considered legitimate, as was the repression of protest crowds that consisted of leftist sympathizers and so-called useful idiots. In the specific case of Trelew, Lanusse and Mayorga emphasized that the prisoners had been treated correctly after their surrender at Rawson airport and that blood had been donated altruistically after the unfortunate shootings.

The accounts by Camps and Vaca Narvaja on the one hand, and Lanusse and Mayorga on the other, were composed out of conflicting historical explanations, ideological worldviews, political interests, and personal emotions. From a legal perspective, one account must be false, as was shown in court. In October 2012, the Federal Tribunal of Comodoro Rivadavia concluded that the shooting was not caused by an escape attempt but was "a premeditated and coordinated action, ordered by senior officers."[27] The court could not establish who gave the order but mentioned two meetings of high-ranking naval officers, one with President Lanusse and the other between Naval Aviation's Commander Mayorga and the Almirante Zar naval base commander Paccagini, on the day before the killing.[28] Captain Luis Emilio Sosa, Lieutenant Emilio Jorge Del Real, and Corporal Carlos Amadeo Marandino were convicted to life imprisonment for the assassination of sixteen people and the attempted assassination of three others. The sentence was confirmed by a Federal Court of Appeals in March 2014. Lieutenant Roberto Guillermo Bravo was detained in the United States in October 2019. By January 2022, the extradition request was still pending in a Miami court. The trial of Rear Admiral Horacio Mayorga was postponed indefinitely because of his poor health. Sosa and Del Real died in 2016 under house arrest. Mayorga passed away that same year. Lanusse had died in 1996.

The verdict of 2012 and its confirmation in 2014 didn't mean that everyone considered the convicted defendants to be perpetrators. Many members of the navy believed that Captain Sosa had been a hero at Trelew and had become a political prisoner of a vindictive government.[29] Furthermore, the court's findings do not make the original testimonies of the naval officers and the three surviving guerrillas irrelevant. The testimonies continue to be important because they show the emotions, motives, and states of mind of those involved in the massacre, especially because four decades later the court was unable to establish who had ordered the killings.

The American historian Robert Potash has suggested that the slaughter might have been caused by an emotionally unstable Captain Sosa who was collapsing under the tense circumstances.[30] Emotions had already run high at Rawson airport. The navy felt humiliated by the spectacular escape from Rawson and was shocked by the death of the prison guard Juan Gregorio Valenzuela. It was eager to reassert its authority. These feelings of frustration, humiliation, and revenge were taken out on the prisoners during their incarceration at the Almirante Zar air base near Trelew. They were harassed, humiliated, and insulted, particularly by Captain Sosa and Lieutenant Bravo. Prisoners had to lie flat on the cell floor or stand with their arms and legs spread against the wall, sometimes naked. Occasionally, they had to sleep without blankets during the cold austral winter, and they were frequently awakened by shouts and insults. Finally, Mariano Pujadas had been forced to sweep the passageway between the cells while naked.[31]

According to the trial records, the officers were tired, bored, and eager to return home. On the night of the massacre, five officers who belonged to different navy branches arrived at the cell block. They were nervous and had been drinking. They carried pistols and submachine guns. Captain Sosa told Corporal Marandino to unlock the cells. In violation of any security protocol, the prisoners were ordered out together. Out of pure revenge, Mariano Pujadas was shot seventeen times. Ana María Villarreal de Santucho was shot three times in her pregnant stomach.[32]

The naval officers at Trelew were imbued with a hatred of leftist ideologies that were said to threaten Argentina's way of life and core values. In fact, former President Lanusse told me that "it is madness from a military point of view in this [counterinsurgency] struggle to leave people like that alive."[33] He was implying that killing the prisoners had ultimately been beneficial for Argentina. The convicted naval officers were thus patriots instead of perpetrators in the eyes of the military. Receptive to the orders of superior officers, they had acted within the chain of command and developed a psychological preparedness to carry out the massacre by dehumanizing the prisoners.

Of Ethnographic Choices and Moral Convictions

Depicting Argentine officers convicted of crimes against humanity as paradoxical figures has been an ongoing challenge because I don't want to relativize their violence. I want to demonstrate their contradictory status as perpetrators according to the courts and most Argentines, and as heroes, scapegoats, and political prisoners to most officers and their civilian sympathizers.

In the case of the Trelew massacre, I have mentioned the Cold War thinking of the Argentine military, and the humiliation and execution of the recaptured guerrilla combatants by naval officers. I did so in the awareness that the Argentine military saw themselves as saviors for winning their self-declared just war against the guerrilla insurgency, and as victims of state persecution when democracy returned to Argentina in 1983.

The existential limits of the perpetrator's paradoxical status have been explored by Albert Camus in his novel *The Stranger*. Camus showed that human beings can be victims to some, perpetrators to others, and bystanders to themselves. In a literary fashion, he amplified these contradictions and human flaws while painting a human condition that preceded good and evil. In doing so, he created a narrative that allowed him to withhold moral judgment.

Camus the author differed from Camus the person. In real life, he was clear about his political choices and moral convictions. A communist until 1937, he joined the French Resistance against the Nazi occupation during the Second World War.[34] What was right, and what was wrong, was obvious to him at that time.

This moral choice gives me pause to reflect on how I as an anthropologist write about perpetrators. I interacted with violent men and tried to understand them through cognitive and affective empathy. Even though I condemn these perpetrators from a moral perspective, I want to understand what moved them. This concern for the complexities and contradictions of human beings is our common ground as anthropologists, irrespective of our political beliefs. It is therefore not the political choice between one side or the other that is hardest to writing about perpetrators, but the decision to take a proper distance. Only once we have come to the limits of our understanding of perpetrators can we assume a moral stance that situates their violence in a human perspective.

———

ALEX: At different points, we have touched a bit on gender and female perpetrators. You note here your interviews with violent men. Did you interview any violent women? And how, more broadly, was the violence in Argentina inflected by gender? There were, you note above, female prisoners and perhaps female guerrilla perpetrators? And there were gendered patterns of violence, such as the shooting of the pregnant woman in the stomach. More broadly, how does the issue of gender inflect perpetration and perpetrator research? The gendered positioning of researchers also impacts their studies in so many ways, opening some doors of inquiry and closing others. It was, for example, very difficult for me as a male researcher to speak to Cambodian victims of rape during DK. I am asking too many questions here, so please pick and choose. But I think a discussion of gender might be useful here.

TONY: You are absolutely right that the social positioning of male researchers influences their ethnographic encounters. Like you, I also avoided questions about rape. Surprisingly enough, I was once asked by a victim-survivor of the navy's ESMA why I hadn't asked her about rape. I more or less apologetically said that this wasn't necessary because I had read her testimony given at the 1985 trial of the junta commanders. She then continued to tell how female captives had been raped frequently by the navy officers, including Alfredo Astiz, with whom we started this book. I asked her how she knew. She explained that she was able to tell by the nervous, aroused way Astiz left the torture room. Still, this unusual interview didn't encourage me to bring up the subject in subsequent interviews.

I spoke with several former female guerrilla members, but I doubt whether they had been armed combatants. It is interesting that the Argentine guerrilla organizations wanted to abolish gender inequality but that in reality women were generally assigned to noncombat duties and had to carry out domestic chores such as cooking, washing, and cleaning.

I didn't interview female perpetrators of the dictatorship, even though they existed. They worked, for instance, in the maternity wards of several secret detention centers, taking care of pregnant captives and delivering their babies. The women who adopted these stolen babies can also be regarded as perpetrators because they were part of a whole system that took possession of the children of the disappeared.

As far as the military attitude toward female guerrillas is concerned, the stereotype of men as rational and women as emotional was regularly brought up. Female guerrillas were portrayed as ferocious and were suspected of becoming pregnant in the hope that the military would treat them less harshly. This didn't help them in the torture room, where pregnant women were given electric shocks in the uterus. One officer told me about one combat operation in which a woman used her small child as a shield in her escape attempt. This incident, true or not, was mentioned to show me that these women were ruthless terrorists who placed the revolution over the well-being of their children. They weren't caring mothers and didn't act how women should.

I believe that anthropology is concerned with the value of human life and people's diverse condition as cultural beings. As an anthropologist, I try to understand violent events from people's point of view without prejudging them. Albert Camus pondered such a balancing act in 1957, the year in which he received the Nobel Prize in Literature and the same year in which French paratroopers developed a counterinsurgency tactics of surveillance, torture, and disappearance against the Algerian liberation movement—an approach that was later taught to the Argentine armed forces.

Camus said about authors writing during the Cold War: "If they speak up, they are criticized and attacked. If they become modest and keep silent, they are vociferously blamed for their silence. . . . The moment that abstaining from choice is itself looked upon as a choice and punished or praised as such, the artist is willy-nilly impressed into service."[35] These words resonate with my aim to understand all sides of Argentina's political violence. I try to write about perpetrators from an empathic point of view while taking a moral position toward their violence that is based on compassion for the victims. I may have learned through decades of research that new revelations may upset earlier interpretations and understandings, but I never lose sight of the atrocities and state terrorism inflicted on the Argentine people.

SIX

Curation

IF EXCAVATION INVOLVES a "hollowing out," curation involves assembly as the artifacts of perpetrator research are reordered and put on display. Of course, the two processes, as I discuss in chapter 4, are highly interrelated, each undertaken with an eye on the other and mediated by desire, spectacular optics, abjection, authority, and so forth. The curation involves the objectification, sublimation, and commodification of ruins as they are transformed into an ethnographic essay, book, report, interview, or other formal display.

Etymologically, curation is related to the Latin term *cūrāre*, which it shares with word *cure*.[1] Indeed, one of its obsolete uses refers to "the action of curing; healing, cure." Along these lines, curation suggests guardianship, such as that of a clergyman—a curate—who oversees the spiritual welfare of a congregation toward certain ends, including the cure of their souls. This idea of guardianship informs the contemporary sense of curation as the selection of and oversight over a collection of materials, which have been excavated and preserved, for a display.

Here we return full circle to the concerns of chapter 1 on spectacle and optics in the sense that a curation may be more or less spectacular. My discussion also follows directly from Tony's previous chapter, which considers strategies for writing about perpetrators that account for ambiguity. If this chapter also discusses ambiguity, it centers more directly on phronesis and craft as I reconsider the "practical wisdom" I gained while seeking new ways to curate the complexities of perpetrator research in a series of writing projects. In doing so, this chapter anticipates some of the guideposts we discuss in the conclusion.

Before turning fully to the analogy I have begun to develop between writing about perpetrators and curation in the sense of selection, guardianship, preservation, and display, I want to pause briefly to note the curation's salutary ("curative") connotation. If linked to care, this sense of *curation* also connotes order in the face of existential threat and experiential fragmentation (of body, soul, mind, and so on).

Along these lines, curation provides the abject perpetrator researcher with a means of containing the difficult content they deal with and emotions they experience during their passage through the ruins of violence. Narrative, of course, does this more broadly, providing meaning in the face of suffering and existential anxiety. Politicized as it was, for example, the Tuol Sleng Genocide Museum offered a narrative that helped Cambodians understand and cope with the DK past.[2] Curation has many inflections, including political messaging intended to produce identities and inflame hate as Tuol Sleng was also meant to do, but it retains this "curative" dimension as well. Curation may also alleviate the abjection of the perpetrator researcher—even if "visitors" to our exhibitions may disturb us with questions like "How can you study *that*?" The coded question "man or monster?" suggests that no normal person would want to study perpetrators and the horrible things they do. Perpetrator researchers carry the stain of their abjection.

Ethnodrama

If the finished curation may be salutary, the process of writing about perpetrators can also be excruciating and amplify the researcher's abjection. The most difficult chapter I have written focused on torture at S-21.[3] As I sought to explicate the process by which S-21 confessions were manufactured, I drew upon Duch's trial testimony, "torture notebooks" from lectures Duch had given, and prisoner confessions that included interrogator remarks detailing their torture.

Ironically, the interrogators used torture to force prisoners to create a narrative of subversion that supported larger DK political discourses about "hidden enemies burrowing from within." *Man or Monster?*, the book in which the chapter appears, illustrates how a similar process of "articulation" and "redaction" structured the production of confession narratives at S-21, a Khmer Rouge Tribunal psychological evaluation of Duch, and law itself as manifest in Duch's trial. I refer to this process as "the banality of everyday thought," playing on Arendt's notion of the "banality of evil."[4] Part of the conundrum I faced in writing *Man or Monster?* was selecting a writing strategy that would allow the "unloosening" of analysis without the "freezing" hypostasis of traditional academic exposition, which often slips into the binaries and reductionisms characteristic of the banality of everyday thought and the articulation-redaction dynamic.

This issue mediated the way I selected, preserved, and curated the artifacts of my research—the "findings" and "data" extracted by my ethnographic excavations—during the writing process. I turned to literary strategies, even if I knew that some scholars, skimming the text for "findings," would miss the heart of the argument as they searched for my pronouncement about whether Duch was "a man or a monster." And indeed some of the reviews of the book asked why I hadn't been clear on this, complained that I didn't provide an answer, or contended that my book argued for the "man" explanation.

There is a risk in such an approach—one I could more readily take since that I was a tenured professor—given an undercurrent of scholarly bias against texts that are not on the surface "academic enough" as evinced by the deployment of overt theory and expository writing. In anthropology, Margaret Mead is iconic in this regard, an anthropological star who wrote beautifully but never made it into the tenured halls of academia.

In the 1990s, there was a turn toward literary experimentation in anthropology that was partly linked to the rise of postmodernism.[5] If the purview of literary anthropology gradually broadened and included significant works, it remained modest for many years. As the introduction notes, there has been a resurgence of interest in experimental ethnography, a tradition within which this book fits and that now includes a range of voices and creative forms, including, more recently, graphic narratives.[6]

What emerged in my book project was an ethnodrama that included poetic forms, one of which appears in interlude II. However, this curatorial choice emerged later in the writing process. Indeed, my original project, as formulated in an early research proposal, was meant to examine whether and how "global justice" would have meaning in a non-Judeo-Christian context like Cambodia. And this ended up being the focus of my second book on the tribunal, *The Justice Facade: Trials of Transition in Cambodia*, published two years after *Man or Monster?*[7] Indeed, I never intended to write a book directly focused on Duch.

At first, the two projects were commingled. As noted in chapter 4, the first draft of the manuscript was 250,000 words (perhaps a six-hundred-page book!). It included extensive material about civil party participation and testimony, including the Buddhist understandings that often informed it. If discussed in *Man or Monster?* I edited out much of this material, which later would become central to *The Justice Facade*. While written in a more traditional ethnographic style, having a more expository tone, and overtly discussing theory, *The Justice Facade* also draws on first-person voice, dialogue, and narrative form. This collaboration with Tony represents a continuation of such experimentation—as does my more recent book on white power in the United States, *It Can Happen Here: White Power and the Rising Threat of Genocide in the US*, which is centered on classroom dialogue and extensively uses first-person voice and creative nonfiction literary strategies.[8]

As I began the process of revision, I sought a form that would echo the institutional process I was examining, Duch's trial, and provoke critical thought about Duch and perpetrators more broadly instead of giving a straightforward exposition about perpetrator motivation. As is the case with all spectacular trials—and many people made the link between Duch and another spectacular perpetrator, the Nazi Adolf Eichmann—people often depicted Duch as either an ordinary man or a monster, a binary that is sometimes colloquially posed by the afore-mentioned question "Man or monster?"

This question about Duch even appeared in a newspaper headline prior to the start of his trial. It was also a binary that undergirded defense and prosecution arguments about Duch. I selected this question as the title of my book to pose a question that simultaneously suggested a partial answer (the banality of everyday thought). To make this argument, as noted earlier, I sought a writing style that "unloosened" instead of "freezing" the reader's gaze, an idea that was conceptually discussed in *Man or Monster?* through the notion of the redactic, or the excess that "frozen" articulations edit out but that remain as a trace, a haunting presence—just like the spirits of the Khmer Rouge victims who many civil parties said haunted the courtroom as well as their everyday lives. I needed a writing style that was subversive, recursive, and "undead" in this manner.

I settled on a dramatic form that I came to call *ethnodrama*.[9] Instead of foregrounding straightforward exposition and exegesis, ethnodrama includes elements of dramatic structure and uses language and narrative structure to raise questions and evoke ambiguities often glossed over in expository writing as Tony discussed in the previous chapter.[10] In keeping with these literary strategies, *Man or Monster?* has a dramatic structure that includes a protagonist (Duch), an agonist (his victims), key roles and characters (defense, prosecution, judges), a stage (the courtroom setting), and dramatic action unfolding before an audience (those seated in the five-hundred-seat public gallery or watching on live stream). Indeed, each morning the start of the proceedings was marked by the drawing of the curtains, and the proceedings were sometimes referred to as "the show." My curation of *Man or Monster?* includes monologues, dialogues, a plot-like structure, scene, suspense, and a denouement. The book's chronology also loosely follows the unfolding of Duch's trial.

While at times using exegesis and more traditional academic expository prose, I draw on other literary techniques, including poetry, to evoke and convey ambiguity, uncertainty, disruption, contradiction, and the redactic. This literary approach also draws on juxtaposition, imagery, and lineation as a way to open as opposed to close reflection, leaving it to readers to consider and reach their own conclusions. As opposed to "telling it as it is," the text seeks to "show, don't tell" as the creative writing imperative goes. I also place myself directly in the narrative, echoing the experimental ethnography traditions discussed in the introduction and noted above that seek to blur genres, convey polyphony versus a singular voice of ethnographic authority, and encourage critique and reflexivity.

In a book forum on *Man or Monster?*, Leigh Payne, who has written extensively about perpetrators in the Southern Cone, asks how a graduate student might read the book and extrapolate potential methodological strategies for their research. What exactly, she asks, is the ethnodramatic method?[11] It is, I respond, a method for writing a book that is "undead" in the sense of not being frozen, embracing ambiguity and tension, and inviting rereading along the lines of Roland Barthes's open and polyphonic "writerly" as opposed to the singular authoritative voice of "the readerly" that curates an authoritative truth displayed in the textual "museum."[12]

The term *method* has an interesting etymology, connoting "pursuit of knowledge" or "mode of investigation" (Gk. *methodos*) and a "way" (*hodos*).[13] A "method" is thus "a particular procedure for accomplishing or approaching something," one that provides an "orderliness of thought and behavior" and thereby enables articulation—to use a conceptual frame that figures prominently in *Man or Monster?* Already, part of the methodological answer is manifest in this very sort of exercise of exploring etymology, definition, articulation, and redaction.

Accordingly, we might define the ethnodramatic method along the lines of an ethnographic approach ("mode of investigation") inspired by performative and dramatic form (giving it apparent "orderliness") that draws on anthropological, literary and dramaturgic conventions while keeping an eye on the redactic and its corollaries (not just articulation, redaction, and dehiscence but also effacement, erasure, afacement, conviction, the double, the uncanny, hauntings, and so forth). Along these lines, ethnodrama embraces multivocality, critique, and iteration and tension while simultaneously enacting and destabilizing given articulations. It affords one path to writing about perpetrators.

Poetic form offers another. *Man or Monster?* includes four hybrid writing pieces, one of which, "Interrogation: Comrade Duch's Abecedarian," is reproduced in interlude II. Two of the poems are collages, the other two, erasures. Indeed, the book begins with an erasure of the ECCC case information profile on Duch, indicated only by the inclusion of the word *redacted* in the title. It passes unnoticed by most readers, which, in the context of the book, signals the themes of articulation, redaction, the redactic, the banality of everyday thought, and framing.

The other hybrid writing pieces are more apparent. The introduction is followed by the aforementioned abecedarian, an ancient poetic form structured by alphabetical order.[14] Later parts of the book include an erasure of the apology Duch offered in court and a collage formed from parts of testimony given by Prak Khan, a S-21 interrogator who also participated in the DC-Cam outreach session I attended prior to the Supreme Court Chamber's final decision on Duch's case (see chapter 4).

I use these hybrid writing pieces for a number of reasons. Poetic form offers a different way to convey the complexity of the materials about which I am writing, one that lets people and texts speak more directly as opposed to being mediated by a voice of scholarly exegesis. Along these lines, the poetic techniques of juxtaposition and condensation provide a way to raise questions and spur thought as opposed to explaining "the answer."

This abecedarian stands out in this regard. It is situated at the beginning *Man or Monster?* to introduce Duch, S-21, and the difficult and even jarring content discussed during his trial, including torture and interrogation. It also offers a way to present Duch as multifaceted as illustrated by the fourth stanza of the abecedarian:

> Duch. Eldest son. Star student. Loner. Math teacher. Meticulous.
> Khmer Rouge Revolutionary. Patriot. Party Member. Dutiful.
> Prison commandant. Brute. Eyes and ears of the Party.
> Obedient. Gave orders. Stoic. Fanatic. Torturer. Father. Cog in

*the machine. Believer. Mass murderer. Prisoner imprisoned. The
Accused. Defendant. Criminal. Convict.*

In short order, this passage juxtaposes information about Duch's background, personality, occupation, S-21 position, and defense—as well as
the way he was sometimes depicted by the prosecution, in the media,
and by the defense. This portrait of Duch is supplemented by other
stanzas focused on torture, Buddhist beliefs about the spirits of the
dead, and the daily routines of interrogators. The use of found language
(for the most part), in turn, allows for multivocality (versus an authorial
monologue) and "showing" (as opposed to "telling").

Finally, I use poetic form, and the placement of it within the book,
for disruption. In keeping with my intent to write in a manner that is
"undead," I use poetic form to interrupt the flow of the ethnodrama
and destabilize readings of it—even as hybrid writing also enables the
reader to more fully enter the experience I am writing about in all its
horrors, complexities, ambiguities, and nuances. To this end, I seek to
build into the text generative ambiguity, tension, and openness as opposed to monologic and foreclosing exposition.

In doing so, I am also inspired by graphic narratives with their
gutter-frame construction, intertwining of image and text, and dis-
ruptions of space, time, and narrative flow. "Man or Monster?" the
book cover caption asks, a question that, as noted earlier, also offers an
answer in terms of its binary framing—a first pointer toward the banality of everyday thought. The book revolves around the words the reader
encounters from cover to finish—starting with the book's title and
ending with the word *haunting*, which is meant to fracture the notion
that there is a definitive "end" and invite rereading. This strategy is inspired in part by the end of Art Spiegelman's groundbreaking graphic
narrative, *Maus*, a text I teach often and that first led me to draw on
graphic narrative form and theory in my writing curations.[15]

———

TONY: You show clearly how you struggled to find the most suitable
narrative style to portray Duch with all his unsolvable contradictions

and mention that writing about torture was your greatest challenge. So was mine. You preferred an ethnodramatic style in *Man or Monster?*, having already written the more conventional book *Why Did They Kill?* I chose an expository style for my book *Political Violence and Trauma in Argentina* because I wanted to convince the reader that torture was intended by the Argentine military to systematically destroy the revolutionary spirit of their captives and traumatize them by disabling the sociality that makes people into and therefore political beings. Torture completed the military victory on the ground into the minds and selves of the armed revolutionaries and political opponents.

I therefore designed the chapter about torture as a chronicle that consisted of the abduction, the beating and the hooding, the journey to the secret detention center, the undressing and blindfolding, the initial interrogation to gather information, and then the torture sessions with electric shocks that might last for days, weeks, and sometimes months on end, complemented by water boarding, rape, and mock executions. I used many quotes from victim-survivors and some from torturers, trying to explain the rationale of the perpetrators and convey the experience of the tortured.

Your chapter in *Man or Monster?* adopts the perspective of the torturers, and how Duch lectured and taught them to extract confessions. Both our approaches offer readers a good depiction and understanding of torture, even though they are written from different perspectives and in other narrative styles. What if we would have switched approaches, and what if we had tried something as radical as the graphic artist Art Spiegelman who told his father's story as a Holocaust survivor by portraying Nazis as cats and Jews as mice? Would these two moves have changed the reader's understanding of torture?

ALEX: In a word: yes! And at one point I considered writing a graphic narrative in partnership with a graphic artist, something the anthropologist Alisse Waterston recently did with Charlotte Corden.[16] Perhaps I will in the future. But with regard to your question, I wanted to do so precisely to convey material on mass violence through an alternative medium that leads to different sorts of understandings while also leaving an openness and reflexivity that often get washed out of academic prose. And the visual elements, supplemented by spare, succinct text and, of course, the gutter-frame construction, offer so much. I have done erasures, including a long series of erasures related to Aleppo that appears at the end of an edited book, *Rethinking Peace*,[17] precisely because the form is visual, has frame-gutter-like construction, encourages reflexivity, and so forth. And I have a surprise at the end of this chapter that speaks to this point.

Writing without Banisters

While it was a struggle to find literary strategies and forms for my curation of Duch's trial in *Man or Monster?*, I also found it liberating. In all disciplinary fields, students must be disciplined or taught given academic vernaculars, histories, and writing tools. To borrow a metaphor from Hannah Arendt, these conventions provide banisters to help academic disciples to think, act, teach, and publish within the given domain. But the key to thinking is ultimately to be able to "unlearn" and let go of these banisters, a process Arendt's referred to as "thinking without a banister."[18] The banister of convention is still present, of course, but the thinker no longer relies upon it, instead branching out in new directions, including moving between genres, disciplines, and literary forms.

While my first single-authored book, *Why Did They Kill?*, is firmly written within the conventions of traditional ethnographic writing, *Man or Monster?* wanders much further afield and convinced me of the importance of, to extend Arendt's metaphor," "writing without banisters." My third single-authored book, *The Justice Facade*, returns to a more traditional style, but the two that followed—along with this coauthored volume and different essays I subsequently wrote—are curated in more experimental forms. I conclude this chapter by briefly discussing three of these efforts in the craft of literary anthropology and experimental writing.

Graphic narratives continue to inspire some of this work. The frame-gutter construction, in particular, serves as a metaphor to think about presence and absence, what is foregrounded and backgrounded, the said and the unsaid—or, as I put it in *Man or Monster?*, articulation and redaction.

Whatever set of terms are used, the gutter-frame construction underscores the point that authorial curations—including those of the perpetrator researcher—are premised on gaps and excesses that haunt them and that, ideally, must be acknowledged. And indeed, all three of the writing pieces I now discuss are centered on exploring such erasures.

Two of these texts are single-authored books that, like *Man or Monster?* and *The Justice Facade*, began as a combined project that sought to put expert witness testimony I gave at the Khmer Rouge Tribunal in 2016 in conversation with the resurgence of white nationalism and white power extremism in the US during the Trump administration. The combined project, which had various titles, including "The Hater" and "The Extremist," was eventually split because the two experiences didn't cohere well enough, a point reviewers noted. One of the most important imperatives of writing is "revise, revise, and revise again" in the sense of re-vision—ruthlessly so if necessary and as was the case with this project.

And so a first curation, "The Hater," was radically reimagined as "It Can Happen Here: Genocide, White Power, and Lessons from Trump's USA" and ultimately published, in keeping with a publisher title suggestion, as *It Can Happen Here: White Power and the Rising Threat of Genocide in the US.*[19] If I let go of the banisters in *Man or Monster?*, I more fully write without them in *It Can Happen Here*. My aim was to craft a book that is accessible and engaging to anyone from an educated lay reader to a senior scholar.

To do so, I set the book in motion with a problematic—the rising threat of atrocity crimes (genocide, crimes against humanity, and war crimes) during the Trump administration—driven by a temporal narrative (chapters narratively set in chronological time), dialogue, character, setting, and first-person voice. The book upends two key conceptual blockages: the "not us" (American exceptionalism and the idea "it can't happen here") and the "not me" (the notion that white power extremism is the result of "a few bad apples" and has little to do with "us").

Along these lines, *It Can Happen Here* contends that Trump was not an exception but instead a symptom of a long history of white supremacy in the US that has taken on new forms including structural racism, a long-standing academic idea that became popularized after the George Floyd protests. This gap is the key "gutter" that *It Can Happen Here* unpacks in making the argument that not just "it can happen here" but "it has happened here," and many times, dating back to settler colonialism, enslavement, lynching, and other violence perpetrated against Black and Brown communities in the United States.

The challenge I faced was writing a book that involves quite a bit of conceptual, historical, and other background information in a clear and engaging manner—what Narayan refers to as "expository lumps."[20] I solve this issue by setting much of the book in the flow of related classes and teach-ins I taught, beginning with chapter 1, "Charlottesville Teach-In." What might have otherwise been dry expository prose written with ethnographic authority is recast more dynamically as classroom dialogue with the voice of students often foregrounded. While drawing upon academic sources and theory, I seek to minimize self-referential, insular academic vernaculars.

The text on my testimony at the Khmer Rouge Tribunal that I edited out of *It Can Happen Here* formed the beginnings of another single-authored book, *The Anthropological Witness: Expert Lessons at the Khmer Rouge Tribunal*.[21] This book project presented a distinct challenge because it centered on my testimony over three and a half days at the Khmer Rouge Tribunal, which culminated in an in-court exchange with "Brother Number Two," Nuon Chea, who at one point supervised Duch and worked hand in hand with Pol Pot to undertake Cambodia's "Super Great Leap Forward" during DK.

This exchange became a pivotal moment toward which the narrative of the book drives. I become a character in the book along with the other courtroom players, such as the prosecution lawyer and Nuon Chea's defense team. Once again, I confronted "expository lumps" that I weave into my courtroom experience and testimony. And once again I curate the book using literary conventions related to voice, setting, dialogue, and narrative.

The conceptual dimensions of the text are another sort of lump I grapple with in the writing, especially since one of the peer reviewers suggested I include more on the epistemological differences between anthropology and law. I had to weave discussion of epistemology into a narrative framed around the question of whether a public scholar can effectively testify in an international criminal tribunal given the different assumptions of social science and law.

This question requires discussion of truth-seeking in both domains, an issue that is all the more critical in this case since the Khmer Rouge have long been involved in genocide denial, which was also a fulcrum of Nuon Chea's defense. To grapple with the question of truth, I draw on Trouillot's discussion of silence, power, and the production of history.[22] Trouillot's analysis of how silences imbue the processes by which facts are reacted, assembled, narrated, and historicized provides a way of thinking about epistemology and the "gutters" of law, which is aimed at testing evidence and producing legal facts that result in the verdict's determination of criminality. The epistemological assumptions of anthropology and law therefore became a key factor in the way I curate *The Anthropological Witness*, informing my selection of dialogue, character, voice, and setting.

———

TONY: You're right in saying that students are disciplined into particular academic styles of writing, but the emotional reception of those conventional texts are seldom addressed. Even though I tried to write about torture as straightforwardly as possible, using several banisters to lessen the impact on the reader, I nevertheless learned that many of my students erected emotional barriers to protect themselves from the existential anxieties evoked by the description of the unworldly reality of Argentina's torture rooms. Some students blamed me for obliging them to read about those horrible scenes, and one student even literally stapled the pages of the chapter about torture together in an act of resistance and repression. To what extent should we pay heed to such reactions?

ALEX: Staples! That is powerful and all the more so given the focus on torture. And yes, it is very difficult to navigate this issue in both our curations and our pedagogies. Perhaps what we, as curators, need to do is to make sure that our audiences are prepared. This can be done with a keyword. Everyone who reads the title of *Man or Monster? Trial of a Khmer Rouge Torturer* knows it will extensively discuss torture. And there are people who won't read texts—and sometimes even talk about—topics like genocide, mass violence, and torture. I understand. It's difficult material. For some, it intersects with personal or family histories of trauma. And to return to our discussion in chapter 4, many readers may share the author's sense of ruin, abjection, and existential anxiety.

But ultimately, it is not possible to undertake perpetrator research if the acts of perpetration are masked. So, we need to make clear to our audiences what our curations are about and why we are undertaking them. The same is true for teaching, although in the classroom we have more space for framing, discussing, processing, and together working through the difficult material. Here, too, the title and introduction to our courses need to be clear that the intellectual journey ahead will involve content that can be upsetting and offer options, ranging from stepping out of the classroom to seeking counseling at student services if needed. And of course, we need to have open conversations about this issue.

Writing with Medusa

If a gutter-frame thread runs through all these recent projects, the connection to graphic narratives is most evident in a more experimental essay I wrote titled "The First Lesson in Prevention."[23] It begins:

Warning
"There's a Medusa in the room!"

Pig in a Poke
In prevention, we tell many tales . . .

Both of these metaphors direct the writers toward critique, a "first lesson" that is premised on a "methodology involving discernment, ambiguation, decentering, genealogy, openness, recursivity, and a look at the unsaid. . . . Analysis if you will—but in the etymological sense of an unloosening. Denaturalization. Contextualization. Multivocality."[24] This initial "giveaway" was included in response to a peer-review request. The first version of the essay sought to make critique implicit and even included a small interlude invoking the peer-review process, which is usually pushed into the gutter (or acknowledgments) of academic essays. It imagines (and challenges) a "social science" prevention researcher peer-review response to an essay that uses experimental writing and related literary strategies—extremely unusual and even at odds with the strong positivist orientation of the field—to decenter the assumptions of prevention research:

Evaluation
Time to change the tone. I'm worried about what reviewers will say (but also that I'll continue to stray from the well-trodden path to prevention). "Post-modern junk." "Boring." "I read *Why Did They Kill? What happened?!*" "Frivolous and foolhardy." "A waste of pen and ink (and my time)." "Too many clichés!" "Nothing to do with prevention." "Can't write." "And I thought *Man or Monster?* was odd! At least it had an explanatory ending." "Passé." "Number One . . . on the top ten list of why I no longer read anthropology." "Retitle *The Hinton Facade*." "Fell asleep while reading." "What's the point?"[25]

More broadly, and as indicated by its opening line, the essay foregrounds Medusa as a metaphor and reminder of the importance of critique.[26] It does so through a discussion of graphic narrative renderings of the myth of Medusa, noting that the compositional style of graphic narratives offers paths to undertake critique—ranging from considerations of space and time (through the layout and visual structures that enable analysis of linear, emplotted moments and places) to the gutter-frame structure highlights the process of foregrounding (whatever is highlighted in the panel) and backgrounding (through the ever-present gap between the frames connoting erasure).

In other words, even as they assert given articulations, such as the popularized Perseus and Medusa myth, graphic narratives structurally and visually suggest the erasure that inevitably accompanies them.[27] Graphic narrative form demands that we always ask what has been edited, existing now only as a trace in the visually present gutters bordering the frames.

———

TONY: The myth of Medusa seems to pose an impossible dilemma to perpetrator researchers: if we look into her eyes then we turn into stone or, as you write below: "The more spectacular the ethnographies, the more they petrify." Yet if we refuse to look, then we will never learn about her secret ocular powers. However, the Greek myth shows an escape. When Perseus entered the cave where Medusa was sleeping, he knew that her eyes could petrify him, so he used his shining shield as a mirror to look at the reflection of her awakening eyes before cutting off her head. Are the different literary styles—conventional as well as experimental—different types of shields that reflect the violence we never saw directly as fieldworkers and protect us and our readers from being emotionally affected by the conjured-up images?

ALEX: Let me answer your question in a roundabout manner. I want to note that, even as I have been discussing gutters and frames, we have created a gutter-frame structure to this book—including these intra-textual dialogues reflecting the sorts of discussions we have had as we have been writing and thinking about our curation. I only realize this, now, at a very late stage of the final revisions we are doing.

And perhaps, as well, we have been seeking to curate this book with an eye on the Medusa in the room, subverting singular authoritative narratives with discussions that rupture the authorial flow and inflect it in new directions. We have included conventional prose, experimental writing, poetry, creative nonfiction, and a bit of memoir. I'm not sure what to call it—perhaps ethnographic pastiche or collage? Perhaps it's better not to have a term since Medusa would warn us that we're becoming petrified.

And along those lines and since you mentioned Perseus, I want to note that Perseus is petrified. He commits a horrible act of violence—creating a singular silence and erasing multivocality—and afterward uses

Medusa's head to kill many other people. He, more than most, could have used Medusa as a guide. Instead, he blindly served as Athena's pawn and indeed ends up giving her Medusa's head, which Athena affixes to her shield, a tool of violence and war.

But circling back to your question, I hope we have modeled and explored a variety of forms for readers to consider as they undertake their own curations of perpetrator violence. The strong emotional content, as you note and as we have discussed throughout this book, needs to be considered throughout the process of perpetrator research.

————————

How does this bear upon perpetrator research? It suggests a lesson to bear in mind—a "first lesson of perpetrator research"—that directly bears upon our curations: the need to constantly search for the "Medusa in the room," a haunting and uncanny presence, often only glimpsed from traces, which needs to be critically discerned. And indeed the myth's emphasis on the gaze is suggestive in this regard: the eye of the Gray Witches, prophecy, the helmet of invisibility, and, of course, Medusa's petrifying gaze.

In both graphic narratives about Perseus and Medusa that I drew on, eyes are also highlighted in the panels, and the petrifying power of Medusa's head is signified by glowing light emanating from her eyes. This motif of the seen and the unseen—which is critical to decentering our "spectacular" optics—is a key current in the myth of Medusa and one the graphic form is able to underscore in visual ways prose usually cannot.[28]

Echoing the theme of silence and power in *Man or Monster?*, *It Can Happen Here*, and *The Anthropological Witness*, "The First Lesson in Prevention" also discusses perpetration in relation to temporality, noting how the myth of Medusa is often articulated as a hero myth in ways that redact a history of violence—such as Medusa's rape by Poseidon in Athena's temple and Athena's transformation of Medusa into a monstrous form.

Medusa, then, raises many questions that inform our writing and curations of perpetrators: how we represent and analyze violence; how our accounts dehistoricize, decontextualize, and even dehumanize others; the gaps in our analyses; the haunting and uncanny conceptual spaces we fear; our tacit assumptions about gendered violence and the legitimation of violence including mass murder; and questions about the intersection of violence, law, power, responsibility, and legitimacy.

If analysis involves an unloosening, curations usually freeze. We select, order, and display our findings, creating our own graphic artifacts, the ruins that we pen. These curations are marked with the stamp of our authority and bound up with objectification and power. Just as I have cast Medusa in a critical light, so too have many others, perhaps most famously Freud. He curated Medusa in terms of castration anxiety, an exegesis Hélène Cixous countered with a feminist optic critiquing Freud's phallogocentrism.[29]

Medusa is a quintessential spectacular perpetrator, to return to the theme of chapter 1. As with Lor, Duch, Prak Khan, and other perpetrators discussed in this book, we seek to explore the ruins of their violence and then curate them in graphic form that may be more or less petrified and spectacular, our own textual ruins. In this latter regard, we may slip into an "Indiana Jones trap," framing our texts in good versus evil narrative terms with the perpetrator researcher as the intrepid hero venturing into the heart of darkness. The anthropologist Napoleon Chagnon's spectacular ethnographic accounts of his encounters with the Yanomami are illustrative in this regard—as are the Perseus-focused narratives.[30]

The more spectacular the ethnography, the more it petrifies, often in dramatic form. Spectacle also masks power, including the authority with which our excavations are undertaken and our curations formed, with artifacts situated within fields in which politics, theory, and status are at stake. Chagnon's use of his data to argue for sociobiology provides one illustration—as does the construction of his narrative in terms of underlying stage theory tropes of the savage and the civilized.

It is easy for perpetrator researchers to fall into such traps. The writing strategies I used in *Man or Monster?*—and later *It Can Happen Here*, "The First Lesson of Prevention," and *The Anthropological Witness*—provide examples and strategies for writing in a manner that unloosens and minimizes petrification. Ethnodrama, poetic form, first-person dialogue, and other literary strategies may be useful to other researchers even if their curated assemblages will in the end unfold from their excavatory desires. Whatever strategies a perpetrator researcher chooses, Medusa can serve as a critical guide. For that reason, it is important for them to always bear in mind a "first lesson for perpetrator research":[31]

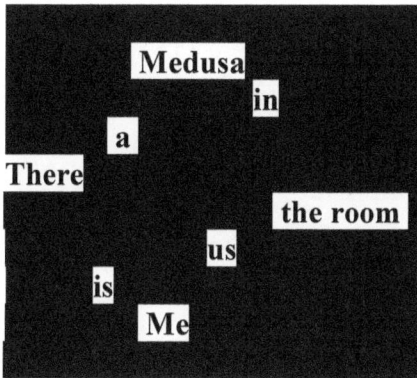

Medusa in
a
There
the room
us
is
Me

CONCLUSION

Six Guideposts for Perpetrator Research

IN THE PRECEDING PAGES, WE have largely focused on the keyword *perpetrators*. We conclude with a consideration of a theme—*phronesis*, the ancient Greek term for practical wisdom—that has been implicit throughout. Indeed, this book is framed as a set of strategies for engaging perpetrators of mass violence based on the experiences of two scholars who have undertaken such research for three decades and in two different parts of the world.

In this sense, the book can serve as a guide, or at least provide some markers, for perpetrator research. Etymologically, the term *guide* connotes sight and knowledge. This origin is linked to the contemporary sense of the term as someone or something that "leads or shows the way," particularly with regard to an unfamiliar place, and provides "guidance" on how to conduct oneself there.[1] Along these lines, perhaps the most iconic guides are those that assist "travelers in a strange country." Guides have knowledge enabling them to "point out objects of interest" and protect travelers from potential harms.

This book is our modest offering in this regard, as we have, drawing on our years of research engaging "humanity's dark side," provided practical advice on perpetrator research to students, scholars, and colleagues. While we offer methodological insight through a sustained reflection on doing ethnographic research with perpetrators, however, this book is not a nuts-and-bolts "how-to" research textbook. There are already useful books that do this.[2]

There are guides to ethnographic research, volumes about fieldwork in violent settings, and a few publications about conducting perpetrator research.[3] This book goes well beyond these helpful studies with a reflexive examination of interviewing, dreaming, and writing about perpetrators. We do so not as distanced researchers but what might be called ethnographic flaneurs whose long walks in the area have yielded phronesis, or practical insights that we hope will be of help and interest to others.

As opposed to a comprehensive mapping, then, we have discussed what we consider some of our most significant observations about perpetrators and perpetrator research. To this end, we finish by reflecting on some of the phronetic guideposts to the practice of perpetrator research that have emerged in this book. Even as we do so, we recognize that our guideposts casts light in certain ways, revealing some areas while shedding less or no light on other "places of interest" that are significant. At the end of this conclusion, we briefly discuss some of these limitations and other paths for future research.

Guidepost 1—Subjectivity

Throughout this book, we have illustrated the ways in which subjectivity informs perpetrator research. By subjectivity, we refer to the backdrop (ranging from historical and sociocultural milieus to personal life history) and sense of self (ranging from conscious being to affect and embodied experience) that researchers bring to their study of perpetrators—as well as that of the perpetrators whom researchers seek to understand, sometimes in direct face-to-face situations. A researcher's gender, age, religion, nationality, and other social markers also influence the relationship with perpetrators who bring their self and social identities to ethnographic encounters.

These different aspects of subjectivity are captured by the term's etymology.[4] On the one hand, there is subjectivity in the sense of its etymon *subject*, which encompasses the ways in which this conscious-ness is formed through history and power (being "a subject" or "subject to"). The oldest English uses of the term *subject* refer to a person who is subordinate to a sovereign or a superior, a point that Marx and Foucault underscored. This subordination consists of the superior's control and power and the subject's allegiance and obedience. On the other hand, the etymon *subjective* connotes the ways subjectivity has the sort of phenomenological and psychodynamic aspects that scholars ranging from Husserl and Merleau-Ponty to Freud and Lacan have explored. Perpetrator researchers are affected by both meanings, as we have tried to show in this book. They need to construct their positionality vis-à-vis perpetrators with whom they may maintain uncomfortable relation-ships. They are grateful for the research collaboration but may also be anxious or even fearful about the personal contact with people accused of horrendous crimes. This ambiguity has interpersonal and psychody-namic consequences that influence the ethnographic research.

Along these lines, we have cautioned at points that, given how loaded the topic of mass violence and trope of the perpetrator are, it is critical for perpetrator researchers to reflect upon their subjectivity and how it mediates their intersubjective encounter with perpetrators. In part I, for example, we discuss how this encounter is informed by personal histories, projection, transference, and "spectacular" assumptions. Part II, in turn, considers this issue in terms of dreams, which provide one path to reflexivity, an issue that Tony considers in detail in terms of his experience of undergoing psychotherapy with an analyst as his "guide," while conducting perpetrator research.

Guidepost 2—Abjection

Such exercises in reflexivity bring the researcher into direct relation with, as the ending of our subtitle puts it, "humanity's dark side." The notion of a side is suggestive here since it implies connection to one or more other sides—in this case a light side. Interestingly, this metaphor has been a recent source of debate within anthropology, with some cri-tiquing "dark anthropology" and suggesting the need for more discus-sion of lighter topics, such as an anthropology of "the good."[5]

While acknowledging the need for scholars to take account of all sides of human experience, we note that in fact there has been little anthropological focus on perpetrators of mass violence—and indeed and more broadly, the related topic of genocide and the Holocaust remains understudied in the discipline.[6] Part of this reticence and hesitation to grapple with such issues, we expect, has to do with the fact that the topic is imbued with the abject, which is another thematic strand running throughout this book.

There is a long and storied literature on abjection. Etymologically, abjection refers to something that is "cast off" or "degraded."[7] Like subjectivity, abjection has historical and sociocultural dimensions related to power and social order, such as when certain sorts of people are stigmatized, distinguished, and marked as "not us" and even as a contaminating threat to "us." The "subject" becomes the "abject" who is demoted from its subordinate position. Judith Butler, Mary Douglas, and René Girard, for example, have explored this dimension in terms of issues like social structure, gender, and the scapegoat.

And like subjectivity, abjection also has phenomenological and psychodynamic aspects. If group belonging and social categories are solidified by "casting off" or "degrading" others, so too is an individual's sense of self and being. Julia Kristeva's *Powers of Horror: An Essay on Abjection*, which builds on Freud and Lacan, has famously explored this dimension of abjection. Researchers are also affected by abjection when the perpetrators persistently deny any wrongdoing. Such denials undermine the researchers' self-image as scholars and make them question the value and validity of their ethnographic knowledge.

Researchers of mass violence may also be regarded as abject, as if contaminated by their association with perpetrators. Having looked into Medusa's eyes, even indirectly, they have learned dangerous knowledge, as Alex explains in chapter 6. Furthermore, people may close their ears to stories of human degradation, as Hannah Arendt experienced during the Second World War: "How often have we been told that nobody likes to listen to all that; hell is no longer a religious belief or a fantasy, but something as real as houses and stones and trees. Apparently nobody wants to know that contemporary history has created a new kind of human beings—the kind that are put in concentration camps by their foes and in internment camps by their friends."[8]

At points in this book, we have discussed how perpetrator research is deeply intertwined with abjection in these sorts of ways. This issue, as we note in the introduction, is an undercurrent in discussions of the perpetrator in terms of good and evil. In chapter 4, Alex discusses the issue of abjection through the metaphor of ruin, in part through a discussion of Kristeva. Tony similarly takes up the topic in chapters 2 and 3 through his discussion of transference, projection, and psychoanalysis. To engage in perpetrator research, we suggest, scholars must directly grapple with the abject while seeking to not fall into the traps of displacement and stigmatization associated with perpetrators, who are readily rendered as both spectacular and abject.

Guidepost 3—Composition

One way perpetrator researchers can grapple with such issues, we have suggested, is by using different writing strategies, some traditional and expository, others experimental and evocative, as Alex has shown with his books about Cambodia's genocide and its aftermath, each of which strikes a different tone. As noted in the introduction, perpetrator research involves an unusually broad range of issues that can best be addressed through different forms of composition. By composition, we are referring to writing strategies. But the use of the term *composition* underscores the process of assembling different elements or how a text is "put together" to form a heterogeneous "compound."[9] We have chosen this term because it may also connote artistic or literary forms, such as musical composition, which are sometimes more suitable for grappling with the issue of perpetration. Few are able to master several styles of writing when they embark on their careers. We recommend young perpetrator researchers to learn about such styles by reading a variety of scholarly and literary texts and perhaps even auditing or taking courses in journalism and creative writing.

As opposed to simply discussing the topic of composition, we have sought to model it in this book. Some of the chapters are written in a more traditional expository fashion. Others are more experimental, including the use of creative writing, dialogue, and nonfiction and poetic forms. For this reason, we have interspersed the different sections of the book with interludes. Indeed, we have sought to write a book that is, to use Roland Barthes' phrasing, more writerly (open-ended and inviting of recomposition and reinterpretation) than readerly (straightforward, authoritative exposition).[10] By juxtaposing different forms of composition, we seek to simultaneously provide analysis and destabilize its authority by suggesting the need for pluralism and multivocality in perpetrator research.

Guidepost 4—Critique

To this end, we have also sought to write a "critical guide" to perpetrator research. By critique we do not mean "criticizing" but instead the act of discernment and parsing that is suggested by the etymology of the term from which *critique* is derived, *critic*.[11] The best sort of perpetrator research, we have argued, takes place in this critical spirit. Indeed, our writing of this book has been an attempt to shed light on a topic that is often obscured by presuppositions about "the dark side" and thus in need of initial illumination by "a guide."

Even as we have offered such guidance based on our experience doing research on and interacting with perpetrators, we have throughout stressed that it is urgent for scholars to constantly reflect on, decenter, and become aware of their conceptual presuppositions. We have discussed how we have sought to do this in ways ranging from psychotherapy to thinking about our findings as a modality of "curation" that inevitably "hollows out." We have also destabilized our own guidance by introducing another guide, the Medusa in the room who demands that we constantly seek to recognize and unloosen our petrified assumptions.

Guidepost 5—Craft

As the Medusa metaphor suggests, this book offers a number of methodological insights into perpetrator research, many of which can be applied more broadly to ethnographic and other forms of research. If a methodology suggests a general theoretical perspective that directs researchers toward certain methods to be used in particular circumstances, our book begins with the particular and proceeds with cautious induction, offering lessons or as we have framed them here, phronetic guideposts.

As noted earlier, we do so in the spirit of phronesis, the practical wisdom the ancient Greeks contrasted with *sophia*, transcendent wisdom. Or, to use a loose anthropological corollary, we have sought to discuss some of the "approaches" that the perpetrator researcher may bring to bear as part of their ethnographic "bricolage." In English, these ideas are captured to an extent by the idea of craft in the sense of the skill and knowledge that are learned over time in a profession or trade, including the work of the craftsperson.[12] And so we offer some limited methodological insights based on our experience learning the "craft" of perpetrator research.

Guidepost 6—Limitation

Indeed, the notion of limitation is a fitting guidepost with which to conclude this book. A limit is a boundary that may be demarcated by landmarks. And so, as we set out our concluding list of guideposts, we have also been laying out a series of markers that, if offering guidance and a generative source of craft and composition, are also in a sense limiting. To subvert the very limits implicit in our perpetrator research guide, we have included discussion of critique, reflexivity, and the writerly— which encourage the reader to strike out in new directions, including ones that destabilize and subvert limitations.

The phronetic guideposts derived from this book's methodological reflections on our fieldwork with perpetrators can be interpreted in various ways and, as is typical of guideposts, steer us away from other places. A fieldworker's awareness of subjectivity and abjection gives insight into cultural notions of perpetratorhood and the interpersonal dynamics of fieldwork, but differs greatly from the way perpetrators are conceptualized in criminal trials and international tribunals. Judicial approaches to perpetrators will search for conclusive, secondary, or exculpatory evidence to establish guilt, innocence, or lack of proof.

The perpetrator's life history and professional environment may be mentioned in the counsel's plea to provide attenuating circumstances, but the court's primary concern is with the crimes committed and not the defendant's subjectivity—let alone those of prosecutors, lawyers, and judges. Furthermore, there is no legal assumption of "the abject" or a "dark side" to humanity—an expression we use to refer to the concealed realities of perpetration and culturally mediated notions of evil—but rather a presumption of the defendant's possible criminal "shady side" that is assessed by documents and witness testimonies resulting in a judicial truth, the judgment.

The text of criminal sentences has a clear structure that includes the defendant's name and alleged crime, the prosecutor's case, the lawyer's defense, the reasoned statement of facts by the bench, and the verdict. Adversarial critique and counterarguments are built into the rhetoric of public defenders and lawyers, whereas the judges are the arbiters who decide about the facticity of the evidence and counterevidence presented in court. Each party, including the judges, uses rhetorical techniques of persuasion and contestation to present a credible truth while masking whatever may detract from the argument.[13]

Ethnographers don't have prescribed procedural accounts—although emerging scholars face pressures to not wander too far beyond the limits of conventional academic prose to obtain tenure—but can experiment with different narratives to communicate knowledge that can be ambiguous and equivocal. They may explicitly point out epistemic gaps and doubts, a self-critique that is deliberately excluded from legal arguments. As authors, we have continuously struggled with how to describe and analyze perpetrators. We realize too well that text and interpretation are interrelated and that our style of writing influences the perpetrator's representation and the reader's understanding. Sometimes we fall short in finding the right words, possibly because they don't exist in our scholarly lexicon. Fiction, creative nonfiction, and other literary genres have therefore been sources of inspiration in contemplating other ways of writing.

The craft of ethnographic research and writing can be learned, just as law students are taught how to construct a judicial plea. Lawyers and prosecutors are more constrained by narrative conventions than anthropologists, but both run up against the limits of their creative talent.

Some lawyers possess a greater rhetorical power to convince juries than others, and an engaging narrative adds to the persuasiveness of an ethnographic text. These limitations are enhanced by the complexity and seeming incomprehensibility of perpetratorhood as manifestations of human agency and social interaction. We have tried to shed some light on perpetrators even as we are unable to reach into the darkest recesses of their perpetratorhood.

We acknowledge that, as is the case with all such projects, there are areas and issues that this book has not fully illuminated. One of them is the issue of gender, which we have touched on but not examined at length. We might also have more fully explored the ways in which perpetrator research has been influenced by the assumptions of Holocaust studies as well as law and criminal justice. Indeed, the idea of perpetration is implicitly linked to notions of criminality and, by extension, victimhood, law, and social order. We might also have also brought to bear the lens of postcolonial and race studies, which provide insight about ways perpetrator research is bound up with history and power.

The good news, as we noted in the introduction, is that other scholars have already begun to explore these issues. Our "guide" nevertheless offers a set of practical insights that a handbook or textbook can't convey: knowledge of the perpetrator researcher landscape with which we are familiar. Our hope is that these insights and the related orienting guideposts we outline here will help perpetrator researchers and other scholars in related fields find their way as they, too, traverse the difficult terrain of the dark side of humanity.

Notes

Introduction

1. Human Rights Watch 1991, 32.

2. See, e.g., Anderson and Jessee 2020; Knittel and Goldberg 2020; Smeulers, Weerdesteijn, and Holá 2019. See also the websites of the Perpetrator Studies Network (https://perpetratorstudies.sites.uu.nl) and the *Journal of Perpetrator Research* (https://jpr.winchesteruniversitypress.org).

3. *Oxford English Dictionary* 2009 s.vv. *perpetrate* and *perpetrator*.

4. See, for example, Hilberg 1992; Jensen and Szejnmann 2008; Khazanov and Payne 2013; Knittel and Goldberg 2020; Schlund-Vials and Martínez 2017; Staub 1989; Williams and Buckley-Zistel 2018.

5. Üngör and Anderson 2020, 11.

6. Hoffman 2011.

7. Hinton 2005.

8. Huggins, Haritos-Fatouros, and Zimbardo 2002, 233.

9. Crelinsten 1993, 40.

10. Gasparini 1988, 149.

11. Jauregui 2016.

12. Arendt 1979, 276.

13. Arendt 1979, 248.

14. Grossman 2019, 217–18.

15. Walzer 1977.

16. Payne 2008, 19. See also Fujii 2021.

17. Berreman 2012, 163.

18. Goffman 1959, 212–18.

19. Payne 2008, 4.

20. Jessee and Anderson 2020, 202.

21. Sageman 2004, ch. 5.

22. Scheper-Hughes 2004.

23. Navaro 2020.

24. For studies on the remnants of massive violence, see Argenti-Pillen 2003; De León 2015; Ferrándiz and Robben 2017; Gordillo 2014; Kwon 2006; Sanford 2003; Theidon 2012; Wagner 2019.

25. Powdermaker 1966; Briggs 1970.

26. Ellis 2004; Okely 1992; Reed-Danahay 1997.

27. Davies and Spencer 2010; Kleinman and Copp 1993; Stodulka, Dinkelaker, and Thajib 2019.

28. Maček 2014a, 2. See also Davies and Spencer 2010; Maček 2014b; Stodulka, Dinkelaker, and Thajib 2019.

29. Bulkeley 2018, 349. For related conceptualizations of the continuity between dreaming and waking, see Domhoff 2017; Mageo 2019.

30. Mageo 2003; Paul 1989; Tedlock 1987.

31. See Davies and Spencer 2010; Devereux 1967; Kleinman and Copp 1993; Kracke 1987; Stodulka, Dinkelaker, and Thajib 2019; Tedlock 1991.

32. Borneman 2011, 234.

33. Borneman 2011; Gammeltoft 2016.

34. Nielsen and Rapport 2017, 3.

35. Beatty 2010, 439.

36. Clifford 1983.

37. Geertz 1973.

38. Clifford and Marcus 1986.

39. Clifford 1986, 2.

40. Geertz 1988, 97.

41. Behar 1995; Mascia-Lees, Sharpe, and Cohen 1989.

42. Elliott 2017; Waterston and Corden 2020; Wulff 2021.

43. Beatty 2010.

44. Narayan 2012.

45. Vesperi and Waterston 2011.

Chapter One: Spectacular Perpetrators

1. See Payne 2008 for a discussion of spectacular perpetrators and public performance. On women as spectacular perpetrators, see Lower 2013; Steflja and Darden 2020.

2. See, for example, Gilbert 1948; Adorno et al. 1950.

3. See, for example, Freud 1990.

4. Arendt 1979; Milgram 1974; Zimbardo 2008; For reviews, see Critchell et al. 2017; Knittel and Goldberg 2020.

5. Reicher and Haslam 2006.

6. Browning 1992.

7. Goldhagen 2001.

8. Hinton 1998.

9. For a review of the anthropological literature on political violence and genocide, see Hinton 2015.

10. Nordstrom and Robben 1995; Robben 1995, 2005.

11. *Shorter Oxford English Dictionary* 2007 s.vv. *spectacular* and *spectacle*.

12. Hinton 2021.

13. Ngor 1988.

14. *Shorter Oxford English Dictionary* 2007 s.v. *exceptional*.

15. Levi 1988.

16. Thayer 1997.

17. Trouillot 2003.

18. Vickery 1984.

19. Hinton 2022.

20. *Shorter Oxford English Dictionary* 2007 s.v. *perpetrate*.

21. See Hinton 2005.

22. The text on my encounter with Lor is adapted from Hinton 2005, 2–3.

Chapter Two: Seductive Perpetrators

1. CONADEP 1986, 59.

2. Almirón 1999, 201–4; Robben 2005, 190–91.

3. Petric 1983, 145–48, 157.

4. Briggs 2007; Staples and Smith 2015.

5. Malinowski 1961, 517–18.

6. Geertz 1973, 27.

7. Malinowski 1961, 22–25.

8. Geertz 1983, 58.

9. Shore 1996, 47.

10. Lanzmann 1985, 76–77.

11. Heyl 2008, 375–76.

12. Robben 2018, 161–62.

13. Grossman 2006, 197.

14. Maibom 2014, 2; Hoffman 2000, 29; Zaki and Ochsner 2016.

15. Throop and Zahavi 2020, 289.

16. "El caso de Graciela Geuna: 3 años desaparecida en La Perla," *El Diario del Juicio*, November 26, 1985.

17. Gillespie 1982: 113; "Argentine Intelligence Officer Is Shot and Killed by Terrorists," *New York Times*, April 5, 1973.
18. Hinton 2005, 280–97.
19. Hollan 2008, 477; Halpern 2001.
20. Hollan 2012, 70.
21. Rapport 2015, 181.
22. Hollan and Throop 2008, 393.
23. Mills 1956; Nader 1974.
24. See Holstein and Gubrium 1995; Skinner 2012; Smith, Staples, and Rapport 2015.
25. Skinner 2012, 9.
26. Berreman 2012.
27. Hathaway and Atkinson 2003.
28. See Robben 1996, 79–81.
29. Devereux 1967; Ewing 2006; Hunt 1989; Robben 1996.
30. *Oxford English Dictionary* 2009 s.vv. *seduce* and *seduction*.
31. Robben 1995, 83–86; Robben 1996, 82–84.
32. Robben 1996, 98–100.
33. Navy Captain Adolfo Scilingo as cited in Robben 2005, 340.
34. Scilingo 2000, 68.
35. Captain Breide Obeid as cited in Grecco and González 1988, 224.
36. Videla as cited in Robben 2005, 171.

The Perpetrator and the Witness
1. This essay is excerpted from Hinton 2004.

"They Were No More. None of Them. They Had Become Disappeared."
1. This creative nonfiction testimony is based on an interview with Matilde Herrera held by Antonius Robben on April 24, 1990, and the publications by Gabetta in 1983, and Herrera in 1986 and 1987. Matilde Herrera died in 1990.

Chapter Three: The Night Stalkers
1. Freud 1964, 556.
2. Agosti 1978, 66.
3. Plotkin 2003, 205–8; Timerman 1981, 95–101.
4. General Acdel Vilas as cited in D'Andrea Mohr 1999, 53–54.
5. Vervaet 2017, 9.
6. The dreams reproduced in this chapter were copied verbatim from the analytic diary in which I wrote down fieldwork dreams and the analytic interventions made during the consulting sessions.
7. Hunt 1989, 25.

8. This chapter includes two dreams that have been previously published in Robben 2020, but their analysis in this chapter emphasizes other aspects and analytic interventions.

9. Kaminsky 1992, 127.

10. Crapanzano 1992, 87–89; Lacan 2013, 28.

11. Crapanzano 1992, 88.

12. Etchegoyen 2002, 34.

13. Jauretche 1997, 194.

14. Borneman 2004, 1, 3.

15. "Murió el reportero gráfico Marcelo Ranea, autor de una foto que hizo historia," *Jornada*, October 14, 2021, https://www.diariojornada.com.ar/311921/sociedad/murio_el_reportero_grafico_marcelo_ranea_autor_de_una_foto_que_hizo_historia/.

16. Devereux 1967, 44–46.

17. Robben 2015.

18. Gianvito 2006, 50.

19. Greenson and Wexler 1969, 28.

20. Kakar 2007, 39–40.

21. Jackson 2010, 49.

22. Lévi-Strauss 1963, 198.

23. Lévi-Strauss 1963, 203.

24. Gianvito 2006, 61, see also 2006, 169.

25. Robben 2018, 183–99.

26. Van Roekel 2019 demonstrates the ethnographic benefit of discussing dreams and day residues with research participants.

Chapter Four: Ruin

1. The text about this dream is adapted from Hinton 2016.

2. *Oxford English Dictionary* 2009 s.v. *ruin.*

3. See, for example, Freud 1990; Foucault 1982; Sebald 2011.

4. Robben 2021.

5. On S-21 and Tuol Sleng, see Chandler 1999; Fawthrop and Jarvis 2004; Hinton 2016.

6. Kristeva 1982, 1989.

7. Douglas 1966.

8. "The Forgotten Island of New York," *Yahoo! News*, https://news.yahoo.com/photos/the-forgotten-island-of-new-york-1328199159-slideshow/.

9. Kristeva 1988, 271.

10. Hinton and Ladson 2007.

11. Parts of this section are adapted from Hinton 2017. See also Hinton 2019.

12. *Concise Oxford English Dictionary* 2011 s.v. *excavate.*

13. *Concise Oxford English Dictionary* 2011 s.v. *drive.*
14. For a discussion of how research on violence involves projection and the need for containment, see Maček 2017.
15. Derrida 1995; see also Johnson 1978.
16. Eisner 2008.

For the Sake of the Fatherland

1. This creative nonfiction testimony by General Ramón Genaro Díaz Bessone has been written by Antonius Robben on the basis of interviews held on June 12, 21, and 26, July 24, August 14, and November 20, 1989, and his publications (Díaz Bessone 1988, 1994, 2001). General Díaz Bessone died in 2017.

Interrogation: Comrade Duch's Abecedarian

1. This abecedarian was previously published in Hinton 2016. Most of the text is taken or adapted from ECCC documents from Duch's trial at the Extraordinary Chambers at the Courts of Cambodia, which took place from 2009 to 2012.

Chapter Five: Nearing the Paradox

1. Robin 2005, 441–42.
2. Robben 2018, 79.
3. Camus 1989, 56.
4. Camus 1989, 56.
5. Camus 1989, 59.
6. Girard 1968.
7. Camus 1989, 59.
8. Camus 1989,101.
9. Castex 1965, 122.
10. Camus 1989, 91.
11. Camus 1989, 84, 96.
12. Daoud 2015, 84.
13. Daoud 2015, 75.
14. Daoud 2015, 105.
15. Winton 1991, 2002.
16. Díaz Bessone 1988, 149; Martínez 1997, 79, 96–97; Mattini 1990, 161–63; Potash 1996, 442; Tapia 1972, 4–6.
17. Díaz Bessone 1988, 150; Martínez 1997, 80; Potash 1996, 443; Urondo (1973) 1988, 53–60.
18. Urondo (1973) 1988, 59–76, 89.
19. Martínez 1997, 132.
20. Urondo (1973) 1988, 225–31.

21. Urondo (1973) 1988, 234.

22. Urondo (1973) 1988.

23. Captain Sosa and Lieutenant Bravo as cited in Urondo (1973) 1988, 108.

24. Cited in Urondo (1973) 1988, 111.

25. See the joint declaration on August 25, 1972, of the six guerrilla commanders who escaped to Chile, reproduced in Sartelli, Grenat, and López Rodriguez 2009, 151–55.

26. Cheren 1997, 202; Petric 1983, 113–15; Anonymous 1974, 20–23.

27. Guanziroli, Cabrera de Monella, and Velásquez 2012, 227.

28. Guanziroli, Cabrera de Monella, and Velásquez 2012, 233.

29. Guanziroli, Cabrera de Monella, and Velásquez 2012, 14.

30. Martínez 1997, 161–64; Potash 1996, 447–48.

31. Guanziroli, Cabrera de Monella, and Velásquez 2012, 39–52.

32. Guanziroli, Cabrera de Monella, and Velásquez 2012, 15, 103.

33. See also Lanusse 1977, 296–98.

34. Bonnier 1959, 58–59.

35. Camus 1974, 249.

Chapter Six: Curation

1. *Oxford English Dictionary* 2009 s.v. *curation.*

2. Ledgerwood 1997. On narrative and meaning, see Bruner 1990.

3. Hinton 2016.

4. Arendt 1979.

5. See Clifford and Marcus 1986; Marcus and Fischer 1999.

6. Atalay et al. 2019; Pandian and McLean 2017; Waterston and Corden 2020; Waterston and Vesperi 2011; Wulff 2016, 2021. See also blogs, social media, and e-zines ranging from *Sapiens* (https://www.sapiens.org) and *Otherwise* to "anthro{dendum}" (https://anthrodendum.org) and *Anthropology and Humanism.*

7. Hinton 2018a.

8. Hinton 2021.

9. The next two paragraphs draw on Hinton 2015, 35–36.

10. After writing the book, I discovered that there was a small anthropological literature on ethnodrama that links it to anthropological concerns with representation, performance, and ethnographic narrative style. This literature, however, has largely focused on ethnotheater, or performative ethnography, which is often scripted and staged (see Hinton 2016).

11. Payne 2018.

12. Barthes 1974.

13. The next two paragraphs draw on Hinton 2018b.

14. "Abecedarian," Poetry Society of America (https://www.poetrysociety.org).

15. Spiegelman 1986, 1992, 2011.

16. Waterston and Corden 2020.

17. Hinton, Shani, and Alberg 2019.

18. Arendt 2021.

19. Hinton 2021.

20. Narayan 2007.

21. Hinton 2022.

22. Trouillot 1995.

23. Hinton 2019a; I discuss the Medusa metaphor directly in relationship to perpetrator research in "Critical Perpetrator Studies," the foreword I wrote to *The Routledge International Handbook of Perpetrator Studies* (Hinton 2020).

24. Hinton 2019a, 128.

25. Hinton 2019a, 131.

26. Part of the discussion that follows is adapted from Hinton 2019a.

27. Hoena and Ferran 2014; Storrie and Yeates 2008.

28. For different readings of the motif of the gaze, see Garber and Vickers 2003.

29. See Garber and Vickers 2003.

30. Chagnon 1977.

31. This erasure, which also concludes "The First Lesson of Prevention," was originally published in Hinton 2019a, 142. As noted, I make extensive use of the erasure form in a companion essay, "Look Again—Aleppo: The Last Lesson in Prevention," published as the final piece of an edited volume, *Rethinking Peace* (Hinton 2019b).

Conclusion

1. *Oxford English Dictionary* 2009 s.v. *guide*.

2. See, for example, Bernard 2017; Knittel and Goldberg 2020. For practical tips about conducting perpetrator research, see Jessee and Anderson 2020.

3. Jessee 2015; Anderson and Jessee 2020.

4. *Oxford English Dictionary* 2009 s.vv. *subjectivity* and *subject*. See also Biehl, Good, and Kleinman 2007.

5. Ortner 2016; Robbins 2013.

6. Hinton 2002; Hinton 2015; Nordstrom and Robben 1995.

7. *Oxford English Dictionary* 2009 s.v. *abjection*.

8. Arendt 1978, 56.

9. *Oxford English Dictionary* 2009 s.v. *composition*.

10. Barthes 1974.

11. *Oxford English Dictionary* 2009 s.vv. *critique* and *critic*.

12. *Oxford English Dictionary* 2009 s.v. *craft*.

13. Amsterdam and Bruner 2000.

Bibliography

Adorno, Theodor, Else Frenkel-Brunswik, Daniel J. Levinson, and R. Nevitt Sanford. 1950. *The Authoritarian Personality.* New York: W. W. Norton.

Agosti, Orlando Ramón. 1978. *Discursos del Comandante en Jefe de la Fuerza Aérea Argentina Brigadier-General Orlando Ramón Agosti.* Buenos Aires: Author's Edition.

Almirón, Fernando. 1999. *Campo Santo.* Buenos Aires: Editorial 21.

Amsterdam, Anthony G., and Jerome Bruner. 2000. *Minding the Law.* Cambridge, MA: Harvard University Press.

Anderson, Kjell, and Erin Jesse, eds. 2020. *Researching Perpetrators of Genocide.* Madison: University of Wisconsin Press.

Anonymous. 1974. "Operación Mercurio." *Militancia* 19: 20–23.

Arendt, Hannah. (1943) 1978. "We Refugees." In *The Jew as Pariah: Jewish Identity and Politics in the Modern Age,* 55–66. New York: Grove Press.

———. 1979. *Eichmann in Jerusalem: A Report on the Banality of Evil.* New York: Penguin.

———. 2021. *Thinking without a Banister: Essays in Understanding, 1953–1975.* New York: Schocken.

Argenti-Pillen, Alex. 2003. *Masking Terror: How Women Contain Violence in Southern Sri Lanka.* Philadelphia: University of Pennsylvania Press.

Atalay, Sonya, Letizia Bonanno, Sally Campbell Galman, Sarah Jacqz, Ryan Rybka, Jen Shannon, Cary Speck, John Swogger, and Erica Wolencheck. 2019. "Ethno/Graphic Storytelling: Communicating Research and Exploring Pedagogical Approaches through Graphic Narratives, Drawings, and Zines." *American Anthropologist* 121 (3): 769–72.

Barthes, Roland. 1974. *S/Z*. New York: Hill and Wang.

Beatty, Andrew. 2010. "How Did It Feel for You? Emotion, Narrative, and the Limits of Ethnography." *American Anthropologist* 112 (3): 430–43.

Behar, Ruth. 1995. "Introduction: Out of Exile." In *Women Writing Culture*, edited by Ruth Behar and Deborah A. Gordon, 1–29. Berkeley: University of California Press.

Bernard, H. Russell. 2017. *Research Methods in Anthropology: Qualitative and Quantitative Approaches*. New York: Rowman and Littlefield.

Berreman, Gerald D. (1962) 2012. "Behind Many Masks: Ethnography and Impression Management." In *Ethnographic Fieldwork: An Anthropological Reader*, edited by Antonius C. G. M. Robben and Jeffrey A. Sluka, 153–74. Malden, MA: Wiley-Blackwell.

Biehl, João, Byron Good, and Arthur Kleinman, eds. 2007. *Subjectivity: Ethnographic Investigations*. Berkeley: University of California Press.

Bonnier, Henry. 1959. *Albert Camus ou la force d'être*. Lyon, France: Vitte.

Borneman, John. 2004. "Introduction: Theorizing Regime Ends." In *Death of the Father: An Anthropology of the End in Political Authority*, edited by John Borneman, 1–31. New York: Berghahn.

———. 2011. "Daydreaming, Intimacy, and the Intersubjective Third in Fieldwork Encounters in Syria." *American Ethnologist* 38 (2): 234–48.

Briggs, Charles L. 2007. "Anthropology, Interviewing, and Communicability in Contemporary Society." *Current Anthropology* 48 (4): 551–80.

Briggs, Jean L. 1970. *Never in Anger: Portrait of an Eskimo Family*. Cambridge, MA: Harvard University Press.

Browning, Christopher R. 1992. *Ordinary Men: Reserve Police Battalion 101 and the Final Solution in Poland*. New York: HarperCollins.

Bruner, Jerome. 1990. *Acts of Meaning*. Cambridge, MA: Harvard University Press.

Bulkeley, Kelly. 2018. "The Meaningful Continuities between Dreaming and Waking: Results of a Blind Analysis of a Woman's 30-Year Dream Journal." *Dreaming* 28 (4): 337–50.

Camus, Albert. 1974. *Resistance, Rebellion, and Death*. New York: Vintage Books.

———. (1942) 1989. *The Stranger*. New York: Vintage Books.

Castex, Pierre-Georges. 1965. *Albert Camus et "L'Étranger."* Paris: Librairie José Corti.

Chagnon, Napoleon A. 1977. *Yanomamo, the Fierce People*. Mountain View, CA: Thomson Learning.

Chandler, David P. 1999. *Voices from S-21: Terror and History in Pol Pot's Secret Prison*. Berkeley: University of California Press.

Cheren, Liliana. 1997. *La massacre de Trelew 22 de Agosto de 1972: Institucionalización del terrorismo de Estado*. Buenos Aires: Ediciones Corregidor.

Clifford, James. 1983. "On Ethnographic Authority." *Representations* 1 (2): 118–46.

———. 1986. "Introduction: Partial Truths." In *Writing Culture: The Poetics and Politics of Ethnography*, edited by James Clifford and George E. Marcus, 1–26. Berkeley: University of California Press.

Clifford, James, and George E. Marcus, eds. 1986. *Writing Culture: The Poetics and Politics of Ethnography*. Berkeley: University of California Press.

CONADEP (Comisión Nacional sobre la Desaparición de Personas). 1986. *Nunca más: The Report of the Argentine National Commission on the Disappeared*. New York: Farrar, Straus & Giroux.

Concise Oxford English Dictionary. 2011. Oxford, UK: Oxford University Press.

Crapanzano, Vincent. 1992. *Hermes' Dilemma and Hamlet's Desire: On the Epistemology of Interpretation*. Cambridge, MA: Harvard University Press.

Crelinsten, Ronald D. 1993. "In Their Own Words: The World of the Torturer." In *The Politics of Pain: Torturers and their Masters*, edited by Ronald D. Crelinsten and Alex P. Schmid, 39–72. Leiden, Netherlands: Center for the Study of Social Conflicts.

D'Andrea Mohr, José Luis. 1999. *Memoria debida*. Buenos Aires: Ediciones Colihue.

Daoud, Kamel. 2015. *The Meursault Investigation*. London: Oneworld.

Davies, James, and Dimitrina Spencer, eds. 2010. *Emotions in the Field: The Psychology and Anthropology of Fieldwork Experience*. Stanford, CA: Stanford University Press.

De León, Jason. 2015. *The Land of Open Graves: Living and Dying on the Migrant Trail*. Berkeley: University of California Press.

Derrida, Jacques. 1995. "Archive Fever: A Freudian Impression." *Diacritics* 25 (2): 9–63.

Devereux, George. 1967. *From Anxiety to Method in the Behavioral Sciences*. The Hague, Netherlands: Mouton.

Díaz Bessone, Ramón Genaro. 1988. *Guerra revolucionaria en la Argentina (1959–1978)*. Buenos Aires: Círculo Militar.

———. 1994. *El futuro de la Argentina*. Buenos Aires: Grupo Editor Latinoamericano.

———, ed. 2001. *In Memoriam*. 3 vols. Buenos Aires: Círculo Militar.

Domhoff, G. William. 2017. "The Invasion of the Concept Snatchers: The Origins, Distortions, and Future of the Continuity Hypothesis." *Dreaming* 27 (1): 14–39.

Douglas, Mary. 1966. *Purity and Danger: An Analysis of the Concepts of Pollution and Taboo*. New York: Routledge.

Elliott, Denielle. 2017. "Writing." In *A Different Kind of Ethnography: Imaginative Practices and Creative Methodologies*, edited by Denielle Elliott and Dara Culhane, 23–44. Toronto: University of Toronto Press.

Ellis, Carolyn. 2004. *The Ethnographic I: A Methodological Novel about Autoethnography*. Walnut Creek, CA: Altamira Press.

Eisner, Will. 2008. *Comics and Sequential Art: Principles and Practices from the Legendary Cartoonist*. New York: W. W. Norton.

Etchegoyen, Alicia. 2002. "Psychoanalytic Ideas about Fathers." In *The Importance of Fathers: A Psychoanalytic Re-Evaluation*, edited by Judith Trowell and Alicia Etchegoyen, 20–41. Hove, UK: Brunner-Routledge.

Ewing, Katherine Pratt. 2006. "Revealing and Concealing: Interpersonal Dynamics and the Negotiation of Identity in the Interview." *Ethos* 34 (1): 89–122.

Fawthrop, Tom, and Helen Jarvis. 2004. *Getting Away with Genocide: Cambodia's Long Struggle against the Khmer Rouge*. London: Pluto.

Ferrándiz, Francisco, and Antonius C. G. M. Robben, eds. 2017. *Necropolitics: Mass Graves and Exhumations in the Age of Human Rights*. Philadelphia: University of Pennsylvania Press.

Foucault, Michel. 1982. *The Archaeology of Knowledge*. New York: Vintage.

Freud, Sigmund. (1900) 1964. "The Interpretation of Dreams." In *The Standard Edition of the Complete Psychological Works of Sigmund Freud*, translated by James Strachey, 4–5: 1–625. London: Hogarth Press.

———. (1930) 1990. *Civilization and Its Discontents*. New York: W. W. Norton.

Fujii, Lee Ann. 2021. *Show Time: The Logic and Power of Violent Display*. Ithaca, NY: Cornell University Press.

Gabetta, Carlos. 1983. *Todos somos subversivos*. Buenos Aires: Editorial Bruguera.

Gammeltoft, Tine M. 2016. "Silence as a Response to Everyday Violence: Understanding Domination and Distress through the Lens of Fantasy." *Ethos* 44 (4): 427–47.

Garber, Marjorie, and Nancy J. Vickers, eds. 2003. *The Medusa Reader*. New York: Routledge.

Gasparini, Juan. 1988. *Montoneros: Final de cuentas*. Buenos Aires: Puntosur.

Geertz, Clifford. 1973. *The Interpretation of Cultures*. New York: Basic Books.

———. 1983. *Local Knowledge: Further Essays in Interpretive Anthropology*. New York: Basic Books.

———. 1988. *Works and Lives: The Anthropologist as Author*. Stanford, CA: Stanford University Press.

Gianvito, John, ed. 2006. *Andrei Tarkovsky: Interviews*. Jackson: University Press of Mississippi.

Gilbert, G. M. 1948. "Hermann Goering, Amiable Psychopath." *Journal of Abnormal and Social Psychology* 43: 211–29.

Gillespie, Richard. 1982. *Soldiers of Perón: Argentina's Montoneros*. Oxford, UK: Clarendon Press.

Girard, René. 1968. "Pour un nouveau procès de L'Étranger." *Revue des Lettres Modernes* 170–174: 13–52.

Goffman, Erving. 1959. *The Presentation of Self in Everyday Life*. New York: Doubleday and Co.

Goldhagen, Daniel. 2001. *Hitler's Willing Executioners*. New York: First Vintage Books.

Gordillo, Gastón R. 2014. *Rubble: The Afterlife of Destruction*. Durham, NC: Duke University Press.

Grecco, Jorge, and Gustavo González. 1988. *¡Felices pascuas! Los hechos inéditos de la rebelión militar*. Buenos Aires: Planeta.

Greenson, Ralph R., and Milton Wexler. 1969. "The Non-Transference Relationship in the Psychoanalytic Situation." *International Journal of Psycho-Analysis* 50: 27–39.

Grossman, Vasily. 2006. *Life and Fate*. London: Vintage.

———. (1952) 2019. *Stalingrad*. London: Harvill Secker.

Guanziroli, Enrique Jorge, Nora M. T. Cabrera de Monella, and Juan Leopoldo Velásquez. 2012. "*Fallo*." Tribunal Oral en lo Criminal Federal de Comodoro Rivadavia, October 15.

Halpern, Jodi. 2001. *From Detached Concern to Empathy: Humanizing Medical Practice*. New York: Oxford University Press.

Hathaway, Andrew D., and Michael Atkinson. 2003. "Active Interview Tactics in Research on Public Deviants: Exploring the Two-Cop Personas." *Field Methods* 15 (2): 161–85.

Herrera, Matilde. 1986. *Vos también lloraste*. Buenos Aires: Ed. Libros de Tierra Firme.

———. 1987. *José*. Buenos Aires: Editorial Contrapunto.

Heyl, Barbara Sherman. 2008. "Ethnographic Interviewing." In *Handbook of Ethnography*, edited by Paul Atkinson, Amana Coffey, Sara Delamont, John Lofland, and Lyn Lofland, 369–83. Los Angeles: Sage Publications.

Hilberg, Raul. 1992. *Perpetrators Victims Bystanders: The Jewish Catastrophe, 1933–1945*. New York: HarperCollins.

Hinton, Alexander Laban. 1998. "Why did the Nazis Kill? Anthropology, Genocide, and the Goldhagen Controversy." *Anthropology Today* 14 (5): 9–15.

———, ed. 2002. *Annihilating Difference: The Anthropology of Genocide*. Berkeley: University of California Press.

———. 2004. "The Perpetrator, the Victim, and the Witness." *Manoa* 16 (1): 137–53.

———. 2005. *Why Did They Kill? Cambodia in the Shadow of Genocide*. Berkeley: University of California Press.

———. 2015. "Violence." In *A Companion to Moral Anthropology*, edited by Didier Fassin, 500–518. Malden, MA: Wiley-Blackwell.

———. 2016. *Man or Monster? The Trial of a Khmer Rouge Torturer*. Durham, NC: Duke University Press.

———. 2017. "Wonder Woman, the Gutter, and Critical Genocide Studies." In *Memory and Genocide: On What Remains and the Possibility of Representation*, edited by Fazil Moradi, Ralph Buchenhors, and Maria Six-Hohenbalken, 165–74. New York: Routledge.

———. 2018a. *The Justice Facade: Trials of Transition in Cambodia*. Oxford, UK: Oxford University Press.

———. 2018b. "Postscript—*Man or Monster?*" *Journal of Genocide Research* 20 (1): 181–92.

———. 2019a. "The First Lesson in Prevention." *Genocide Studies and Prevention* 13 (3): 128–44.

———. 2019b. "Look Again—Aleppo: The Last Lesson on Prevention." In *Rethinking Peace: Discourse, Memory, Translation, and Dialogue*, edited by Alexander Laban Hinton, Giorgio Shani, and Jeremiah Alberg, 221–38. New York: Rowman and Littlefield.

———. 2020. "Foreword: Critical Perpetrator Studies." In *The Routledge International Handbook of Perpetrator Studies*, edited by Susanne C. Knittel and Zachary J. Goldberg, xvi–xix. London: Routledge.

———. 2021. *It Can Happen Here: White Power and the Rising Threat of Genocide in the US*. New York: New York University Press.

———. 2022. *The Anthropological Witness: Expert Lessons from the Khmer Rouge Tribunal*. Ithaca, NY: Cornell University Press.

Hinton, Alexander Laban, Giorgio Shani, and Jeremia Alberg, eds. 2019. *Rethinking Peace: Discourse, Dialogue, Translation, and Memory*. New York: Rowman & Littlefield.

Hinton, Ladson. 2007. "Black Holes, Uncanny Spaces and Radical Shifts in Awareness." *Journal of Analytical Psychology* 52: 433–47.

Hoena, Black A., and Daniel Ferran. 2014. *Perseus and Medusa: A Graphic Novel*. North Mankato, MN: Capstone.

Hoffman, Danny. 2011. *The War Machines: Young Men and Violence in Sierra Leone and Liberia*. Durham, NC: Duke University Press.

Hoffman, Martin L. 2000. *Empathy and Moral Development: Implications for Caring and Justice*. Cambridge, UK: Cambridge University Press.

Hollan, Douglas. 2008. "Being There: On the Imaginative Aspects of Understanding Others and Being Understood." *Ethos* 36 (4): 475–89.

———. 2012. "Emerging Issues in the Cross-Cultural Study of Empathy." *Emotion Review* 4 (1): 70–78.

Hollan, Douglas, and C. Jason Throop. 2008. "Whatever Happened to Empathy? Introduction." *Ethos* 36 (4): 385–401.

Holstein, James A., and Jaber F. Gubrium. 1995. *The Active Interview*. Thousand Oaks, CA: Sage Publications.

Huggins, Martha K., Mika Haritos-Fatouros, and Philip G. Zimbardo. 2002. *Violence Workers: Police Torturers and Murderers Reconstruct Brazilian Atrocities*. Berkeley: University of California Press.

Human Rights Watch. 1991. *Truth and Partial Justice: An Update*. New York: Human Rights Watch.

Hunt, Jennifer C. 1989. *Psychoanalytic Aspects of Fieldwork*. Newbury Park, CA: Sage Publications.

Jackson, Michael. 2010. "From Anxiety to Method in Anthropological Fieldwork: An Appraisal of George Devereux's Enduring Ideas." In *Emotions in the Field: The Psychology and Anthropology of Fieldwork Experience*, edited by James Davies and Dimitrina Spencer, 35–54. Stanford, CA: Stanford University Press.

Jauregui, Beatrice. 2016. *Provisional Authority: Police, Order, and Security in India*. Chicago: University of Chicago Press.

Jauretche, Ernesto. 1997. *Violencia y política en los 70: No dejés que te la cuenten*. Buenos Aires: Ediciones del Pensamiento Nacional.

Jensen, Olaf, and Claus-Christian Szejnmann, eds. 2008. *Ordinary People as Mass Murderers: Perpetrators in Comparative Perspective*. Basingstoke, UK: Palgrave Macmillan.

Jessee, Erin, ed. 2015. "Special Section: Perpetrators." *Conflict and Society* 1: 4–124.

Jessee, Erin, and Kjell Anderson. 2020. "Conclusion: Toward a Code of Practice for Qualitative Research among Perpetrators." In *Researching Perpetrators of Genocide*, edited by Kjell Anderson and Erin Jessee, 199–220. Madison: University of Wisconsin Press.

Johnson, Barbara. 1978. "The Critical Difference." *Diacritics* 8 (2): 2–9.

Kakar, Sudhir. 2007. "Culture and Psychoanalysis: A Personal Journey." In *Explorations in Psychoanalytic Ethnography*, edited by Jadran Mimica, 25–44. New York: Berghahn.

Kaminsky, Marc. 1992. "Meyerhoff's 'Third Voice': Ideology and Genre in Ethnographic Narrative." *Social Text* 33: 124–44.

Khazanov, Anatoly M., and Stanley G. Payne. 2013. *Perpetrators, Accomplices and Victims in Twentieth Century Politics: Reckoning with the Past*. London: Routledge.

Kleinman, Sherryl, and Martha A. Copp. 1993. *Emotions and Fieldwork*. Newbury Park, CA: Sage Publications.

Knittel, Susanne C., and Zachary J. Goldberg, eds. 2020. *The Routledge International Handbook of Perpetrator Studies*. London: Routledge.

Knittel, Susanne C., Uğur Ümit Üngör, Emiliano Perra, and Kara Critchell. 2017. "Editors' Introduction." *Journal of Perpetrator Research* 1 (1): 1–27.

Kracke, Waud. 1987. "Encounter with Other Cultures: Psychological and Epistemological Aspects." *Ethos* 15 (1): 58–81.

Kristeva, Julia. 1982. *Powers of Horror: An Essay on Abjection*. New York: Columbia University Press.

———. 1988. *Étrangers à nous-mêmes*. Paris: Fayard.

———. 1989. *Black Sun: Depression and Melancholia*. New York: Columbia University Press.

Kwon, Heonik. 2006. *After the Massacre: Commemoration and Consolation in Ha My and My Lai*. Berkeley: University of California Press.

Lacan, Jacques. 2013. *On the Names-of-the-Father*. London: Polity Press.

Lanusse, Alejandro A. 1977. *Mi testimonio*. Buenos Aires: Lasserre.

Lanzmann, Claude. 1985. *Shoah: An Oral History of the Holocaust*. New York: Pantheon Books.

Ledgerwood, Judy. 1997. "The Cambodian Tuol Sleng Museum of Genocidal Crimes National Narrative." *Museum Anthropology* 21 (1): 82–98.

Levi, Primo. 1988. *The Drowned and the Saved*. New York: Summit Books.

Lévi-Strauss, Claude. 1963. *Structural Anthropology*. New York: Basic Books.

Lower, Wendy. 2013. *Hitler's Furies: German Women in the Nazi Killing Field*. New York: Houghton Mifflin Harcourt.

Maček, Ivana, ed. 2014a. *Engaging Violence: Trauma, Memory and Representation*. London: Routledge.

———. 2014b. "Engaging Violence: Trauma, Self-Reflection and Knowledge." In *Engaging Violence: Trauma, Memory and Representation*, edited by Ivana Maček, 1–24. London: Routledge.

———. 2017. "Communicating the Unthinkable: A Psychodynamic Perspective." In *Memory and Genocide: On What Remains and the Possibility of Representation*, edited by Fazil Moradi, Ralph Buchenhorst, and Maria Six-Hohenbalken, 107–21. New York: Routledge.

Mageo, Jeannette Marie. 2003. "Theorizing Dreaming and the Self." In *Dreaming and the Self: New Perspectives on Subjectivity, Identity, and Emotion*, edited by Jeannette Marie Mageo, 1–22. Albany: State University of New York Press.

———. 2019. "Mimesis versus Simulation: Contemporary Dream Theory and the Nature of Dream Mentation." *Dreaming* 29 (4): 370–87.

Maibom, Heidi L. 2014. "Introduction: (Almost) Everything You Ever Wanted to Know about Empathy." In *Empathy and Morality*, edited by Heidi L. Maibom, 1–40. Oxford, UK: Oxford University Press.

Malinowski, Bronislaw. (1922) 1961. *Argonauts of the Western Pacific.* New York: E. P. Dutton & Co.

Marcus, George E. and Michael M. J. Fischer. 1999. *Anthropology as Cultural Critique: An Experimental Moment in the Human Sciences.* Chicago: University of Chicago Press.

Martínez, Tomás Eloy. 1997 (1973). *La pasión según Trelew.* Buenos Aires: Planeta.

Mascia-Lees, Francis E., Patricia Sharpe, and Colleen Ballerino Cohen. 1989. "The Postmodernist Turn in Anthropology: Cautions from a Feminist Perspective." *Signs: Journal of Women in Culture and Society* 15 (1): 7–33.

Mattini, Luis. 1990. *Hombres y mujeres del PRT-ERP.* Buenos Aires: Editorial Contrapunto.

Milgram, Stanley. 1974. *Obedience to Authority: An Experimental View.* New York: Harper & Row.

Mills, C. Wright. 1956. *The Power Elite.* New York: Oxford University Press.

Nader, Laura. 1974. "Up the Anthropologist—Perspectives Gained from Studying Up." In *Reinventing Anthropology*, edited by Dell Hymes, 284–311. New York: Vintage Books.

Narayan, Kirin. 2007. "Tools to Shape Texts: What Creative Nonfiction Can Offer Ethnography." *Anthropology and Humanism* 33 (2): 130–44.

———. 2012. *Alive in the Writing: Crafting Ethnography in the Company of Chekhov.* Chicago: University of Chicago Press.

Navaro, Yael. 2020. "The Aftermath of Mass Violence: A Negative Methodology." *Annual Review of Anthropology* 49: 161–73.

Ngor, Haing S. 1988. *Surviving the Killing Fields: The Cambodian Odyssey of Haing S. Ngor.* London: Pan Books.

Nielsen, Morten, and Nigel Rapport. 2017. "On the Genealogy of Writing Anthropology." In *The Composition of Anthropology: How Anthropological Texts Are Written*, edited by Morten Nielsen and Nigel Rapport, 3–12. London: Routledge.

Nordstrom, Carolyn, and Antonius C. G. M. Robben, eds. 1995. *Fieldwork under Fire: Contemporary Studies of Violence and Survival.* Berkeley: University of California Press.

Okely, Judith. 1992. "Anthropology and Autobiography: Participatory Experience and Embodied Knowledge." In *Anthropology and Autobiography*, edited by Judith Okely and Helen Callaway, 1–28. London: Routledge.

Ortner, Sherry. 2016. "Dark Anthropology and Its Others: Theory since the Eighties." *Hau: Journal of Ethnographic Theory* 6 (1): 47–73.

Oxford English Dictionary. 2009. 2nd ed. Oxford, UK: Oxford University Press.

Pandian, Anand, and Stuart J. McLean, eds. 2017. *Crumpled Paper Boat: Experiments in Ethnographic Writing*. Durham, NC: Duke University Press.

Paul, Robert A. 1989. "Psychoanalytic Anthropology." *Annual Review of Anthropology* 18: 177–202.

Payne, Leigh A. 2008. *Unsettling Accounts: Neither Truth nor Reconciliation in Confessions of State Violence*. Durham, NC: Duke University Press.

———. 2018. "Overcoming Blindness in the Study of Perpetrators." *Journal of Genocide Research* 20 (1): 175–80.

Petric, Antonio. 1983. *Así sangraba la Argentina: Sallustro, Quijada, Larrabure*. Buenos Aires: Ediciones Depalma.

Plotkin, Mariano. 2003. "Psychiatrists and the Reception of Psychoanalysis, 1910–1970s." In *Argentina on the Couch: Psychiatry, State, and Society, 1880 to the Present*, edited by Mariano Plotkin, 175–209. Albuquerque: University of New Mexico Press.

Potash, Robert A. 1996. *The Army and Politics in Argentina, 1962–1973: From Frondizi's Fall to the Peronist Restoration*. Stanford, CA: Stanford University Press.

Powdermaker, Hortense. 1966. *Stranger and Friend: The Way of an Anthropologist*. New York: W. W. Norton.

Rapport, Nigel. 2015. "Extraordinary Encounter? The Interview as an Ironical Moment." In *Extraordinary Encounters: Authenticity and the Interview*, edited by Katherine Smith, James Staples, and Nigel Rapport, 175–87. New York: Berghahn.

Reed-Danahay, Deborah E., ed. 1997. *Auto/Ethnography: Rewriting the Self and the Social*. Oxford, UK: Berg.

Reicher, Stephen, and S. Alexander Haslam. 2006. "Rethinking the Psychology of Tyranny: The BBC Prison Study." *British Journal of Social Psychology* 45: 1–40.

Robben, Antonius C. G. M. 1995. "The Politics of Truth and Emotion among Victims and Perpetrators of Violence." In *Fieldwork under Fire: Contemporary Studies of Violence and Survival*, edited by Carolyn Nordstrom and Antonius C. G. M. Robben, 81–103. Berkeley: University of California Press.

———. 1996. "Ethnographic Seduction, Transference, and Resistance in Dialogues about Terror and Violence in Argentina." *Ethos* 24 (1): 71–106.

———. 2005. *Political Violence and Trauma in Argentina*. Philadelphia: University of Pennsylvania Press.

———. 2015. "How to Scale Factional Divisions in Conflict Situations: Finding Perpetrators and Switchboard Operators in Post-Authoritarian Argentina." *Conflict and Society* 1: 81–91.

———. 2018. *Argentina Betrayed: Memory, Mourning, and Accountability*. Philadelphia: University of Pennsylvania Press.

———. 2020. "Does the Unconscious Influence Our Ethnography? Psychoanalysis during Fieldwork in Argentina." *Anthropology and Humanism* 45 (2): 339–53.

———. 2021. "Metonyms of Destruction: Death, Ruination, and the Bombing of Rotterdam in the Second World War." *Journal of Material Culture* 26 (3): 324–43.

Robbins, Joel. 2013. "Beyond the Suffering Subject: Toward an Anthropology of the Good." *Journal of the Royal Anthropological Institute* 19 (3): 447–62.

Robin, Marie-Monique. 2005. *Escuadrones de la muerte: La escuela francesa.* Buenos Aires: Editorial Sudamericana.

Sageman, Marc. 2004. *Understanding Terror Networks.* Philadelphia: University of Pennsylvania Press.

Sanford, Victoria. 2003. *Buried Secrets: Truth and Human Rights in Guatemala.* New York: Palgrave Macmillan.

Sartelli, Eduardo, Stella Grenat, and Rosana López Rodriguez. 2009. *Trelew, el informe.* Buenos Aires: Edicones ryr.

Scheper-Hughes, Nancy. 2004. "Parts Unknown: Undercover Ethnography of the Organs-Trafficking Underworld." *Ethnography* 5 (1): 29–73.

Schlund-Vials, Cathy J., and Samuel Martínez, eds. 2017. *Interrogating the Perpetrator: Violation, Culpability, and Human Rights.* London: Routledge.

Scilingo, Adolfo Francisco. 2000. *¡Por siempre, nunca más!* Buenos Aires: Editorial del Plata.

Sebald, W. G. 2011. *Austerlitz.* New York: Modern Library.

Shore, Bradd. 1996. *Culture in the Mind: Cognition, Culture, and the Problem of Meaning.* New York: Oxford University Press.

Shorter Oxford English Dictionary. 2007. Oxford, UK: Oxford University Press.

Skinner, Jonathan. 2012. "A Four-Part Introduction to the Interview: Introducing the Interview; Society, Sociology and the Interview; Anthropology and the Interview; Anthropology and the Interview—Edited." In *The Interview: An Ethnographic Approach,* edited by Jonathan Skinner, 1–50. London: Bloomsbury.

Smeulers, Alette, Maatje Weerdesteijn, and Barbara Holá, eds. 2019. *Perpetrators of International Crimes: Theories, Methods, and Evidence.* New York: Oxford University Press.

Smith, Katherine, James Staples, and Nigel Rapport, eds. 2015. *Extraordinary Encounters: Authenticity and the Interview.* New York: Berghahn.

Spiegelman, Art. 1986. *Maus I: A Survivor's Tale (My Father Bleeds History).* New York: Random House.

———. 1992. *Maus II: A Survivor's Tale (And Here My Troubles Began).* New York: Random House.

———. 2011. *MetaMaus: A Look Inside a Modern Classic Maus.* New York: Pantheon.

Staples, James, and Katherine Smith. 2015. "The Interview as Analytical Category." In *Extraordinary Encounters: Authenticity and the Interview*, edited by Katherine Smith, James Staples and Nigel Rapport, 1–18. New York: Berghahn.

Staub, Ervin. 1989. *The Roots of Evil: The Origins of Genocide and Other Group Violence*. Cambridge, UK: Cambridge University Press.

Steflja, Izabela, and Jessica Trisko Darden. 2020. *Women as War Criminals: Gender, Agency, and Justice*. Stanford, CA: Stanford University Press.

Stodulka, Thomas, Samia Dinkelaker, and Ferdiansyah Thajib, eds. 2019. *Affective Dimensions of Fieldwork and Ethnography*. Cham, Switzerland: Springer.

Storrie, Paul D., and Thomas Yeates. 2008. *Perseus: The Hunt for Medusa's Head*. Minneapolis, MN: Graphic Universe.

Tapia, José Carrasco. 1972. "La fuga que conmovió al continente." *Punto Final* 166: 1–15.

Tedlock, Barbara. 1987. "Dreaming and Dream Research." In *Dreaming: Anthropological and Psychological Interpretations*, edited by Barbara Tedlock, 1–30. Santa Fe, NM: School of American Research Press.

———. 1991. "The New Anthropology of Dreaming." *Dreaming* 1 (2): 161–78.

Thayer, Nate. 1997. "'Am I a Savage Person?' Denials from Pol Pot." *Phnom Penh Post*, October 24.

Theidon, Kimberly. 2012. *Intimate Enemies: Violence and Reconciliation in Peru*. Philadelphia: University of Pennsylvania Press.

Throop, C. Jason, and Dan Zahavi. 2020. "Dark and Bright Empathy: Phenomenological and Anthropological Reflections." *Current Anthropology* 61 (3): 283–303.

Timerman, Jacobo. 1981. *Prisoner without a Name, Cell without a Number*. New York: Alfred A. Knopf.

Trouillot, Michel-Rolph. 1995. *Silencing the Past: Power and the Production of History*. Boston: Beacon.

———. 2003. *Global Transformations: Anthropology and the Modern World*. New York: Palgrave Macmillan.

Üngör, Uğur Ümit, and Kjell Anderson. 2020. "From Perpetrators to Perpetration: Definitions, Typologies, and Processes." In *The Routledge International Handbook of Perpetrator Studies*, edited by Susanne C. Knittel and Zachary J. Goldberg, 7–22. London: Routledge.

Urondo, Francisco. (1973) 1988. *Trelew: La patria fusilada*. Buenos Aires: Editorial Contrapunto.

Van Roekel, Eva. 2019. "Interpretation of Dreams and Humor in Affective Fieldwork on State Violence in Argentina." In *Ethnography as Risky Business: Field Research in Violent and Sensitive Contexts*, edited by Kees Koonings, Dirk Kruijt, and Dennis Rodgers, 139–49. Lanham, MD: Lexington Books.

Vervaet, Stijn. 2017. *Holocaust, War and Transnational Memory: Testimony from Yugoslav and Post-Yugoslav Literature*. London: Routledge.

Vesperi, Maria D., and Alisse Waterston. 2011. "Introduction: The Writer in the Anthropologist." In *Anthropology off the Shelf: Anthropologists on Writing*, edited by Alisse Waterston and Maria D. Vesperi, 1–11. Malden, MA: Wiley-Blackwell.

Vickery, Michael. 1984. *Cambodia 1975–1982*. Boston: South End Press.

Wagner, Sarah E. 2019. *What Remains: Bringing America's Missing Home from the Vietnam War*. Cambridge, MA: Harvard University Press.

Walzer, Michael. 1977. *Just and Unjust Wars: A Moral Argument with Historical Illustrations*. New York: Basic Books.

Waterston, Alisse, and Charlotte Corden. 2020. *Light in Dark Times: The Human Search for Meaning*. Toronto: University of Toronto Press.

Waterston, Alisse, and Maria D. Vesperi, eds. 2011. *Anthropology off the Shelf: Anthropologists on Writing*. Malden, MA: Wiley-Blackwell.

Williams, Timothy, and Susanne Buckley-Zistel, eds. 2018. *Perpetrators and Perpetration of Mass Violence: Action, Motivations and Dynamics*. London: Routledge.

Winton, Tim. 1991. *Cloudstreet*. London: Picador.

———. 2002. *Dirt Music*. London: Picador.

Wulff, Helena, ed. 2016. *The Anthropologist as Writer: Genres and Contexts in the Twenty-First Century*. Oxford, UK: Berghahn.

———. 2021. "Writing Anthropology." In *The Cambridge Encyclopedia of Anthropology*, edited by Felix Stein, Sian Lazar, Matei Candea, Hildegard Diemberger, Joel Robbins, Andrew Sanchez, and Rupert Stasch. https://doi.org/10.29164/21writing.

Zaki, Jamil, and Kevin Ochsner. 2016. "Empathy." In *Handbook of Emotions*, edited by Lisa Feldman Barrett, Michael Lewis, and Jeannette M. Haviland-Jones, 871–84. New York: Guilford Press.

Zimbardo, Philip. 2008. *The Lucifer Effect: Understanding How Good People Turn Evil*. New York: Random House.

Index

Abjection, 140–41, 142–43, 144, 145, 149, 150, 190, 211–13
Actis, Omar, 116
Adorno, Theodor, 31
Affective empathy, 70–72, 74, 75, 77, 78, 83
Agosti, Orlando Ramón, 106
Algeria, 173, 174 (fig.), 187. See also *The Stranger*
Al-Qaeda, 16
American Anthropological Association: Principles of Professional Responsibility, 17–18; statement on human rights, 46
Amnesty International, 20
Anderson, Kjell, 7, 8, 11, 13, 15
The Anthropological Witness (Hinton), 168, 200–201, 206
Anthropology: cultural relativism, 59–60; culture and personality school, 125; "dark," 211; ethics code, 17–18; feminist, 27–28;

lack of research on genocide, 46; literary, 191–92; of political violence, 46; postmodern, 27, 28, 31, 191; study of unconscious, 25. *See also* Empathy; Ethnography; Fieldwork
Anxiety: existential, 133, 140–41, 144, 148, 190, 201; in fieldwork, 116, 117–19; of historical situations, 126–29
Anxiety dreams, 117–18, 119, 124, 126–29
Aramburu, Pedro, 66, 154, 176, 182
Archaeology, *see* Excavation
Arendt, Hannah, 10, 14, 45, 191, 198, 212–13
Argentina: dictatorships, 74, 95–96, 97, 107–8, 112–14, 127; dream analysis in, 25; Federal Court of Appeals, 3–4; Federal Tribunal of Comodoro Rivadavia, 183; human rights organizations, 65,

Reinventing Human Rights
Mark Goodale
2022

The Subject of Human Rights
Edited by Danielle Celermajer and Alexandre Lefebvre
2020

#HumanRights: The Technologies and Politics of Justice Claims in Practice
Ronald Niezen
2020

The Grip of Sexual Violence in Conflict: Feminist Interventions in International Law
Karen Engle
2020

When Misfortune Becomes Injustice: Evolving Human Rights Struggles for Health and Social Equality
Alicia Ely Yamin
2020

The Politics of Love in Myanmar: LGBT Mobilization and Human Rights as a Way of Life
Lynette J. Chua
2018

Branding Humanity: Competing Narratives of
Rights, Violence, and Global Citizenship
Amal Hassan Fadlalla
2018

Remote Freedoms: Politics, Personhood and Human
Rights in Aboriginal Central Australia
Sarah E. Holcombe
2018

Letters to the Contrary: A Curated History of
the UNESCO Human Rights Survey
Edited and Introduced by Mark Goodale
2018

Just Violence: Torture and Human Rights in the Eyes of the Police
Rachel Wahl
2017

Bodies of Truth: Law, Memory, and Emancipation
in Post-Apartheid South Africa
Rita Kesselring
2016

Rights After Wrongs: Local Knowledge and Human Rights in Zimbabwe
Shannon Morreira
2016

If God Were a Human Rights Activist
Boaventura de Sousa Santos
2015

Digging for the Disappeared: Forensic Science after Atrocity
Adam Rosenblatt
2015

For a complete listing of available titles in this series, visit
the Stanford University Press website, www.sup.org.

The authorized representative in the EU for product safety and compliance is:
Mare Nostrum Group
B.V Doelen 72
4831 GR Breda
The Netherlands

www.ingramcontent.com/pod-product-compliance
Lightning Source LLC
Chambersburg PA
CBHW020844270326
41928CB00006B/543

* 9 7 8 1 5 0 3 6 3 4 2 7 5 *